Ghetto at the Center of the World

Chungking Mansions, Hong Kong

GHETTO

at the Center of the World

GORDON MATHEWS

The University of Chicago Press
Chicago and London

GORDON MATHEWS is professor of anthropology at the Chinese University of Hong Kong. He is the author of *What Makes Life Worth Living? How Japanese and Americans Make Sense of Their Worlds* and *Global Cultural/Individual Identity: Searching for Home in the Cultural Supermarket*, among other books.

The University of Chicago Press, Chicago 60637
The University of Chicago Press, Ltd., London
© 2011 by The University of Chicago
All rights reserved. Published 2011
Printed in the United States of America

20 19 18 17 16 15 14 13 12   3 4 5

ISBN-13: 978-0-226-51019-4 (cloth)
ISBN-13: 978-0-226-51020-0 (paper)
ISBN-10: 0-226-51019-0 (cloth)
ISBN-10: 0-226-51020-4 (paper)

Library of Congress Cataloging-in-Publication Data

Mathews, Gordon.
    Ghetto at the center of the world : Chungking Mansions, Hong Kong / Gordon Mathews.
        p. cm.
    Includes bibliographical references and index.
    ISBN-13: 978-0-226-51019-4 (cloth : alk. paper)
    ISBN-13: 978-0-226-51020-0 (pbk. : alk. paper)
    ISBN-10: 0-226-51019-0 (cloth : alk. paper)
    ISBN-10: 0-226-51020-4 (pbk. : alk. paper) 1. Chungking Mansions (Hong Kong, China) 2. Multipurpose buildings—China—Hong Kong. 3. Guesthouses—China—Hong Kong. 4. City dwellers—China—Hong Kong. 5. Minorities—China—Hong Kong. 6. Hong Kong (China)—Commerce. I. Title.
    DS796.H78C48 2011
    951.25—dc22

                                                    2010036533

All photos are the author's own except as noted here. Frontispiece and pp. 24, 25, 42, 45, 79, 110, 122, 150, 190, and 215 courtesy of Jacqueline Donaldson; p. 65 courtesy of Jose Rojas; p. 67 courtesy of Maggie Lin; and maps courtesy of Alice Hui. The cover photo, by Shin Kusano, depicts Chungking Mansions as photographed from its third floor looking skyward.

♾ The paper used in this publication meets the minimum requirements of the American National Standard for Information Sciences—Permanence of Paper for Printed Library Materials, ANSI Z39.48-1992.

To the people in Chungking Mansions

CONTENTS

ACKNOWLEDGMENTS

The Chinese University of Hong Kong and the Hong Kong government have made this research possible through an RGC Earmarked Research Grant, "Chungking Mansions as a 'Global Building,'" project ID 2110148. This book would not have been written without this funding, which has ultimately come from Hong Kong taxpayers' hard-earned dollars. I hope that those of you from Hong Kong who read this book will not feel that your money has been wasted. I might add, to answer a question occasionally addressed to me in Chungking Mansions, that the Hong Kong government has had no input as to any of my research findings and has had no say over anything I report in this book—these findings are strictly my own.

I owe a great debt to my research assistants, recent graduate or undergraduate students in anthropology at the Chinese University of Hong Kong, who have provided an extraordinary amount of work, often above and beyond the relatively meager wages I paid them: "I'm not doing this for the money," I was told, and indeed they weren't. My assistants have been Inez Siu, Jojo Ng, Jo Yung, Ingrid Tang, Amy Fung, Yip Ping, Jose Rojas, Ocean Chan, Simon Tu, and Maggie Lin. Jose, Maggie, Ocean,

Amy, and Ingrid, in particular, have provided essential research help, investigating areas beyond those that I myself was able to investigate. Christian Lo, Catherine Wong, Elaine Hui, Luisa Mok, Claire Chan, and Yang Yang, while never formally working for this project, also provided aid.

I am indebted to the Incorporated Owners of Chungking Mansions, particularly Mrs. Lam Wai Lung, its chairperson; Joe Ng, of its membership committee; and David Leung and Anthony Wong, its managers. They have been unstintingly generous; I owe special thanks to Mrs. Lam and to Anthony Wong, who patiently answered my unending questions. My research assistants and I are grateful to the security guards at Chungking Mansions for their information and help. I am indebted to Christian Action and its staff, operating on the sixteenth and seventeenth floors, Block E, Chungking Mansions. Lisa Lee, Sarah Cornish, Jonathan Harland, Sharmila Gurung, Jonnet Bernal, Julia Mayerhofer, and other staff who have served there enabled me to become involved in the lives of asylum seekers by providing space and encouragement for our weekly class over the past four years.

There are an extraordinary number of people who have spoken to me and to my research assistants within Chungking Mansions or concerning Chungking Mansions, and who have helped us in multitudes of ways. Many of these people I or my assistants know only through their first names, or surnames; some prefer to be fully identified, while others seek to be identified only partially. I alphabetize on the basis of first name where possible, except for some Cantonese names with the surname first. People who have aided us include Abacha (Sany Garba), Abannawa, Abdi, Abdullah, Abiola, Abraham Orume Nangia, Abrar Ahmad, Ahmed, Aladdin, Alex, Ali, Ali Baba, Alsaneidi Abu Zaid, Amin Ezat, Anda, Andy, Asad Ali, Aman, Mr. An, Anderson, Anne Quain, Aqmad, Aris, Asghar, Austin, Auto Sam, Awais, Awais Ejaz, Ayishah, Baron, Ben, Ben Hui, Bettina, Biggy, Bilbab, Billy, Binai, Biola, Bissnu, Bobby, Boniface, Bore, Brian, Bupe, Chain, Mr. Chan, Chantel, Charlotte Walsh, Mrs. Cheng, Cheung Yuk-man, Chiboy, Chibuzor, Chidi, Chikibei, Chimako, Christian Lo, Cliff Atkins, Coco, Connie P. Y. Tang, Cosmo, Dan K., Daniel, Danielle Stutterd, Danny, Darpan, David, Dede, Deltaman, Dhillon, Dhom, Diallo M. Ali, Dixon, Edgar, Ejaz, Elias Zakir Hussein, Emmanuel, Enock, Eqbal, Eva, Ezra, Fatih, Fatuma, Fawaz, Fayez, Fezel, Fred, Fritz, Ms. Fung, Ganeth, Gege, George, Godwill, Golem, Gurdev Singh, Gurdu, Gurjit, Gurung, Hamid, Haseeb, Hawg, Helal, Henry, Henry Wilson, Him, Hunayam, Hermias, Mr. and Mrs. Hugh Baker, Ishaan Tharoor, Ishmael, Ismael, Jack, Jack Chander, Jack Qiu, Jacob, Jacqueline Tsui, James Joseph Keezhangatte, Jamir, Jean, Jean-Louis Schuller, Jeylani, Jhonny, Jimmy, Joe, John, John Lyarua, Jonathan Yip and his mother, Joseph, Joy, Julian, Julius,

Kandiah, Kasmin, Kelvin Chan, Khem Gurung, Kingston, Kit Lam, Kumari, Mr. Lam, Lanka, Larry, Lawrence Au Kwong-yui, Mr. Li, Lucky, Mahmood, Majeed, Manan, Manuel, Mark, Martin, Mama, Mary, Mrs. Mary, Mahmet, Mahmood, Mashan, Masheed, Matthew, Max, McToby, Michael from Ghana, Michael from Hong Kong, Mike, M. M. Khan, Mohammed, Moon, Moses, Mukasa, Muna, Mustafa Alzainy, Nathan, Nelson, Nicholas, Nimaga Aguibou, Obinna, Ovie, Papa and his wife, Papi, Paul, Pauline, Peter, Peter Lau, Phoebe Tsui, Piera Chen, Mr. Poon, Qanni, Rahman, Raiz, Raj, Raja, Rajesh, Rakesh, Ramos, Ramsey, Ransom, Raya, Rita, Robert, Roland, Ron Clayborn-Dyer, Roy, Sabita, Sachu, Said, Salem, Sally, Sanda, Santa, Shabih, Mr. Shah, Shane, Sibi Malamin, Simon, Simon To, Sinh, Stan Dyer, Steve, Steve Goldman, Suba, Sulamen, Sunny, Tabah, Thaddius, Thomas, Tim Elwell-Sutton, Mr. To, Toby, Tony, Tsaijer Cheng, Tseheye, Tseten Kutsabpa, Mrs. Tsui, Ulfat, Vicky, Victor, Mr. Wang, Watson, Wazed Ali, William, Mr. Wong, Mr. and Mrs. Yip Woon-ming, Xuxi, Yogesh, and Zed.

Please forgive me if you do not see your name here. I seek to preserve the anonymity of some of those who appear in this book, particularly those whose full accounts are included. Nonetheless, the above list, although regrettably partial, indicates my debts. To all the people I came to know in Chungking Mansions, the hundreds of people who took their time to speak with me and tell me about their lives, whether your name is listed here or not, I owe you, and I dedicate this book to you.

Several people have helped me in the writing of this book. Lynne Nakano kindly reviewed the manuscript before it was fully finished and gave it an essential critical reading, shaping my subsequent rewriting. My research assistants Jose Rojas and Maggie Lin both read the manuscript and corrected a number of significant errors. Woody and Rubie Watson reviewed the manuscript at a slightly later stage and gave a valuable reading, enabling me to see the manuscript more clearly. Michael Herzfeld, at a dinner in Chungking Mansions, came up with something very close to the title of this book. I thank T. David Brent, Laura J. Avey, and Rhonda L. Smith at the University of Chicago Press and Michael Duckworth of the University of Hong Kong Press for their encouragement and professionalism, as well as three anonymous referees for their valuable suggestions for revision. I also thank Jacqueline Donaldson for taking professional-quality photographs of Chungking Mansions and generously contributing them to this book and Alice Hui for providing the book's maps.

Finally, I thank my wife Yoko, who put up with my being absent many evenings and every weekend for almost four years with never a word of complaint, and indeed, with nothing but love.

A Note on Hong Kong

Chungking Mansions, the subject of this book, is the haunt of South Asian merchants, African entrepreneurs, Indian temporary workers, African and South Asian asylum seekers, and penurious travelers from across the globe. It is, as I discuss in the pages that follow, a ramshackle building in Hong Kong's tourist district that is a hub of "low-end globalization," tightly linked to the markets of Kolkata (Calcutta), Lagos, and Dar es Salaam, among other cities across the globe. Although Chungking Mansions is seen by many in Hong Kong as a mysterious world of otherness strangely set in Hong Kong's very heart, it is nonetheless distinctly shaped by Hong Kong. In order to properly situate Chungking Mansions, I here briefly sketch Hong Kong's history and geography in relation to Chungking Mansions.

Hong Kong was a colony of Great Britain from 1841 until its return to China in 1997. Throughout its colonial history, it served as an entrepôt between China and the world beyond—first as a settlement where British companies managed their opium shipments into China and subsequently, throughout much of its history, as a center of free trade, with minimal customs duties. Throughout its history, its population was a global mix, with the vast majority Chinese but also including an array of other peoples. A late nineteenth-century source speaks of a downtown street as "filled with Britishers, Germans, Anglo-Indians, Chinese from Canton, Armenians from Calcutta, Parsees from Bombay, and Jews from Baghdad"[1]—a mix not utterly different from what is found in a Chungking Mansions corridor today. Another late nineteenth-century account discusses how Hong Kong is "allowed to be the most cosmopolitan city in the world. Representatives of races far in excess of the Pentecostal catalogue, may be encountered in its streets in any hour's walk; men of all shades of colour and of every religious creed live here side by side in apparent perfect harmony."[2] This is the case in Chungking Mansions today as well—although then, as now, there were ethnic tensions and ethnic discrimination.[3]

Hong Kong, throughout much of its history, was an impoverished place for most of its residents. In 1949, the People's Republic of China was founded. During this era, large numbers of Chinese fled the mainland and came to Hong Kong, leading to a massive population explosion in the territory. By the 1970s, Hong Kong had emerged as a manufacturing hub, and from the late 1980s on as a center for Chinese goods being shipped around the world. At the same time, a sense of a distinct Hong Kong identity, separate from that of China, gradually emerged.[4] By the 1990s, Hong Kong had become wealthy—far wealthier in its per capita income than China and wealthier, too, by this measure, than its colonizer, Great Britain. As of 2007, Hong Kong had a per capita income in actual purchasing power that was 93 percent that of the United States, considerably higher than that of most European nations and some eight times that of mainland China,[5] although the gap between the rich and the poor is one of the largest in the world. This makes Chungking Mansions' role, as a ramshackle home of the developing world in Hong Kong, seem incongruous. Much of the disdain and fear that many Hong Kong Chinese feel toward Chungking Mansions, as I later discuss, stems from the subliminal sense that "We Hong Kongers have recently left the developing world and become wealthy. Why should these Africans and South Asians be staying in the midst of our newly wealthy home?"

By the same token, the disdain toward mainland China expressed by some of the Chungking Mansions' merchants and traders in this book, whether African, South Asian, or Hong Kong Chinese, echoes a more general Hong Kong sense of unease toward one's fellow citizens from the north. Mainland Chinese are seen by many as Hong Kong's unchosen political masters and also as economic inferiors, although wealthy mainlanders have an increasingly visible presence in Hong Kong in recent years and the mainland increasingly seems to be overtaking and perhaps leaving behind Hong Kong as the land of the future. Chungking Mansions, an island of otherness in Hong Kong, is nonetheless very much a part of Hong Kong in the attitudes of the people who live and work there. Indeed, the people who fled China to make a better life for themselves in Hong Kong are remarkably similar in their values to those who more recently have left South Asia and Africa to seek a better life for themselves in Chungking Mansions, even though the two groups have almost no understanding of or sympathy for one another.

Hong Kong's 150 years as a British colony have had a great impact in shaping Chungking Mansions. Most important is the prominent presence of South Asians in Hong Kong since the early days of its colonial history and remaining ever since.[6] Were it not for the initial presence of South Asians in Chungking Mansions when the building opened in 1962, Chungking Mansions would almost certainly not have evolved into the global mart that it has become. An astute journalist accompanying me to Chungking Mansions remarked that what he saw, among its many different ethnicities and nationalities, was not just globalization but also an echo of British colonialism. Indeed, while many of the different groups in the building were never the victims or beneficiaries of British colonialism, East Africans and South Asians are very prominently represented. This is partly because these people are more likely to speak English, Chungking Mansions' lingua franca, and partly because visa-free entry for an extended period is, even today, easier for members of these societies to obtain than for members of other societies. Hong Kong's colonial era lives on in this sense.

Many non-Hong Kong readers may assume that since the handover of Hong Kong to China in 1997, everything in Hong Kong has changed—China now controls Hong Kong. Certainly global mass media over the past several decades have focused on Hong Kong's departure from British colonial control and return to China as the single dominant theme of "the Hong Kong story." This is important, but it is also essential to remember that after the handover, life in Hong Kong has remained remarkably stable. Mass media continue to freely criticize China, although there are ongoing worries over self-censorship, and freedom of speech remains firmly ensconced. Hong Kong retains its own legal system and immigration controls. Although it is now part of China, its internal administration is largely independent. There are significant ongoing problems in Hong Kong, not least the fact that the government seems largely in the pocket of business magnates, especially property developers. However, this was true both before and after the handover. For Chungking Mansions, the return of Hong Kong to China has had very little effect. Massive changes have indeed happened to the building since 1997: the coming of African traders, which began around 2000; the

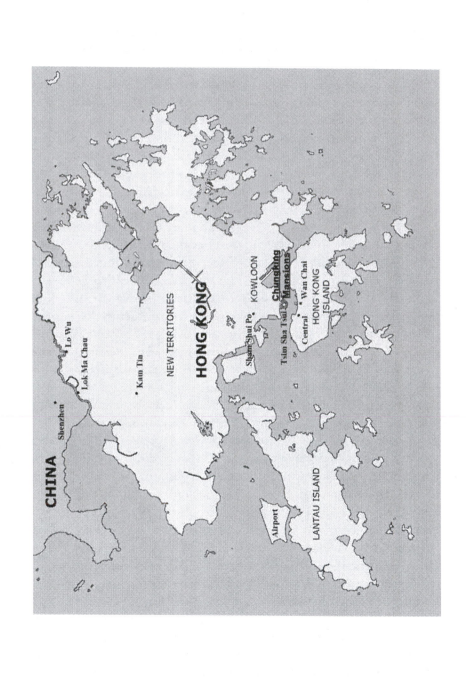

upsurge of asylum seekers; the building's improved maintenance and security; and the increase in mainland Chinese tourists. But these—even the last of these—have little to do with Hong Kong's return to China, which was a nonevent. "Chungking Mansions," as shopkeepers occasionally have reiterated to me, "is the same as it ever was."

Chungking Mansions is located in Tsim Sha Tsui, Hong Kong's major tourist district, at the tip of the Kowloon Peninsula. Hong Kong consists of four major areas: the outlying islands, including Lantau, where the airport is located; Hong Kong Island, where Hong Kong's financial center as well as many of its older buildings can be found; Kowloon, somewhat less upscale than Hong Kong Island but more heavily populated and containing Hong Kong's touristic heart as well as its most crowded districts; and the New Territories, closer to the Chinese border, where over half of the population of Hong Kong now lives. This is all in a relatively small area of a little over four hundred square miles. Because Hong Kong as a whole is so tightly linked by mass transit, these different areas are generally reachable in under an hour and are well known to many of those in Chungking Mansions.

To mention just a few of Hong Kong's neighborhoods, there is Sham Shui Po, a working-class area some two miles north of Chungking Mansions, full of cut-rate stores where African traders often go to buy clothing especially designed and manufactured for the African market and where others, such as asylum seekers, go to buy used goods for sale with no questions asked at prices that undercut even those of Chungking Mansions. There is Wan Chai, a well-known nightlife district across the harbor from Tsim Sha Tsui, where some in Chungking Mansions go in search of wine and women, and many more, intimidated by the prices, only dream of going. There is Kam Tin, a town in the New Territories that tourists go to for its walled village but that Chungking Mansions traders go to in order to buy used car parts from automobiles junked by their Hong Kong owners. And there is Lo Wu, at the Hong Kong-Chinese border, where traders go to make their passage to the marts and factories of south China and where temporary workers go to renew their visas for another few weeks. Merchants in Chungking Mansions live all over Hong Kong, but the sites just outlined are known to most of the people within Chungking Mansions, regardless of why they are in the building and what they are doing there.

In chapter 1 I describe the particular locale of Chungking Mansions in more detail, but let me provide a brief sketch here. Chungking Mansions is located at 36–44 Nathan Road, the street which is Hong Kong's main tourist drag. The building is adjacent to a Holiday Inn and a block from the Peninsula Hotel, perhaps Hong Kong's fanciest. It is little more than a hundred

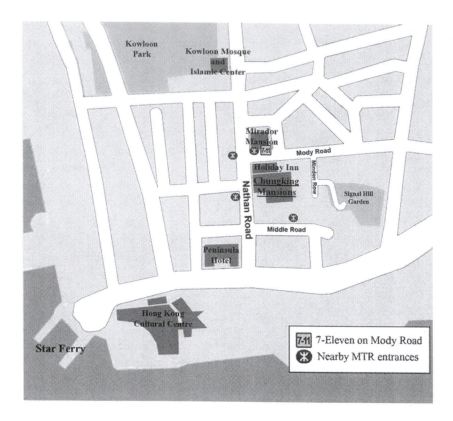

yards from two of Hong Kong's newest and glitziest shopping malls, and just a ten-minute walk from the famous Star Ferry, a touristic icon of Hong Kong, taking passengers across Hong Kong harbor every few minutes. It is surrounded by entrances to the MTR, Hong Kong's mass transit trains, which whisk passengers to the Chinese border every five minutes or so, a forty-minute journey. Chungking Mansions, as this brief depiction reveals, is in the thick of downtown Hong Kong, smack in the middle of hotels, malls, and skyscrapers—some of the most expensive property in the world. Its location in the heart of Hong Kong is what makes the building's reputation as "a heart of darkness" so extraordinary.[7]

The photographs in this book, unless otherwise specified, were all taken in or around Chungking Mansions. These photographs, as a rule, do not depict the people or the businesses discussed in the text but are offered in order to provide a more generic picture of the building and what goes on within its walls.

place

ONE

Introducing Chungking Mansions

Chungking Mansions is a dilapidated seventeen-story structure full of cheap guesthouses and cut-rate businesses in the midst of Hong Kong's tourist district. It is perhaps the most globalized building in the world. In Chungking Mansions, entrepreneurs and temporary workers from South Asia, sub-Saharan Africa, and across the globe come to seek their fortunes, along with asylum seekers looking for refuge and tourists in search of cheap lodging and adventure. People from an extraordinary array of societies sleep in its beds, jostle for seats in its food stalls, bargain at its mobile phone counters, and wander its corridors. Some 4,000 people stay in Chungking Mansions on any given night. I've counted 129 different nationalities in its guesthouse logs and in my own meetings with people, from Argentina to Zimbabwe, by way of Bhutan, Iraq, Jamaica, Luxembourg, Madagascar, and the Maldive Islands.

Chungking Mansions is located on the Golden Mile of Nathan Road, famous, according to the guidebooks, for "its ability to suck money from tourists' pockets."[1] If you approach Chungking Mansions from across Nathan Road, you will see a row of

glitzy buildings towering on the other side of the street bearing an array of stores, including a Holiday Inn, many electronics places, several entrances to shopping arcades, a number of fashionable clothing outlets, a couple of steak houses, and several bars. This looks like the Hong Kong of postcards, particularly if you approach in the evening and are bathed in the gaudy sea of neon that Nathan Road is famous for. However, in the midst of these fancy buildings is one that looks plainer, more disheveled and decrepit. Its lower floors, seen from across the street, hardly seem part of the building since they too are fancy shops and malls, physically part of the building but inaccessible except from outside and a world away. But then, in the middle of these stores, you see a nondescript, dark entrance that looks like it belongs somewhere else. As you cross Nathan Road on a butterfly crosswalk and draw closer to this entrance, you will notice that the people standing near the entrance to this building don't look like most other people in Hong Kong, certainly not like the throngs of shoppers elsewhere on Nathan Road. As you enter the building, if you are Chinese, you may feel like a member of a minority group and wonder where in the world you are. If you are white, you might instinctively clutch your wallet while feeling trepidation and perhaps a touch of first-world guilt. If you are a young woman, you may feel, very uncomfortably, a hundred pairs of male eyes gazing at you.

If you approach Chungking Mansions from the same side of Nathan

Road walking from the nearest underground MTR railway exit on Mody Road, just around the corner from the building (see map on p. 6), you will get a somewhat fuller introduction to the place. You will first see a 7-Eleven that in the evenings may be full of Africans drinking beer in its aisles and spilling outside its entrance. You may also see a dozen Indian women resplendent in their saris who, if you are male and look at them, will offer you a price and then follow you closely for a few paces to make certain that you truly aren't interested in their sexual services. After passing the 7-Eleven, you may, if you are male, be accosted at the corner of Nathan Road by other young women, from Mongolia, Malaysia, Indonesia, and elsewhere. You will also be accosted by a number of South Asian men offering to make you a suit—"A special deal just for you." They may be joined by copy-watch sellers, offering various brands of watches for a small fraction of the price of the original. If you hesitate and show interest, they will lead you to any of the numerous shadowy emporiums in nearby buildings.

Once you cross Mody Road and are on the same block as Chungking Mansions (whose entrance is now some one hundred feet away), the restaurant touts may be in wait if it is the right time of day, shilling for a half dozen different Chungking Mansions curry places. You must either ignore them or decide to follow one tout to his restaurant; otherwise you will be mobbed. You may also—especially if you are white—find a young man quietly sidling up to you and whispering, "Hashish?" and if you query further, numerous other substances as well. Once you reach the steps at the entrance to Chungking Mansions, the guesthouse touts will set upon you if it is late afternoon or evening, with a South Asian man saying, "I can give you a nice room for HK$150" (US$19),* and a Chinese man saying, just out of earshot of the South Asian, "Those Indian places are filthy! Come to my place! It's clean"—possibly so, but at a considerably higher price.

After you have passed through this gauntlet of attention, you will find yourself in the midst of Chungking Mansions' swirl, at times more people crowded in one place than you have seen in your entire life. It is an extraordinary array of people: Africans in bright robes or hip-hop fashions or ill-fitting suits; pious Pakistani men wearing skullcaps; Indonesian women with *jilbab*, Islamic head coverings; old white men with beer bellies in Bermuda shorts; hippies looking like refugees from an earlier era; Nigerians arguing confidently and very loudly; young Indians joking and teasing with their arms around one another; and mainland Chinese looking self-contained or

* US$1 = HK$7.78 as of this writing.

stunned. You are likely to find South Asians carting three or four huge boxes on their trolleys with "Lagos" or "Nairobi" scrawled on the boxes' sides, Africans leaving the building with overstuffed suitcases packed with mobile phones, and shopkeepers selling everything on earth, from *samosas* to phone cards to haircuts to whiskey to real estate to electrical plugs to dildos to shoes. You will also see a long line of people of every different skin color waiting at the elevator, bound for a hundred different guesthouses.

You may wonder, upon seeing all of this, "What on earth is going on here? What has brought all these different people to Chungking Mansions? How do they live? Why does this place exist?" These are the questions that led me to begin my research in Chungking Mansions. I first came to Chungking Mansions in 1983 as a tourist, staying for a few nights before moving on. I came to Hong Kong to live in 1994, visiting Chungking Mansions every couple of months to eat curry and to take in the world there. In 2006, I began formally to do anthropological research in Chungking Mansions, finding out all I could about the place and the people in it and seeking to understand Chungking Mansions' role in globalization. I have been living in Chungking Mansions for one or more nights each week over the past three and a half years and have spent my every available moment there (it is a thirty-minute train ride from the university where I live), seeking to answer the questions posed above and, more than that, to understand Chungking Mansions' significance in the world.

Over the past few years I have found some answers. Let me describe a typical walk of late from the train station exit to Chungking Mansions. The Indian sex workers are already out this early evening but know that I'm not a customer, so they ignore me, except for the new ones who see in a white face the chance to make a lot of money; their seniors tell them not to bother. A copy-watch salesman friend waves hello from behind his dark glasses. He was partially blinded by the police in his South Asian country, he has told me, when they taped open his eyelids and forced him to gaze at the sun all day. But the United Nations High Commissioner for Refugees (UNHCR), the arbiter of his case and his fate, may not believe him, he worries, because he cannot provide proof. So he illegally works, attempting to save up enough money to eventually be able to receive cornea transplants. Meanwhile, he looks out for undercover police as best he can and accosts every likely customer: "White people are the best. They buy more than anyone else." But sales are bad this month, and he can hardly pay his rent, let alone save for his longed-for transplants. Whether he was blinded by the police in his country, or by a congenital problem or an accident of some sort, is an open ques-

tion—how much of his account is true is not for me to judge. But it's good to come across him again.

A few steps later, a restaurant tout greets me effusively. I haven't seen him for two months because he's been back in Kolkata, his home—he is illegally working in Hong Kong as a tourist. He proudly shows me a picture of his baby son, born last month, but says that he's happy to be back in Hong Kong. "I have to support my family! . . . I miss my family, but the pay's much better here in Hong Kong, so . . ." But he spends a significant portion of his money calling home on his mobile phone, he tells me ruefully.

At the entrance to Chungking Mansions, I meet a Nigerian trader I haven't seen for six months. He says that he couldn't return to Hong Kong because the exchange rates back home were exorbitant, and he couldn't get the dollars he needed. "Now I finally can come back. I had an order for 4,000 phones, but I couldn't come here to pick them up. Now I can do that. I can make money again." He flies back home the day after tomorrow, after checking every phone as closely as he can. His friend, whom I meet for the first time, is going into south China the day after tomorrow—"It's better to buy clothes there than in Hong Kong now. I can get 30,000 shirts made following my own style"—after picking up his visa. Both are worried that exchange rate fluctuations might kill any chance of making a profit, not to mention the vicissitudes of customs back home and the dangers of getting cheated in China and in Chungking Mansions. "It's so hard to make any money," they say, the continuing refrain of so many traders I have spoken with.

A few steps later, I meet an Indian friend standing near the guard post, He works for a large Hong Kong corporation by day and by night comes back to help his family at their guesthouse. His agony at present is not simply that he has no time, but more that he has a Hong Kong Chinese girlfriend that his parents refuse to recognize. He wonders what he should do—choose his girlfriend or his parents—but at present, he just can't decide and only waits.

I then meet a West African friend who until recently ran a business in south China. He, unlike almost every other African trader I've met, has had the capital to obtain a Hong Kong ID card in return for a US$200,000 investment, which he has made by renting and outfitting an electronics store in Chungking Mansions, one that his fellow Africans and fellow Muslims will patronize, he hopes. His wife and children have recently come to Hong Kong, and he looks forward to making a new life for them here, as against what he feels to be the lawlessness of China. "You can trust Hong Kong." Of course, whether he can make money remains to be seen, especially in the economic downturn that has affected Chungking Mansions as much as anywhere else in the world; but he believes that by being an honest Muslim merchant, he can succeed in the building.

Another few steps later, I meet a young South Asian whom I've only met once before. He tells me that he has lost his job and is desperate. "What am I going to do? I have no money! Everyone in my family depends on me!" I don't know if he is telling the whole truth, but he certainly seems frantic. I don't know him, so I only give him HK$100 and wish him luck. I hate playing God this way, but what can I do? There are so many like him. The next time I come back to Chungking Mansions, I don't see him; in fact, I have never seen him again.

These people are all denizens of Chungking Mansions, the subject of this book. In the book's first chapter, I explore Chungking Mansions as a place: its reasons for existing, its significance, and its architecture, history, and organization. In its second chapter, I depict the different groups of people in Chungking Mansions, from African traders to Chinese owners to South Asian shopkeepers to asylum seekers, sex workers, heroin addicts, and tourists, and my interviews and travels around the globe with various of these people. In its third chapter, I describe the goods that pass through the building and the shopkeepers and traders who buy and sell these goods in their global passages. In its fourth chapter, I examine the web of laws that constrain all in the building and particularly consider asylum seekers, with their lives placed in limbo. Finally, in its fifth chapter, I explore the building's significance, for those within it and for the world as a whole, and speculate as to its future.

This book is about Chungking Mansions and the people within it, but it is also about "low-end globalization," a form of globalization for which Chungking Mansions is a central node, linking to an array of nodes around the world, from Bangkok to Dubai to Kolkata, Kathmandu, Kampala, Lagos, and Nairobi. Low-end globalization is very different from what most readers may associate with the term *globalization*—it is not the activities of Coca-Cola, Nokia, Sony, McDonald's, and other huge corporations, with their high-rise offices, batteries of lawyers, and vast advertising budgets. Instead, it is traders carrying their goods by suitcase, container, or truck across continents and borders with minimal interference from legalities and copyrights, a world run by cash. It is also individuals seeking a better life by fleeing their home countries for opportunities elsewhere, whether as temporary workers, asylum seekers, or sex workers. This is the dominant form of globalization experienced in much of the developing world today.

Chungking Mansions flourishes in a small space through which enormous amounts of energy, people, and goods flow, but this is nonetheless tiny in volume compared to the scale of the developed-world economy that surrounds it. It is one dilapidated building compared to all the financiers' skyscrapers in Tsim Sha Tsui and especially across Hong Kong harbor in the Central District, Hong Kong's concentrated wealth as a center of high-end globalization ten minutes away by train and a universe distant. This book is about Chungking Mansions, but it is also about all the world, in its linkages, its inequalities, and its wonders.

"Ghetto at the Center of the World"

Chungking Mansions is a place that is terrifying to many in Hong Kong. Here are some typical comments from Chinese-language blogs and chat rooms: "I feel very nervous every time I walk past [Chungking Mansions]. . . . I feel that I could get lost in the building and kidnapped."[2] "I am . . . afraid to go [to Chungking Mansions]. There seem to be many perverts and bad elements there."[3] "I saw a group of black people and Indian people standing in front of a building. I looked up and saw the sign 'Chungking Mansions.' Just as the legend goes, it is a sea of pitch darkness there."[4] "I went with some classmates for curry today. It was my very first time going to Chungking

Mansions. I felt like I was in another country. The curry was all right, but I was scared when I entered the building . . . because my dad told me I should never go in."[5] As this last quotation indicates, some Hong Kong Chinese, particularly young people, are attracted to Chungking Mansions because of its half dozen semifashionable curry restaurants on its higher floors, but many more are afraid to even enter the building.

This fear of Chungking Mansions extends beyond Hong Kong—it is apparent among commentators from the developed world as a whole. Consider the following passages, largely written by American and European journalists, also taken from the Internet:

> Chungking Mansions is the sum of all fears for parents whose children go backpacking around Asia. . . . In the heart of one of the world's richest and glitziest cities, its draw card of cheap accommodation has long been matched by the availability of every kind of vice and dodgy deal, not to mention its almost palpable fire and health risks.[6]

> Chungking Mansion is the only place I have ever been where it is possible to buy a sexual aid, a bootleg Jay Chou CD and a new, leather-bound Koran, all from the same bespectacled Kashmiri proprietor who can make change for your purchase in any of five currencies. It is also possible, while wandering the alleys, hallways and listing stairwells of Chungking Mansions, to buy a discount ticket to Bombay, purchase 2,000 knock-off Tag Heuer watches or pick up a counterfeit phone card that will allow unlimited calls to Lagos, Nigeria. . . . You can disappear here. Thousands have. Most of them by design.[7]

> Chungking Mansions offers very cheap accommodation for backpackers and is a hideout for illegals such as those who have overstayed their visas. It is a den of crime, of drug trafficking, prostitution and generally all the nastiness that goes on in the world you can find in Chungking Mansions. . . . Personally I go there for the curry.[8]

This dodgy reputation dates from the 1970s, when Chungking Mansions emerged as a hangout for Western hippies and backpackers. It grew during the 1980s and early 1990s, as confirmed in the dark portrayal in Wong Kar-wai's famous 1994 film *Chungking Express*, a film about Hong Kong Chinese postmodern romance that takes place, in part, in Chungking Mansions. The film depicted Chungking Mansions misleadingly. Hong Kong Chinese did not usually come to Chungking Mansions in the early 1990s, and those who did stuck out so obviously that they probably couldn't have engaged in the kinds of activities the film depicts. Nonetheless, the film does accurately convey the seedy atmosphere of the place at that time. This dodgy reputation of Chungking Mansions continues today, largely because of the massive presence of South Asians and Africans in the building, as seen through the quasi-racist lenses of Hong Kong Chinese and other rich-world peoples who don't quite know how to interact with their poor-world brethren.

The biggest reason why so many people in Hong Kong and in the developed world are terrified of Chungking Mansions is simply that they are afraid of the developing world and the masses of poor people who come to the developed world for some of the crumbs of its wealth. The quotations above exaggerate Chungking Mansions' dangers—I have been told by police officials that there is less crime in Chungking Mansions than in some other buildings its size in Hong Kong, because of its central location and the prominent presence of security guards and police. Nonetheless, they do reflect a basic truth of the place. Chungking Mansions is *in* Hong Kong, but it is not *of* Hong Kong. It is an alien island of the developing world lying in Hong Kong's heart. This, not its crime and vice, is the major reason why it has been so feared. And this is why I have titled this book "Ghetto at the Center of the World."

A ghetto is defined as "a quarter of a city in which members of a minority group live especially because of social, legal, or economic pressure."[9] Chungking Mansions is a building and not a quarter of a city; its residents do not consist of a single minority group, but of members of multitudes of such groups. Nonetheless, Chungking Mansions is indeed a ghetto in the sense that the minority groups who stay there (all but the whites and Hong Kong Chinese) are to at least some extent economically blocked from Hong Kong as a whole and are socially discriminated against through racism or fear of the developing-world unknown. Chungking Mansions is seen by many, such as the authors of our earlier quotations, as a transgressive other in the heart of Hong Kong. To many Hong Kong Chinese, living in one of the world's richest cities, Chungking Mansions is a "heart of darkness."*

---

*Chungking Mansions has been linked in some accounts to Kowloon's Walled City, demolished in 1993. The Walled City, several kilometers from Chungking Mansions, was an area never fully under colonial British control and was throughout the twentieth century a haven in Hong Kong for illicit activity, such as prostitution and drug dealing. Largely impenetrable by police, it was long controlled by Chinese organized crime groups. Chungking Mansions has never been quite as off-limits to external authorities as the Walled City was reported to have been, and the comparison of the two sites is historically incongruent. Nonetheless, both the Walled City and Chungking Man-

But if Chungking Mansions can be characterized as a ghetto, it is an unusual sort of ghetto. Most of the people in the building, operators of the various wheels and cogs of low-end globalization, are remarkably bourgeois in their outlooks on life. They represent the striving middle class of the developing world in South Asia and Africa. Hong Kong people may see Chungking Mansions as a hellhole of danger and vice, as do some of the tourists in the building, but for most of the people residing or working in Chungking Mansions, this "ghetto at the center of the world" is a beacon of hope. It is their best chance to climb out of developing-world poverty and make a prosperous life for themselves. Among many of the Muslims, Hindus, Sikhs, and evangelical Christians from South Asia and Africa who work or trade in Chungking Mansions, Max Weber's "Protestant Ethic" lives on—hard work and savings, as well as a little or a lot of luck, can buy them a ticket to a better life.[10]

Why, then, does Chungking Mansions, this "ghetto at the center of the world," this island of the developing world in Hong Kong's heart, exist?

Why Chungking Mansions Exists and Why It Matters

There are three reasons for Chungking Mansions: (1) the building's cheapness, (2) the ease of entry into Hong Kong for many in the developing world, and (3) the emergence of south China as a manufacturing powerhouse.

The first and most practical reason why Chungking Mansions exists is simply that food and accommodations there cost so little. Even wealthy people from the developing world may recoil in shock at the prices of a city like Hong Kong. But Chungking Mansions itself is remarkably inexpensive, with single rooms costing as little as HK$100 (US$13) each night and with prices of meals and goods among the cheapest in Hong Kong. Why is there such a discrepancy?

For one thing, there has been no real unified ownership of Chungking Mansions. Until recently, the ownership organization has been remarkably weak, and the building has steadily deteriorated. But this explanation is insufficient—there are many buildings throughout Hong Kong that have lacked a unified ownership structure, but none has deteriorated as spectacularly as Chungking Mansions over the decades. The most essential reason for Chungking Mansions' cheapness is the play of particular historical circumstances.

_____

sions have been seen over the years as Hong Kong's "others"—Hong Kong's "hearts of darkness"—and in that sense there is indeed a parallel.

I will later discuss Chungking Mansions' history, but let me set forth a few factors here. The building began with a significant South Asian presence, which increased over the years—in a Hong Kong all too prejudiced against South Asians, this served as a black mark for many of the Chinese in Hong Kong, keeping most Chinese out and keeping the building's property values low. In the 1970s, the building became famous, via *Lonely Planet*, for its hippies and backpackers staying in its rock-bottom-priced guesthouses, and many Chinese living in apartments in the building began converting them into guesthouses with a dozen or so miniscule rooms. By the 1980s and early 1990s, fires and extended blackouts took place. By the early 2000s, African traders became a prominent presence in Chungking Mansions, generally seeking, like their hippie forebears, the cheapest possible prices. These factors supported a situation in which property owners could maximize profits by keeping prices low. Chungking Mansions, exactly because it is decrepit and thus cheap, remains a draw throughout much of the developed world. Mention Hong Kong in Kathmandu, Kolkata, or Dar es Salaam, as I myself have done, and there is a reasonable chance that you will hear in response, "Chungking Mansions."

A second reason why Chungking Mansions exists as an island of the developing world in Hong Kong is the territory's comparatively relaxed visa regulations.* In most developed countries, visitors from the developing world must obtain a visa prior to arrival, or they will not be allowed to board the airplane. If, upon arrival, they are found to lack a visa, they will be sent directly home. In Hong Kong, visitors from many countries in the developing world are allowed in without visas for periods of fourteen, thirty, or ninety days. This enables entrepreneurs from many countries in Africa and Asia to come to Hong Kong without prior paperwork. With a thirty- or even a fourteen-day visa-free period, they can come to Chungking Mansions, inspect various goods, conduct their business, make their purchases, and return home in good time.

Many of these entrepreneurs remain in Hong Kong, but many more seek to go into China. In Hong Kong, particularly through expeditious travel agents in and around Chungking Mansions, visas for China can generally be obtained quickly. Accordingly, developing-country entrepreneurs can go into China to visit wholesalers, come back to Hong Kong, and depart with

---

*China does not control Hong Kong's visa regulations; these are Hong Kong's own responsibility. Generally speaking, when matters of police, government, or laws are discussed in this book, these are matters dealt with not by China but by Hong Kong itself.

their goods in their luggage or in air freight or container, depending on the goods bought and the wealth of the entrepreneur, in a matter of a few days or weeks. Since flights to Hong Kong are more frequent and convenient than flights to most cities in China, it is easier for many businesspeople and other visitors to come to Hong Kong first, although in recent years more have been going directly into China. Because it is so cheap and because it serves as a de facto clearing house and information center, Chungking Mansions is where theycome.

In recent years, the Hong Kong government has been tightening entrance restrictions. Citizens of Nigeria, Pakistan, Bangladesh, Ghana, and Nepal, among other countries, are now required to get visas as they did not in the past. In some cases, this has been due to an apparent increase in drug and other offenses among nationals coming to Hong Kong. In other cases, it has been because of an increase in nationals of these countries seeking asylum. These restrictions have had a significant effect on Chungking Mansions, with the presence of Nigerians, Ghanaians, and Bangladeshis, among others, diminishing in recent years. However, by overstaying their visas or, as is often the case for those in Chungking Mansions, applying for asylum-seeker status through the UNHCR or the Hong Kong government, those already in Hong Kong can often prolong their stay indefinitely. Because of an increase in asylum seekers in Hong Kong, there is pressure on the government to further tighten entrance restrictions. But as of this writing, this has not happened, at least not formally, and so Chungking Mansions continues to be the beneficiary of an unusual policy: a government in the developed world that allows many arrivals from the developing world to enter unimpeded, for at least a limited period. This enables Chungking Mansions to exist.

A third reason is the emergence of China, and especially south China, as a world manufacturing center. Entrepreneurs from throughout the developing world flock to Chungking Mansions so that they can buy Chinese goods, whether in Hong Kong or over the border in China. These goods range from mobile phones, used or copied, to garments to watches to building materials to furniture to such exotic products as whirlpool baths (bought by wealthy East Africans such as government ministers, I have been told) and mounted opals (mined in Australia, sent through Chungking Mansions to south China to be mounted, and then returned to Australia for sale to Chinese tourists). Hong Kong, as it has been throughout its history, continues to serve as the gateway to China for these entrepreneurs, who may either venture into south China themselves to make their orders or rely on Hong Kong middlemen to sell them made-in-China products. These goods tend to be of cheap price and low quality, but this is what consumers in the developing world can afford.

For these three reasons, Chungking Mansions exists, but why does it matter? Why is it worth writing a book about? The simplest reason is that it contains an extraordinary array of people from throughout the world. How do they interact? More than this, what can Chungking Mansions teach us about how globalization works in the world today?

As previously noted, I am an anthropologist. The forte of anthropology as a discipline is ethnography: the on-the-ground depiction of the interactions and daily lives of a small number of people, described in great detail on the basis of many months or years of intensive fieldwork. Globalization is a vast and abstract field, analyzed most typically by economists. While anthropologists have also made important theoretical contributions, such as those of Arjun Appadurai and Ulf Hannerz,[11] their major contribution lies in their ethnographies, which serve to show how globalization's abstractions shape the lives of very particular people in very particular places.

There have been hundreds of ethnographies written about the effects of globalization on particular groups of people around the world, but there have been remarkably few written about places of global interchange. I am thinking not of international airports and big-city hotels, which, although globalized spaces, are typically full of people who do not interact. Rather, I am thinking of those sites in which people from places across the globe do indeed interact for business and pleasure, sites that embody and exemplify an "intensification of global interconnectedness" on a human-to-human scale.[12] These kinds of ethnographies, depicting sites of global interchange, are very much needed, I think, in that they can show how globalization works on the ground, in the ongoing cross-cultural give-and-take of actual people.

Chungking Mansions is, of course, exactly such a site. Despite the claims of the *Lonely Planet* guidebooks that "there is probably no other place in the world like Chungking Mansions," we should perhaps not think of it as unique.[13] Flushing in New York City, Brixton or Willesden in London, and Roppongi in Tokyo, to mention just a few neighborhoods, offer different and yet parallel depictions of globalization and certainly some of what can be seen in Chungking Mansions can be found in these neighborhoods as well.[14] But Chungking Mansions is not just a center of globalization, but rather globalization of a particular kind: low-end globalization, as I previously mentioned.

I define low-end globalization as the transnational flow of people and goods involving relatively small amounts of capital and informal, sometimes semilegal or illegal, transactions commonly associated with "the developing world." This is the globalization of African traders returning to their homelands clutching a few hundred phones in their luggage, and of South Asian temporary workers bringing home to their families a few hundred dollars of needed money and extraordinary tales from a world their families can only imagine. Multinational corporations, and indeed a great deal of the discussion on the financial pages of the world's newspapers, have only a limited impact upon the consciousness of much of the world's population. Globalization for these people consists, in large part, of the goods, ideas, and media brought in by small traders and illegal workers, such as those living and working in Chungking Mansions.

Marts of low-end globalization can be found in sites across the globe. They can be found in Bangkok, Kolkata, and Nairobi as well as in Paris, London, and New York City. They may also be found in such places as Ciudad del Este, at the confluence of Argentina, Brazil, and Paraguay,[15] and, geographically closer to Chungking Mansions, in the Yuexiu and Sanyuanli districts of Guangzhou, in southern China, and in such Chinese cities as Yiwu. In the course of this research, my research assistants and I have journeyed to a number of these sites for days or weeks to talk to traders and merchants. We traveled to Guangzhou, Kolkata, Dubai, Nairobi, Mombasa, Dar es Salaam, Kampala, and Lagos, tracing out through multisited ethnography the webs of low-end globalization linking Chungking Mansions to the developing world across Asia and Africa.

Ethnographers in recent years have emphasized that ethnographies based in a single site may be increasingly insufficient to enable full anthropological understanding of the world; multisited ethnography is necessary in order to understand the world's interlinkages.[16] Although we have been limited by inevitable insufficiencies of time and money, we have tried, using Chungking Mansions as a base, to trace out its linkages across the globe. A global ethnography could have been written from within Chungking Mansions alone; however, our travels enriched our understanding of Chungking Mansions, in revealing how the transactions and interactions within the building are apparent in nodes across the developing world to which they are linked in complex and multilayered ways. Chungking Mansions' linkages extend throughout the world, just as the world as a whole is in Chungking Mansions.

Chungking Mansions offers a particularly concentrated milieu in which to observe all the world in its transactions and interactions. It may well be that in the vast diversity of people in such a small place and in the multiplicity of intercultural activities they engage in—from business dealings to philosophical conversations over chapattis to sex with the array of multicultural professionals in this line of work—there is indeed no place in the world quite like Chungking Mansions, although it no doubt has its parallels. What Chungking Mansions offers is a very concentrated picture of low-end globalization in a very small place. We need to understand the building and its people because the globalization at Chungking Mansions is, in essence, the globalization experienced by the majority of the world's people. What is really going on in Chungking Mansions? How do so many people from so many different societies get along there? How do these people make their globalized livelihoods? Where do they go and what do they do? What are their global routes, techniques, and practices? And how do they understand their transnational lives? This book is devoted to exploring these questions.

The Building

Chungking Mansions is unusual in that rather than being a global neighborhood, it is a single global building. Anthropologists have only rarely studied buildings. Gelberto Velho depicts a building in Copacabana in Rio de Janeiro and the efforts of its white-collar residents to escape stigmatization; Laura Ring explores how "everyday peace" is maintained between families living in an apartment building in Karachi, Pakistan; and Theodore Bestor depicts a building in some respects parallel to Chungking Mansions, the Tsukiji Fish Market in Tokyo, Japan, in all its global linkages.[17] Despite these notable exceptions, anthropologists have generally neglected buildings, simply in that it is unusual for a single building to be analytically noteworthy. Like the buildings mentioned above, Chungking Mansions is an exception.

The building has a first and second floor—or ground floor and first floor in the British locution generally used in Hong Kong (I will use this British locution from here on out)—of 280 by 190 feet, which are retail and wholesale shopping areas. On the second floor of Chungking Mansions is a shopping mall consisting of various boutiques called "Chungking Express" that is physically part of the building but in all other senses a world apart. Shoppers enter it via an escalator from the crowded sidewalks of Nathan Road; it is linked to the rest of Chungking Mansions only through always-locked back doors. An upscale basement mall opened in 2009 is similarly physically part of and yet closed off from Chungking Mansions. Then, from the third floor up, there are three blocks rising up to the seventeenth floor, reachable

by staircases (such as the one depicted above) but most commonly by cramped elevators rising from the ground floor.*

Each of these high-rise blocks has several light wells, open holes of varying dimensions but typically seven by fifteen feet, descending from the seventeenth floor on down to the third floor. These light wells are no doubt a good idea in theory, bringing outside air and ventilation to cramped inner-building apartments; however, the experience of looking down these shafts, descending into black, trash-strewn holes, is extraordinary. As a writer told me, with only a bit of hyperbole, "That's like staring into hell. It's like the repressed consciousness of Chungking Mansions!" I lost a shirt in 1983, when I first stayed in Chungking Mansions as a tourist; my shirt fell from a laundry pole into the depths of one of these air shafts. I've sometimes wondered if it is still there today, although I haven't had the stomach to check (I have

*It is commonly thought that Chungking Mansions has five blocks: A, B, C, D, and E. But B and C blocks are part of the same high-rise tower, as are D and E blocks. There are, in fact, only three blocks. A Block is more open architecturally than B-C and D-E blocks, with the halls twice as spacious. Accordingly, it is busiest and has the most guesthouses. There are five separate elevators, A, B, C, D, and E, serving these three blocks.

seen cleaning crews cleaning the bottoms of these shafts, so perhaps my shirt is long gone).

Chungking Mansions is often mentioned in tandem with Mirador Mansions, a building one block north of Chungking Mansions that also has a significant number of South Asian residents and guesthouses for tourists, at slightly more expensive rates. Mirador Mansions is far less bustling with people than Chungking Mansions and caters more to low-budget European and mainland Chinese tourists than to developing-world businesspeople, so I do not much discuss the building in these pages. But it is worth noting the different forms of architecture of the two buildings.

Chungking Mansions was built using a fairly typical vernacular design of Hong Kong in the 1960s, utilizing a two-level plinth and tower blocks rising above it. A recent architectural survey of Chungking Mansions shows that its basic design was paralleled in a number of other Hong Kong buildings constructed in that era.[18] However, Chungking Mansions' architectural particularity becomes clear when it is compared to Mirador Mansions, which was built around the same time. Mirador Mansions follows the same general concept as Chungking Mansions but with a central open space at its third floor—subsequent floors, up to its top floor, are ringed around this space. This means that different guesthouses and other businesses on the same floor can easily be reached, once one is on that floor, since they have a common, open environment. This is not true of Chungking Mansions, where the three blocks and five separate elevators each link to their own separate worlds that cannot be reached except by returning to the ground floor.

Chungking Mansions is often described as a maze or a labyrinth, and its architecture explains why. "You can't get there from here" is a statement that largely applies to Chungking Mansions' different blocks vis-à-vis one another. One can indeed melt away and vanish in Chungking Mansions. I know a number of guesthouse workers whom I have never seen except in the tiny area of their own guesthouse and its environs—they may rarely come downstairs and cannot be reached, if they are on an upper floor, except through what might be a five- or ten-minute wait for an elevator. Ambulance crews, firemen, and police also must wait, with, inevitably, a significant effect on the building's security.

When one goes in the main entrance to Chungking Mansions, on Nathan Road, one first passes eight or so money-changing stalls of varying size and reputation. Some of the stalls are reputed to offer the worst rates in Hong Kong despite their misleading exchange-rate postings, while others offer some of the best rates, with Cathay Pacific flight attendants, among many others, venturing into Chungking Mansions to change money at such

places. Many money-changing stalls, as well as some other Chungking Mansions establishments, now have a major part of their business in remittances, sent by traders from Africa and elsewhere through Chungking Mansions and then into mainland China and back—business that is quite lucrative.

After this promenade of currency stalls, one encounters the information post, where guards wait, largely to show lost or confused Hong Kong Chinese the route to where they want to go. The guards have a good reputation in Chungking Mansions for being reasonable, but many speak limited English, and few of the international parade of people in Chungking Mansions speak Cantonese, so the guards are of limited help to them. At this point a corridor filled with shops branches to the left and right; perpendicular to this corridor are four additional corridors, also filled with shops and people. In the middle two of these corridors are the five elevator blocks, A, B, C, D, and E spaced at intervals, which during much of the day and evening may have lines of a half dozen or a dozen people, particularly block A, where the largest number of guesthouses are found. These elevators can carry no more than seven or eight people, or fewer if the elevator is also carrying some of the goods and supplies that must constantly be transported to and from higher floors. When the alarm signifying overcrowding sounds, the last passenger must exit, but by wiggling and changing the position of one's feet, the alarm may be silenced—a skill that everyone staying in Chunking Mansions for long learns, to avoid having to wait for the elevator to ascend or descend the heights and return.

The 140 or so shops on the ground floor offer a dizzying array of merchandise. To give a 2009 portrait, there are around a dozen phone card stalls featuring bargains for calling Nigeria or Tanzania or Pakistan, and there

are five Internet cafés. There are twelve restaurants and snack bars, with names like Punjab Fast Food and Lahore Fast Food, mostly tiny places with a few tables and stools and basic South Asian food at rock-bottom prices. However, there are also two glass-enclosed restaurants seeking to be more deluxe. There have been occasional attempts at upgrading the food offerings on the ground floor. A 24-hour sports bar occupied by bemused African customers wondering just why they were watching cricket at 2 a.m. folded quickly, but as of 2009 several Turkish-Pakistani restaurants have become quite popular among African traders who cannot stomach the spiciness of South Asian food.

There are some fifteen mobile phone stores and thirty clothing stores, some selling retail hip-hop clothes but most selling wholesale Western or African-styled clothing as well as shoes. There are fifteen watch stores, largely wholesale; ten or so retail and wholesale electronics stores; and three South Asian video outlets. There is a souvenir shop selling Buddha figurines and Swiss Army knives and a news emporium in a corridor extending out front that sells pornography as well as a few high-end books for those with a sudden craving for literature. There are several packing and shipping stores, a dozen stands selling canned soft drinks and juice as well as South Asian sweets, and eight grocery stores mostly specializing in South Asian food; some also do a brisk business in whiskey. Stores often have a very rapid turnover, but sometimes have astonishing longevity. I know of four stores whose owners have been running them since the 1970s.

The first floor of Chungking Mansions, with some 120 shops, differs from the ground floor in the massive proliferation of mobile phone stores. There are other stores too—a number of money changers, travel agents, and sari emporiums, as well as Internet cafés, barber shops, a half dozen restaurants, including Chungking Mansions' lone Chinese place, and an Islamic bookstore. But the large majority of stores, some eighty in all, are wholesale phone stalls, selling a wide variety of phones—returned, used, refurbished, or copied—to developing-world buyers, primarily from Africa. The first floor is quieter than the ground floor, but it is where most of the more consequential deals, the purchases of thousands of phones, are made.

This trade in mobile phones is quite new, dating from the late 1990s. Indeed, stores on the first two floors of Chungking Mansions have been significantly changing even during the three years of my fieldwork. Whereas in September 2006, there were forty-seven stores on the first two floors dealing primarily in cloth and garments, by April 2009, there were just thirty-three. In September 2006, there were seventy-nine mobile phone stores, but by April 2009, there were ninety-eight. This may reflect the herd mentality of shopkeepers, but even more it reflects the desires of consumers in sub-Saharan Africa, for whom the mobile phone, more than watches or jewelry or clothing, has come to be seen as the lifeline to modernity.[19]

As noted earlier, it is amazing how much can be obtained in Chungking Mansions, from lodging to a haircut to *halal* barbeque, to whiskey of all price ranges, to sex, to computer repairs, to TV remotes, to spy cameras installed in pens and glasses, to stationery, to groceries, to laundry service, to medicines, to legal advice for asylum seekers, to spiritual sustenance for Christians and Muslims. As one well-read informant explained, "There is a self-sufficient ecosystem in Chungking Mansions." One might never leave the building for weeks or months on end, since virtually all that one might need is in the building itself.

Within this ecosystem, there is a very distinct ethnic division of labor. Many of the stores in Chungking Mansions are owned by mainland Chinese who came to Hong Kong over the past forty years. These owners now come to Chungking Mansions infrequently, leaving management of their stores to South Asians or, of late, to a new wave of mainland Chinese migrants. Despite the fact that many of the faces one sees in Chungking Mansions are African, there are very few Africans working behind the counters of any stores. This is because few Africans have legal residency in Hong Kong. Many South Asians either have had such residency for generations, or obtained such residency in the years before 1997 and the end of British colonial rule. Since then, other South Asians have obtained Hong Kong residency as close relatives of these people. While many of the South Asians working in Chungking Mansions are either admitted as tourists or are asylum seekers, they can all work with a degree of safety in numbers against the potential incursions of the immigration police because many other South Asians are entirely legal. Africans, on the other hand, are instantly visible; thus very few ground-floor or first-floor employers hire them unless they are among the few who legally live in Hong Kong. There are innumerable exceptions, but at its simplest, the ethnic picture of Chungking Mansions' first two floors is this: Hong Kong-based Chinese owners, South Asian managers and clerks, and customers from Africa and the world over.

It is surprising to me how little a sense of overall community exists in the first two floors of Chungking Mansions, its open shopping area. Although news of pivotal events rapidly spreads ("I hear there was a robbery on C block this afternoon."), few shopkeepers have a full sense of the building as a whole. Each ethnic group may to some extent keep to itself, with, for example, Punjabis knowing other Punjabis but knowing almost nothing about the Chinese man whose shop lies just thirty feet away or the Filipina who runs the store around the corner. There are exceptions, of course. More gregarious shopkeepers may know a great deal of what is going on around the building, but many don't. Especially in those stores encased in glass walls, the proprietor may be entirely shielded. I know of one Chinese shopkeeper on the ground floor who rails against asylum seekers and Africans, but in his enclosed retail shop, he never encounters them. I know several other Chinese shopkeepers who say they have never eaten South Asian food. South Asians and Africans are more likely to have had a multitude of cross-cultural interactions, but here too some may know little of the world of Chungking Mansions as a whole. Most shopkeepers are largely confined to the area around their shop of maybe no more than thirty feet square; this is the world of Chungking Mansions that they intimately comprehend.

Each of these small worlds has its own set of strategies and stories. To relate just a few, there is the Hong Kong Chinese owner of a grocery store that used to make much of its profits selling particularly large bottles of whiskey to sailors docked at the nearby Ocean Terminal, who were allowed to carry just one bottle back with them to their ships. Because that trade diminished, a few years ago he converted much of his store to racks of shoes to be sold wholesale to African traders, so now his stock in trade is fresh groceries, whiskey, and shoes. There is the Filipina in her fifties married to an older Pakistani man who watches over her customers like a mother. During the week she serves South Asian food, but mostly tea, particularly to the Somali asylum seekers who make her shop their public square, but on Sundays she switches to Filipino fare for the many Filipina maids enjoying their day off from work.

There are the two aging Hong Kong brothers running an electronics store selling cheap goods but not knock-offs or copies, unlike many of the stores around them, which they cannot bring themselves to do. They bemoan the poor state of their business and lament the ever-dwindling number of Hong Kong Chinese shopkeepers: "There are just a few of us left now." And there is the Punjabi owner of a food stall who sunk all his savings into a new enclosed restaurant and watched disconsolately as no customers came. "You are a professor. Why can't you bring the cameras and newspapers to take pictures of my restaurant?" he asked me. Fortunately customers eventually began trickling in without my help. These are just a few of the hundreds of stories I've heard over the years about Chungking Mansions' businesses.

Let us now turn to upper floors. The dominant business of all the blocks in Chungking Mansions are guesthouses, small hotels of six to twelve rooms each (with a number of larger places as well), of which there are about ninety in Chungking Mansions. There are well over a thousand beds available for guests in the building on any given night. All these rooms are amazingly small, although this varies with the price. Rooms typically consist of no more than a bed and, in a separate enclosure, a toilet with a shower nozzle directly over it. The larger rooms may have a nightstand of some sort or two twin beds. Most rooms have a mounted television and an air conditioner, and many have a telephone. The majority of the guest rooms are tiled, making them look like bathrooms but also keeping potential vermin at bay. Cheaper rooms that have not been tiled may be bedeviled with the cockroaches living within Chungking Mansions' walls, but I have yet to see a cockroach in one of the tiled rooms.

Over the years, I have found these rooms to be quite comfortable in their womb-like enclosure, with the single problem being that because many rooms do not have windows, or have only windows facing into the perpetual-night

light wells, the sleeper never knows whether it is night or day. The danger of fire always has led me to keep a flashlight close to my bed, but I have never had to use it, nor have I ever had to rouse to the insistent knocks of immigration police checking my status—I've heard much about this but have never experienced it myself.

Television is the staple of most guesthouse rooms and is distinctly different from that in the rest of Hong Kong. Television in Chungking Mansions consists of sixteen channels, including separate channels from India, Pakistan, and Nepal; the BBC; the French channel TV5MONDE, watched by many Africans; and a number of Hong Kong and mainland Chinese stations. These channels have a significant effect on life in Chunking Mansions, with each nationality more or less immersed in life on its own particular screen. Next door in Holiday Inn, one may watch CNN and HBO, but only in Chungking Mansions are the channels of South Asia so readily available, with many guesthouse managers and shopkeepers constantly attuned to goings-on in their home countries. In each guesthouse room, one can get an idea of the nationality of the previous occupant simply by noting which channel the TV has been turned to.

Guesthouses generally do not practice racial discrimination but do have different kinds of customers as their targets. There are some guesthouses that have been elaborately renovated, in search of the tourist and upscale-businessperson market; their rooms run from HK$180 to HK$300 or more per single room (but are more expensive in April and October, the peak seasons because of trade fairs in Hong Kong and Guangzhou). Although cramped, these rooms are usually clean and well taken care of, sometimes, for really deluxe rooms, bearing amenities such as pictures on the wall, flat-screen TVs, and refrigerators. Some guesthouses have bought nearby private flats as well and converted them to informal guesthouses to house the overflow from their main, legal guesthouse. Some of these guesthouses target mainland Chinese as customers, the newly emergent tourist market increasingly coming to Chungking Mansions. There are also a number of guesthouses that primarily target Western travelers, including one dirt-cheap place that is the favorite of backpackers, as if in a thirty-year time warp (a few of its guests have stayed there for decades). In 2008, I was startled to find that for the first time, a few guesthouses had started accepting credit cards, in conjunction with their increased presence on the Internet—the websites of some of these guesthouses downplay their presence in Chungking Mansions, not even mentioning the building.

There are other guesthouses that target more cost-conscious business-people. Many of these have not been renovated in years and often feature forty-kilogram scales on their premises, for traders to weigh their bags against their airlines' weight limits: small entrepreneurs who buy mobile phones or clothing must worry greatly about not exceeding the weight limit, and the scales are there for their benefit. Single rooms with attached toilet at these guesthouses generally cost from HK$100 to HK$150; many traders stay two or three people per room.

I have stayed in many of these places, and they are generally serviceable, if basic; only twice have I been so discouraged that I departed before morning. Once I asked the proprietor of a guesthouse for a pair of flip-flops to use in my bathroom, since the shower and toilet share the same small space and guesthouses generally provide them, and he took the pair off his own feet and gave them to me. Very often in these lower-end guesthouses, the clerk sleeps on the floor next to the front door and may be tripped over by any guest departing early or coming back late.

There are guesthouses that target long-term stayers and are still cheaper and dingier. Some of these are legal and marked, but more are unmarked and can't easily be discovered. In one such place I know of, a very small room costs HK$2,000 per month. Its renters usually seek one or two additional occupants for the room, to reduce expenses. The apartment as a whole has six rooms and fifteen residents, ever shifting month by month as their visas expire or their money runs out—or, more rarely, they make a business deal that enables them to move to better quarters.

There are numerous other businesses aside from guesthouses in these blocks, including travel agents, often specializing in visas to China that can be obtained in just a few hours; clothes wholesalers; and a number of gem merchants, especially those dealing in opals. There are also several hundred private residences, although how many are de facto guesthouses is an open question. There are also several ministries and charitable nongovernmental organizations (NGOs) serving asylum seekers or heroin addicts.

In the upper floors of Chungking Mansions, the most well-known businesses are the twelve or so legal restaurants, serving South Asian food, and several more unlicensed places, mostly serving various types of African food. The best-known and busiest restaurants are those with touts out in front of Chungking Mansions grabbing customers. These restaurants are the only places in Chungking Mansions that actually appear to be in Hong Kong, often with Cantonese-speaking waiters and with the typical volume of Cantonese speakers enjoying themselves as in restaurants throughout Hong Kong. They are the only businesses in Chungking Mansions that manage to bring many Hong Kong people to their doors. The other less well-known restaurants cater to almost no Hong Kong people but to their own nationals instead, whether Bangladeshi, south Indian, Pakistani, Nepali, or African. These last restaurants serve various kinds of African cuisine and are often owned by the Hong Kong wives of Africans. They often have video monitors at their entrance in case immigration police seek to enter to search for over-stayers. It is ironic that despite the large numbers of African businesspeople in Chungking Mansions making the building prosperous, most of the res-taurants in Chungking Mansions with food that Africans find palatable are unlicensed and thus illegal.

Turning to the building's immediate surroundings, Chungking Mansions, at its ground-floor level, is surrounded by concrete walkways, inhabited by a few dozen heroin addicts living in shacks made of cardboard. There are also a few stores off these walkways: several South Asian grocery stores, a mobile phone repair place, and most well-known, a stall serving what African drink-ers call "tears of the lion," Indian bottled whiskey poured into Styrofoam cups for HK$5 (US 65¢) a shot. African and South Asian businesspeople and passersby congregate here after hours, often including some of the more down-and-out. This is the only place in Chungking Mansions where I have been threatened; it is also the only place in Chungking Mansions where I have known of someone to simply drop dead. At the same time, it is prob-ably the most sociable spot in all of Chungking Mansions, where conversa-tion with friendly strangers is pretty much the norm—this is Chungking Mansions' neighborhood tavern.

Right next to this stall is a narrow walkway leading away from Chung-king Mansions. This is the major passageway for goods being taken by hand trolley to a back street where numerous vans manned by South Asians wait to transport customers and their goods to the airport. This back street leads into a fashionable street of bars a world away from Chungking Mansions. It also leads, in a different direction, to the entrance to an all-but-secret park, Signal Hill Garden, ascending up a high hill to a signal tower built in 1907, a brick structure redolent of British colonialism.[20] Little more than a hundred yards from Chungking Mansions, via a narrow back passageway, one can be on tree-shrouded sidewalks in the thick of an empty forest.

Unlike the back of Chungking Mansions, Nathan Road, in the front of the building, is at all hours full of people. The hundred or so feet surround-ing Chungking Mansions' front entrance represent a concentrated swirl of culture shock: Africans and Indian Muslims cheek by jowl with fashionable Hong Kong patrons of nearby bars, boutiques, and restaurants. Late on any given night, there may be twenty Africans seated on the railing dividing the sidewalk from Nathan Road and twenty South Asians seated on the steps of stores that have closed early, as well as a few Hong Kong Chinese guesthouse proprietors seeking customers. Between them pass Hong Kong Chinese girls in short skirts clutching their boyfriends' arms and Europeans having drunk their fill and now wondering where on earth they are.

Passing by Chungking Mansions at 11 p.m. on Saturday night is, for these Hong Kong people, a matter of running a gauntlet of foreign eyes, but the incomprehension is mutual. I have seen a young African man tell a young Hong Kong woman to whom he had never before spoken that he loved her, whereupon she fled down the street in terror, and I have heard young Indian Muslims fulminate against the immorality they behold—"Those girls are wearing almost nothing. And if you ask them for their phone number, they'll maybe give it to you. I would hate for my family to see this!"—but they keep on looking. Certainly the fears of Chungking Mansions held by many in Hong Kong stem in part from these late-night mutually uncomprehending gazes.

Around the corner from this scene is Mody Road, the site of a 7-Eleven that is a rendezvous point for African businesspeople exchanging tips of their trade: as one African trader told me in 2007, "This is where we all come to meet one another. This is where we Africans come to help each other out with business in a foreign place. This is our bar and our office." Mirador Mansions is just to the north of this 7-Eleven, on the same block, and the Kowloon Mosque, where many of Chungking Mansions' Muslims worship, is farther north, across the street. The nearest McDonald's is immediately west of Chungking Mansions, as is the nearest supermarket, both often frequented by businesspeople who stay in Chungking Mansions. This, along with the well-known touristic icons mentioned in the prelude, is the environment of Chungking Mansions. But the real environment of Chungking Mansions is the entire world.

History

The history of Chungking Mansions has never been written and, except for certain crucial facts, is a matter of reconstructing oral history. It was built in 1961 and was, by many accounts, a high-class building in its initial years. As a scholar of Hong Kong real estate told me, "Chungking Mansions was famous from day one in Tsim Sha Tsui. It was high-class in the 1960s because it was so tall—that area didn't have tall buildings then, and Chungking Mansions definitely stood out." In its early years, its lower floors contained a shopping mall with escalators and a nightclub, along with a number of high-end jewelry shops. Several local Hong Kong celebrities apparently lived in the building, it is said, as well as British Army officers.[21]

However, others I have spoken with dispute Chungking Mansions' high-class origins. A British man who lived in Chungking Mansions from 1962 to 1964 said, "It didn't seem high-class at all. . . . It had a seedy atmosphere. It was built cheap." A well-known Hong Kong Chinese writer who lived near Chungking Mansions in her childhood in the mid-1960s succinctly described it to me as being, at that time, "a dump." One reason for the apparently rapid disintegration of Chungking Mansions was probably its initially shoddy construction—hardly surprising, since Hong Kong itself was still an impoverished society in the early 1960s.[22] A second reason was the building's architecture; as we have seen, it seems almost to have been designed to become a rabbit warren.

From the start, there was a significant South Asian presence in Chungking Mansions. The British man quoted above said, "When we were [living in Chungking Mansions], most stores were Chinese. But there were quite a few Indian shops. . . . I would say that 20 percent of the shops were run by Indians, but they seemed to be present, more than the silent Chinese in the background." South Asians had been a presence in Tsim Sha Tsui from the mid-nineteenth century on, with Indians employed by the colonial government as policeman and soldiers.[23] The Kowloon Mosque was built in the late nineteenth century in the neighborhood where Chungking Mansions came to be built and was rebuilt in 1964 at a new site across Nathan Road, just two blocks north of Chungking Mansions. This no doubt had a significant effect in contributing to the Muslim presence in Chungking Mansions.

By the late 1960s, the Vietnam War came to have an impact on Chungking Mansions: in effect it transformed the neighborhood of Tsim Sha Tsui into a red-light district for American military personnel. A policeman working near Chungking Mansions in this era described to me how American serviceman would stand outside the building to meet sex workers; the writer Xuxi also described Chungking Mansions in this era in her novel *Chinese Walls*, whose nine-year-old protagonist describes at length her fascination for a sex worker soliciting American sailors in "Chung King Mansions' dingy cavernous mouth."[24] By 1969, backpackers and hippies had also begun to appear. An American described to me how by 1969,

It was already a flophouse, for Europeans, Americans, Australians, mostly students; there were a lot of hippies, some druggies. . . . The thing I remember most is the curry joints, Indian restaurants in private apartments. . . . Chungking Mansions was a little dodgy, a little worrying then—my concern was never assault or anything; it was fire. There were many locked exits, and the place was like a labyrinth.

Indeed, by the late 1960s, fires were already a regular occurrence in Chungking Mansions; as the policeman told me, "Fire trucks had some trouble getting in there, since fire exits were all blocked."

In the 1970s Chungking Mansions emerged as a backpacker haven. Many of the Hong Kong Chinese families who had originally lived in Chungking Mansions moved elsewhere, often leaving day-to-day management of their property to Shanghainese and other mainlanders who had newly emigrated to Hong Kong, as well as to South Asians. These mainlanders increasingly began buying into Chungking Mansions, since prices there had already become cheaper as compared to elsewhere in Hong Kong. In this period, residential flats in Chungking Mansions increasingly were turned into guesthouses for travelers, since so much profit could be made.

The role of the newly ascendant *Lonely Planet* guides was essential in this process. Tony Wheeler's *Southeast Asia on a Shoestring* had a pivotal role in bringing Chungking Mansions to the attention of many young Western travelers. It was first published in 1975, and its 1981 edition states that "there's a magic word for cheap accommodations in Hong Kong—*Chungking Mansions.*"[25] The ongoing problem this created for Chungking Mansions was the overburdening of its electrical system, which was designed around 1960, a time with few air conditioners or TVs. Whenever a private apartment was converted into a guesthouse, each room would require its own lights and air conditioner and perhaps a television, using up a magnitude more of power; this became increasingly dangerous over the years.

I myself, as a young traveler, stayed for a week in Chungking Mansions in late 1983, finding myself among a large throng of Europeans and Japanese bedding in dormitories and endlessly trading tips on what to see in Delhi, where to go in Thailand, and how to get a visa to Burma. I was amazed at the tininess of the single room in which I stayed, the randiness of my fellow travelers ("You're the first man I've ever met who admits that he's married," a young British woman squawked at me—I was traveling alone), and the wonderful noisiness of the birds of Tsim Sha Tsui at dawn, something also true in 2009. An Australian who traveled in the mid-1980s told me twenty years later of the "gold run" that existed in Chungking Mansions at that time, with notices posted on guesthouses' walls seeking recruits. This involved travelers receiving gold in Hong Kong and taking it into Nepal, where owning gold was illegal, by hiding it in their rectums. In late 1985, the Nepalese police corralled a group of young travelers and made them squat and jump until the heavy tubes of gold came out; some apparently received substantial prison terms. The "gold run" nonetheless continued, I have been told by old-time travelers.[26]

Fires too continued. Most notably, in February 1988 a fire broke out on the eleventh floor of Chungking Mansions; a Danish traveler died as he attempted to escape by diving out of the building on a mattress, and nine others were injured.* Fires had happened before with considerable frequency, but in this case, the incident attracted worldwide media attention. Following this fire, there were numerous calls for Chungking Mansions to be more tightly regulated. Newspaper headlines from the era read, "High-Rise Menace Needs Urgent Action by Govt," "Chungking 'to Remain a Firetrap,'" and "Facelift Fails to Improve Fire Safety at Chungking."[27] In July 1993, the electrical power system, after years of warnings, became critically overloaded, and an explosion and blackout resulted. Chungking Mansions was without electricity and water for seven days.[28] Eventually public outcry in Hong Kong led to stringent new requirements for guesthouse licensing—by 1994, sixty-one guesthouses had been closed down in the building, although new ones soon enough emerged to take their places.[29]

Through the 1980s and 1990s, it is remarkable that there was little penetration of Chungking Mansions by Chinese triad gangs, which apparently controlled much of the surrounding neighborhood in Tsim Sha Tsui. There was apparently a triad plot to blow up a nightclub in Chungking Mansions in 1994 that was foiled by police (a nightclub that was in the basement, I've heard, physically within Chungking Mansions but inaccessible from inside the building), but this is the only mention I have been able to find of triads, and none of my informants mentioned the presence of Chinese gangs.[30] Pakistani gangs filled the void—harassing Hindu shopkeepers after the destruction of the Babri Mosque in northern India by Hindu extremists and extorting protection money from South Asian businesses.[31] This apparently ended in the early 2000s, when a prominent gang leader was deported. By all accounts, there has been no organized gang presence in Chungking Mansions in recent years. As one Pakistani shopkeeper told me, "Why should anyone extort money? They can make money much more easily by selling mobile phones!"

In 1997, a hundred or more Nepalese who were living on the roof of

---

*There are several reports on the Internet claiming that eleven people were killed in this fire; these are erroneous.

CHECK IN RECEIPT
1254 Southwestern University Bookstore
04/29/2024 02:53:30 PM
12540000002410353210EJ

ITEM	QTY	FEE
GHETTO AT THE CENTER OF THE WORLD		
9780226510200	[SURPLUS]	
CHECKED IN	1	0.00

	QTY	TOTAL
TOTAL:	1	0.00

Patron Name: JOSHUA MACON
Patron ID: 15049504

Associate: 140877
Transaction Date: 04/29/2024

CUSTOMER COPY

ITEM	QTY	FEE
GHETTO AT THE CENTER OF THE WORLD	1	0.00
9780226510200 [SURPLUS]		
CHECKED IN		

	QTY	TOTAL
TOTAL:	1	0.00
		0.00

Patron Name: JOSHUA MACON
Patron ID: 15049504

Associate: 140877
Transaction Date: 0

Chungking Mansions were evicted, I have been told by Chungking Mansions security staff who recall the event. These Nepalese were the relatives—most often sons—of Gurkhas who had been employed by the colonial government. Most returned to Nepal after the handover of Hong Kong to China, but some remained, living in tents and connecting electric appliances to Chungking Mansions' power lines. The police would not help because the roof was private premises and the Nepalese there had not committed any crimes, so the building management itself and its private guards forced the Nepalese from the roof, in a confrontation that was apparently never reported in the mass media. Subsequently, many Nepalese left the area, but a few stayed in Chungking Mansions' back alley, where they remain today.

Throughout the 1990s, mass media reported on police raids, in which dozens or a hundred or more people from Bangladesh, India, Pakistan, and Nigeria, among other countries, were arrested for not having proper documentation.[32] These were only the largest of a multitude of immigration raids that have taken place in the building over the years and that continue today. In the early 2000s, a guesthouse owner, a guesthouse employee, and a sex worker were murdered in separate incidents in Chungking Mansions.[33]

Already by the 1990s, the number of backpackers was dwindling, but numbers of South Asians—Indians, Pakistanis, and Nepalese—continued to increase, aided by the British colonial regime's relatively lenient visa policy. From the late 1990s and early 2000s on, a new population began to be seen at Chungking Mansions: Africans, drawn by the opportunity to buy goods in Hong Kong and China and resell them for a profit in their home countries. The stores on the first two floors of Chungking Mansions increasingly came to reflect the changing needs of African merchants—from watches to African-style clothing to cut-rate mobile phones, the new "must have" commodity for many African consumers. By the early 2000s, the majority of people staying in Chungking Mansions were African. By 2007, more and more mainland Chinese began appearing in Chungking Mansions, drawn in by the extraordinarily cheap guesthouses advertised on websites. Particularly on Chinese holidays, such as National Day, some guesthouses had entirely mainland Chinese customers, who came to Chungking Mansions because it was so close to the waterfront of Tsim Sha Tsui and the fireworks displays above Hong Kong harbor.

Since 2005, the newly reinvigorated Incorporated Owners of Chungking Mansions has made an effort to upgrade the building, installing over two hundred closed-circuit television cameras, providing uniformed guards, and creating more regular garbage collection—leading some reporters to hail a new dawn for Chungking Mansions and others to remain skeptical.[34]

In subsequent years, the dangers of crime and especially of fires do seem to have significantly diminished as compared to previous eras. As the manager of Chungking Mansions' security unit told me, "Ten years ago, there were lots of fires, mostly in restaurants' kitchens. Now all the restaurant owners have smoke sensors. If a fire broke out, the control center would know immediately through the sensors."[35] He said that there are indeed fires, and so the danger remains, but less so than in the past. In addition, Chungking Mansions now has its own extensive fire equipment.

As of this writing, many of Chungking Mansions' decades-old problems remain. Fires continue to take place, albeit small, killing no one, and the Incorporated Owners of Chungking Mansions, which I discuss below, continues to worry about the ongoing construction of guesthouses and the strain this places on the power grid. By most accounts, the building has become salubrious as compared to ten and twenty years ago. Nonetheless, barring a major transformation of the place—which seems unlikely—Chungking Mansions will never become just one more shopping mall, like the hundreds of others throughout Hong Kong, but will retain its unique international character, along with its seediness. This book describes Chungking Mansions and the people in it during a particular period, 2006 to 2009. All of the information I set forth in this book, ranging from the prices of mobile phones to the treatment of asylum seekers, is necessarily bound by the dates of my research and two or ten years from now may no longer be the case. From a broader perspective, whether in twenty years Chungking Mansions will be an icon of worldwide tourism, a second-rate Hong Kong shopping mall, a den of iniquity, or a fading memory, remains to be seen.

Owners' Association

There are 920 holders of ownership shares of Chungking Mansions; as of 2008, 549 involve residences and 371 involve businesses, according to Anthony Wong, manager of the Incorporated Owners of Chungking Mansions. Of these, seventy percent are Chinese, some born in Hong Kong but many more in China. The remaining thirty percent are South Asian.

In April 2007, I attended, along with two of my research assistants, the first annual Incorporated Owners of Chungking Mansions' dinner and beheld table after table of ethnic Chinese—twelve tables in all, of ten to twelve seats each—with only one table of non-Chinese, consisting of one African and a half dozen South Asians, all Cantonese speakers. It seemed remarkable that the most multiethnic, non-Chinese site in Hong Kong should here be monoethnic and Chinese. As the dinner proceeded, the language of its speechmakers was Cantonese, the dominant language of Hong Kong but distinctly not the dominant language of Chungking Mansions, where one is more likely to hear English or Urdu and as likely to hear Mandarin, Hindi, Swahili, French, Bengali, and Punjabi.

At the close of the dinner, the assembled group of owners sang, in accented Cantonese, "Under the Lion Rock," a song that is emblematic of being a Hong Konger. These immigrants from China were singing a song to proclaim their Hong Kong identity, in a Hong Kong that in the 1980s and 1990s, and today to some extent as well, has often looked down upon mainland immigrants[36]; the owners were in effect saying, "Through decades of struggle, we too have become Hong Kongers." The irony is that they have made their livings and lives in the one place in Hong Kong where most Hong Kong people dare not go. They proclaim their Hongkongness through belonging to a building that Africans and Indians may love, but that many Hong Kong people are ashamed of. Ironies thus abound, but this too is Chungking Mansions. Subsequent years' dinners have followed a similar pattern. These dinners in 2008 and 2009 have become more multicultural, with food provided, buffet-style, by various Chungking Mansions' South Asian restaurants, but the pattern remains. I have found myself in long conversations with an array of people (most notably property owners in the building, high-ranking police officers, and local politicians) whom I have never met in Chungking Mansions itself.

These dinners, like so much else that has happened in Chungking Mansions, were the brainchild of the indefatigable Mrs. Lam Wai Lung, the chairperson of the Incorporated Owners of Chungking Mansions and the person shaping Chungking Mansions' recent transformations. Mrs. Lam, a stout, smiling, energetic woman in her late sixties, grew up in Fukien, in mainland China, and first came to Hong Kong in 1979. After working in an electronics factory and various other jobs, in 1988, she set up a guesthouse in Chungking Mansions and has become a Chungking Mansions fixture. She first became chairperson of the Incorporated Owners of Chungking Mansions in 1994. The last British governor of Hong Kong, Chris Patten, came to Chungking Mansions for the opening ceremony of the new electrical supply system at that time. No Chinese chief executive of Hong Kong has visited Chungking Mansions since then. She indignantly says, "Don't they value Chungking Mansions as the most international place in Hong Kong?" In recent years, she has spearheaded the placement of CCTV cameras around the building and the upgrade of the fire-alarm system and cleaning services.

Ms. Lam and I have a complex relationship, partly because of language (my Cantonese is at least as bad as her English) and partly because of our different perspectives on the building. Mrs. Lam is a remarkably effective advocate for Chungking Mansions and has played an indispensable role in making it as successful an environment as it is today. At the same time, because she is focused on formal business activities in the building, she does not see much of what actually goes on—she does not appreciate the vital role that illegal workers play in enabling Chungking Mansions to survive, nor does she understand the complex position of asylum seekers or of drugs in Chungking Mansions, with "white people" rather than Africans making up the dominant market for hashish. I have often told her that if illegal workers vanished from Chungking Mansions, the place would die, becoming like any other Hong Kong shopping mall, since the Africans would all leave, recoiling from the high prices. She in turn tells me that I need to remember the needs of everyone in Chungking Mansions—implying that I am not paying enough attention to the desires of Hong Kong Chinese property owners. She has been unwittingly racist in some of her comments, telling Chinese reporters and travel writers—as I learned from their later phone calls—that South Asian guesthouses are dirty and that guests should stay in Chinese-run guesthouses. She has also been unstintingly generous toward me, blessing my research at every turn and helping me in every possible way.

Many of the business owners in Chungking Mansions have great respect for Mrs. Lam. As one Hong Kong Chinese owner said,

> We really like that woman for being so good at organizing. The elevators used to be old and crowded—they used to stop midfloor—it was awful. Today, the elevators are different: they're still small but new. That's a really big achievement. Even the men's toilet: that's been really upgraded. Now, there are public facilities, like the lights, the elevator, the toilet—these are much, much better—this is good for everyone. Also, the closed-circuit cameras—they make it safer. Getting all the different owners to pay the money for this—that's impressive.

Others, particularly South Asians, have a darker view. In one store owner's words: "The management committee: it's a Chinese mafia, and they control everything. They just get contracts for other Chinese people." Still others accuse her of using her position as chair of the Ownership Committee to expand her own holdings. These views indicate ethnic tension, which is real, especially given language differences. As I have heard from some South Asian owners, "Why should I pay attention to her? She doesn't even speak English!" But much of the tension is that which might be directed at any holder of authority toward which others may be envious. She has indeed done a remarkable job in making Chungking Mansions a more salubrious place in which to live and work, even if she retains a degree of sinocentric ethnocentrism—as the most recent *Lonely Planet* guide to Hong Kong describes her, she has "the political correctness of a Ming emperor."[37]

Business

Despite the lack of a central nervous system in the building—the lack of a full community in most senses of the word[38]—businesses across Chungking Mansions are generally run in a more or less common manner. A vast gap remains between those who own their property and those who rent it. I know South Asian owners and renters better than I know most Chinese, who tend not to be present in Chungking Mansions, so I write using their words. For those who own, property values have been going up in recent years. The South Asian owner of one popular upstairs restaurant told me that when he bought the place some five years earlier, his restaurant was worth HK$1,500,000, but by 2007, it was worth HK$2,500,000. Another spoke of how a 700-square-foot flat he seeks to buy has increased in price from HK$800,000 to HK$1,400,000. He mentioned one of the most prominent South Asian entrepreneurs in Chungking Mansions, whom he asked, "Why are you buying all these properties?" The answer was "Because it's so valuable—it's worth so much." But as another guesthouse manager told me, "To buy needs lots of money. Big money! Four million, five million, one flat. It's better to rent. HK$15,000, HK$20,000, HK$17,000 . . ." In a time of economic downturn, such as that which took place in late 2009, owners tend to be better able to weather out the storm than renters, since their expenses are lower and pockets deeper. Renters facing several consecutive months of sales that do not even meet rental costs may be forced to close up shop. Rents in Chungking Mansions on the ground-floor shops may range from HK$8,000 for a particularly small stall to HK$40,000 or more for a particularly well-located and spacious one, as of 2008.

Some of the owners and proprietors of shops in Chungking Mansions vociferously complain about the more lucrative businesses around them. As a watch shop owner said, "I've seen some people here become rich very quickly. But when I do my honest business here, I don't make much money." Indeed, it is difficult, although not impossible, to profitably run a business in Chungking Mansions without to some extent eliding the law (as is true of small businesses throughout Hong Kong). A number of businesses on the ground and first floors sell, among other types of goods, mainland-China-made cop-

ies of European and Japanese originals, most often of mobile phones but also of computers and other goods. (Shops that naïvely sell new phones, not knowing the market, may go out of business in a matter of weeks, as I've seen.) The buyers of these goods, mostly African entrepreneurs, generally know exactly what they are purchasing, so few complaints ever arise. Some employees hired by these businesses, and by businesses throughout Chungking Mansions, are either temporary workers coming to Hong Kong as tourists or asylum seekers. They can be paid at a fraction of the rate of legal Hong Kong residents (typically at HK$3,000 to HK$3,500 per month rather than HK$5,000 to HK$8,000 per month) and tend to accept this without complaint, since these wages may be very good indeed in the context of their home countries, to which they may be sending earnings home. Some of the upstairs restaurants are unlicensed and have video-camera monitors in part to screen out undesirable prospective diners, and some guesthouses have unlicensed auxiliary guesthouses to handle overflow guests without the bother of official procedures.

These extra-legal business dealings are what make Chungking Mansions possible as a world center of low-end globalization. Only in the context of low-end globalization can we understand how businesses tend to be run in Chungking Mansions. Let me describe the economics of one food stall, from what I have been able to glean. The rent is HK$23,000 per month; the food stall cannot easily afford to hire legal employees with that kind of rent, since an experienced Hong Kong resident cook would cost HK$8,000 to HK$10,000 a month to hire. All of the eight employees of the restaurant entered Hong Kong as tourists, meaning that they must remain in their home country of India 180 days a year and can be jailed in Hong Kong if caught working. The restaurant's prices range from HK$20 to HK$50 for a meal, serving some one hundred customers per day. Accordingly, the restaurant may gross HK$100,000 a month on average. Subtracting from that the employees' salaries, the raw food costs, and the rent, the owner may make HK$20,000 in a bad month, HK$30,000 to HK$40,000 in a good month. These profits dwarf the salaries of the illegal workers, but are hardly exorbitant in the context of Hong Kong small businesses. If the owner were forced to hire legal workers, the food stall would have to double its prices, driving away most of its current customer base, who regularly count out their change to the last hard-earned dollar in paying their bills.

The economics of a guesthouse are broadly similar. An owner told me that she makes about HK$30,000 a month profit on average on a guesthouse of nine rooms. This guesthouse, relatively upscale by Chungking Mansions' standards, charges around HK$200 a room and has 75 percent occupancy on average. It can thus make some HK$1,400 a night, minus expenses. It has a Filipina worker, who often deals with customers as well as doing the laundry and cleaning the rooms, who makes HK$3,500 per month. This place too is based on semilegal or illegal labor*; these guesthouses would significantly raise their prices without such labor. As one owner told me, "Our business couldn't survive if we didn't hire illegal workers!"

There are some businesses that insist on being upscale and entirely legal. I know of one guesthouse owner, a Hong Kong Chinese man, who does all the cleaning and washing himself and is sometimes out at Chungking Mansions' entrance trolling for guests at 1 a.m. Paradoxically, he takes delight in African and South Asian businesspeople who refuse to stay in his guesthouse given its high prices—HK$250 to HK$300 per room. He tells me, in a voice concordant with that of Mrs. Lam, "I want to make Chungking Mansions a place for a higher class of guests!" It remains to be seen how long

---

*Filipina and Indonesian domestic helpers are a Hong Kong fixture, with some 220,000 in Hong Kong, hired primarily by middle-class Hong Kong employers. These helpers are supposed to be working in their employers' homes, but in Chungking Mansions are sometimes left to run guesthouses.

he can survive in Chungking Mansions, or, conversely, how long Chungking
Mansions can survive with many proprietors like him.

This leads to the question of why some businesses succeed and others
fail in Chungking Mansions. There is a huge rate of turnover at Chungking Mansions. This is because with rents as cheap as they are, despite their
significant rise in recent years (continuing up through the economic downturn of 2009, since so many mainland Chinese seek to invest), a company
or individual can enter and, if necessary, exit in a matter of months without an exorbitant loss of capital. Many business owners I spoke with be-
moaned how Africans were no longer steady customers, given the lure of
mainland China. In the words of a guesthouse owner, "They used to stay
for a month but now they stay for just one or two days back and forth
from China, where they've relocated their business." An electronics wholesaler said, "The Africans can get into China easily now, and prices are less,
though the quality isn't good. . . . There's a direct flight from Addis Ababa
into Guangzhou now, and a lot of Africans just take that rather than coming to Hong Kong."

The businesses that succeed (at least up until the downturn of 2009,
guesthouses and restaurants, as well as the majority of mobile phone stalls,
have done quite well, while retail stores of any kind have done comparatively
badly) are those that (1) have a good knowledge of the market and (2) are
flexible enough to change with changing times. This is Business 101, but I
have often been surprised by how many business owners and managers (particularly newly arrived mainland Chinese) don't fully understand the nature
of Chungking Mansions, for example, seeking to sell new top-of-the-line
mobile phones or having no understanding of Chungking Mansions' ethnic
mix. These businesses are often doomed from the start.

Businesses, in response to changing circumstances, have indeed changed
with the times. Upstairs restaurants have managed to survive by reaching
out to a Hong Kong Chinese clientele. Whereas in the early 1990s they had
predominantly British, backpacker, and South Asian customers, by adroitly
changing their focus through advertising, through touts at the entrance to
Chungking Mansions, and by lessening the degree of spiciness of their dishes
to suit a Hong Kong palette, they have succeeded in transforming their customer base. More recently, guesthouses have attracted many new customers
through the Internet, bringing in guests from mainland China and Europe
who may have no idea what Chungking Mansions is but who are attracted
by rooms at cheap prices.

Let me now turn to the accounts of two Hong Kong Chinese in Chung-

king Mansions: a man who grew up in a Chungking Mansions guesthouse and a woman working at a ground-floor restaurant.*

Andy Mok

My family runs a guesthouse in Chungking Mansions. There's lots of money to be made. Before the handover, from a two-bed room you could make HK$400 to HK$500 a night. One flat, ten rooms, occupied every night. In the account books, of course you keep another set of figures. There are a lot of Filipina maids and Thais—they're lesbians or are having a date with

*These names, like those in all informants' accounts in this book, are pseudonyms.

their boyfriends on Saturday or Sunday; you rent them rooms a short time, for two or three hours, and make a lot of money there. That's why a lot of people—Hong Kong Chinese and now Indians—want to open a guesthouse. There's no special skill required; all you have to do is work hard. My mom asked me why I should work so hard earning a master's degree and being a secondary-school teacher—I could make as much money running the guesthouse, she said.

My mother came to Hong Kong from Shanghai in 1982, worked for some relatives in Chungking Mansions at a guesthouse, saved some money, and then opened her own guesthouse in 1985. People in Chungking Mansions businesses always have some connections—we know each other. We're competitors but we also cooperate. When I have too many customers, I send them to you; tomorrow you do the same for me, and so on. When I was a kid, I'd take phone messages for our guests and sometimes get tips because of that. Once an African guy was washing something in the bathroom and making a lot of noise. I asked him what he was doing, and he showed me—he was washing unpolished diamonds! Some traders get rich and don't need to stay in Chungking Mansions, but they do anyway. They want to stay in the same room as before, because they think it brought them good fortune. Also, they stay in Chungking Mansions because they can talk to people there. The information exchange is quite easy.

Hong Kong people are afraid of Chungking Mansions partly because in 1988 there was a serious fire in A block, on the eleventh floor. That was my neighborhood then; as a kid I lived there! There was a tourist from Denmark—because of the smoke, he climbed out a window, fell, and died. Before then, the government hadn't paid any attention to Chungking Mansions and its fire danger. From then on, people began thinking that Chungking Mansions was a dangerous place. After 1988, because the press, especially the international press, began to pay attention, inspections began. Before then, Indians had gotten hurt in fires, but it's as if that didn't matter! Finally, restrictions became stricter; all the guesthouses were regularly inspected for fire dangers—that was new. Now there are fire alarms everywhere.

There are hidden rules. The Chinese and Indian owners will usually never rent a room to a Hong Kong Chinese. Before we give them a room, they have to register. If they have a Hong Kong ID, "Sorry, good-bye." We were worried that the triad societies—Chinese gangsters—would come in and try to take some protection money. When you're local Chinese and walk into Chungking Mansions, you're so obvious! You can never hide yourself! Even the CID, the undercover police, if they walk in we can recognize them immediately, in one second.

The police in Tsim Sha Tsui do not want to touch Chunking Mansions, it seems. If you send a hundred police to Chungking Mansions for a midnight action, they can't find anything. Whenever they come in, the people they want all just run away. The police are just doing a show for the media and the public. There are many regular residents in Chungking Mansions; the police can't knock on every apartment door, because residents would get angry. So they knock on the doors only of those guesthouses with licenses. But illegal guesthouses don't have signs—they can't find those. If the illegal workers stay there, they're safe. They look like ordinary residences, so the police don't tend to enter. The police don't like Chungking Mansions because they don't speak English very well, and the Chungking Mansions' residents often don't speak English very well either. It's very difficult to find an interpreter for all the different languages they'd need, so they don't bother. But all in all, there's little conflict in Chungking Mansions: just make money and keep quiet. The Indians and Pakistanis don't fight—there's no nationalism. Everything is money.

As a guesthouse owner, you're most afraid of people not paying. Guests might pay for one night and then stay a week; you're afraid they'll slip off. We prefer people who stay quietly and pay their money on time—that's all. We refuse people with just one bag, or who are dressed poorly; we don't think they have the money and won't let them stay. Or else we make them pay everything in advance. But if they're white and dressed well, with passports from Europe, then we don't worry. Of course we could say, "Pay in advance." But they may say, "Oh, I don't have Hong Kong dollars now. Could I pay later?" What can you do?

We hate people from Nepal, Pakistan, and Bangladesh, and Africans too, who want to cook. We have our kitchen for our own family, but they want to use it! And people with a lot of friends who come visiting. And fighting between guests. We once had a white guy get drunk and fight a yellow guy— we hate that. We also don't want single women who stay a long time. If she stays a few nights, that's all right. But two weeks, three weeks, it usually means she's a prostitute. If any woman ever brings customers back, "No. You must go." Smoking is OK, but taking drugs? No, they must go. We get people to leave by packing their bags for them. We wouldn't make them pay for the time they hadn't paid for, and we'd send their luggage to another guesthouse, a cheaper place that we'd recommend to them. The other guesthouse would take them because it lacked customers. One American—he was getting social security from the US; this was before e-mail and he was writing long letters home—he gave me some American stamps. But he was taking drugs, and so my mother decided he had to go. We clean the rooms—we can tell, or at least suspect, what he's doing. He had just gotten a divorce and came to Hong Kong to refigure out his life.

People in Hong Kong don't value Chungking Mansions enough. They should—it's an example of globalization! The government should try to protect it. I have some worry about Chungking Mansions twenty or thirty years from now. Can they tear it down? There are so many owners, it's so complicated. The government just hopes there's no crime, no illegal workers, peace and harmony.... Mostly it is peace and harmony! It's a really safe place. Crimes sometimes happen in rooms—there's been cheating and murders in incidents between sex workers and customers—but these are personal matters, not Chungking Mansions per se. The travelers just want to do business; they won't break the laws. They don't want the police involved, that's the last thing they want. And the locals are afraid to come in Chungking Mansions; they can't hide. Local people are so afraid of Africans!

I remember sitting in the lobby of our guesthouse when a Turk and an American and some other people were watching a movie about World War II. The American general in the movie did something stupid, and the Turk and the American began to argue, with the Turk asking why the Americans always wanted to interfere in the Middle East, and the American saying, "No we don't." Eventually they decided, "It's stupid to argue over ideologies. We're people of the world, and we should respect each other." That's the meaning of globalization. There's no difference between you and me. That's the value of Chungking Mansions.

Another personal story, that of a restaurant manager new to Chungking Mansions, was told, in Cantonese, to my research assistant, Maggie Lin.

Amy Leung

I am Hong Kong Chinese; I'm divorced and in my thirties. I manage this restaurant. I'm happy that I can do this job well. I made a bit of money in my earlier job, so I can afford this for a while. But I can't do this for too long, or else I'll be broke!

Some of the staff in this restaurant, Pakistanis, go to pray at the mosque five times a day. They're crazy! Well, not crazy, but very devoted. Their attitude toward work is very different; they don't put work as a top priority. They can be very simple and innocent. Once the cook left the restaurant and went to the mosque without telling me. I was angry. But I gradually learned that this was the way he was.

Before I started working here, I'd been coming to Chungking Mansions to help my Indian friend who owns a mobile phone shop. I started bringing silver jewelry and small accessories from Shenzhen to sell at his shop. Once when we were visiting a restaurant in Chungking Mansions, two Pakistani guys kept looking at us. My Indian friend hated how they tried to pick me up. He explained that the two Pakistanis belong to a low caste, and he didn't want me to spend time with them.* But I was curious and ended up talking to them anyway, to learn about business opportunities in the building. One of them subsequently became my boss. He came to Hong Kong many years ago and earned his first big profit from mobile phones in Chungking Mansions. He then got more ambitious and bought five shops in the building before the economy crashed. He doesn't have much money to support his business now. Because he's in need of help, I manage his restaurant for him. My friends say I'm crazy to be helping out here for free.

My boss acts very tough, trying to be on top of everything; he has to be that way. He has a very good friend to whom he rented out part of his shop. The friend's business was slow and he couldn't afford to pay the rent; my boss took back the shop. Business is business—he wouldn't mix it with friendship. That's why sometimes he feels very lonely, he tells me, often in text messages. When I see those messages, I can no longer be mad at him, at his behavior at work. One time, he looked upset after I talked to a Pakistani boy who works here. He overheard something and thought I wanted to invite the boy back to my apartment to spend the night, although I was only asking him whether he was taking his medicine—I wanted him to rest well. My boss was angry and asked whether I liked the boy and if I did, he'd move the boy to another shop. I told him he was wrong. He doesn't like me giving my phone number to customers. But I think it's OK, I'm just being friendly—I don't go out with my customers. Other than that, even though I don't get paid, I have the freedom to do whatever I want at the restaurant, and I enjoy that.

I've seen so much in here, experiences beyond my imagination. I've had Africans coming to the restaurant to eat without paying. This guy, after finishing his food, told me he didn't have money, so he'd only pay half. He can see the prices on the menu when he orders! He said he'd pay me next time. He never did, but he still came back to the restaurant, joining his friends without ordering any food. I told his friends about it and his friends paid for him. Really, it's just a few dozen dollars. Next time he ate at the restau-

---

*Caste is something that the South Asians in Chungking Mansions mostly insisted was irrelevant. In one Indian man's words, "Most of the Indians here are Muslim, so caste doesn't matter"; he claimed he did not know the caste of most South Asians around him. But these words show that caste does matter, in at least some contexts.

rant, he also tried to leave without paying. He took out a US$100 note, saying he had no Hong Kong dollars. I examined the note; it made him angry, and he grabbed it back. I told him I could treat him if he couldn't afford to pay for the meal, but he'd have to tell me in advance; he couldn't just refuse to pay after the meal. He said, "I don't need you to buy me food, I have enough money to buy the whole restaurant!" Hong Kong is not easy for these traders.

There are men who try to pick me up. They're very direct. Yesterday a man told me "I love you." If you like the tall and muscular type, there are plenty of them here. Maggie [the research assistant], you need to be careful. You're like sugar to these men in Chungking Mansions! They're all interested in you! You know what they want? Many of these people want to marry you to get Hong Kong residency.

During my first month of working here, two girls were caught by Immigration, one from India, the other from Nepal. They have Hong Kong residency but are on the waiting list to getting a working visa. They both have "husbands" who are old Hong Kong men from false marriages, but they also have boyfriends in their home countries. The immigration police came twice. The first time, they only came to see the place and to locate the girls. The second time, they took away the girls and me as well. It should turn out OK since there's no proof that they actually worked for the restaurant.

There's a new Pakistani boy who just started working at the restaurant a few days ago. He told me he has sisters who need to get married, and he has to earn money for their dowries. He came to Hong Kong illegally in a ship's cargo and due to a typhoon went three days without food or water. I'd like to help him if I could by allowing him to work here. Those two girls who got caught by Immigration told me, "Madam, you should open a restaurant and we will work for you." I sometimes think about whether I should do that. I'm very happy to be here; I've learned so much in Chungking Mansions. But at the same time, these stories are heartbreaking.

My Own Involvement

As earlier noted, I began doing research in Chungking Mansions in June 2006. Despite the predominant mythology in Hong Kong of Chungking Mansions as a dark and deviant place, from the very first day I began my research, I found that most people were happy to talk with a passing stranger. However, as my presence there continued week after week, a problem emerged. I told people I met and spoke with that I was an anthropologist, but that wasn't clear or believable to some. While few people that I met were engaged in anything morally depraved, many were violating the law in ways that my questions sometimes exposed. I quickly learned that the best strategy was to freely hand out my name cards giving my academic position to everyone I met. Of course name cards can lie, but my own name cards were never questioned. Soon, the standard form of address with which I was called in Chungking Mansions was "professor." In many ethnographic niches, this would be a disaster, but in Chungking Mansions, it was a godsend. The South Asians and Africans and Chinese viewed me as a highly respectable person, entitled to ask impertinent questions. In one informant's words, "Of course I'm illegal! You're a professor, so you won't tell the police—I know that!" I was lucky that a profession scorned by informants in some realms should be treated with such respect in Chungking Mansions.

I was also fortunate to be white, something that might have been a great disadvantage in other places, but that clearly helped this research. Had I been Chinese, I would have been assumed to have been a government agent. Had I been South Asian, I would have been assumed to have been a potential business competitor, the fate of one hapless American-educated graduate student I met seeking to do research on Chungking Mansions and able to find out very little.

Basically, my research method has been to simply "hang out" in Chungking Mansions. I talk to customers at different food stalls throughout the day and night, walk the corridors, stand at the building's entrance, and wander up and down its different blocks, talking to everyone I meet. I drink tea with South Asian storekeepers in various ground-floor restaurants, or at their business stalls; I drink beer with the African traders in the 7-Eleven around the corner from Chungking Mansions. I also lead weekly discussions of current events with a class of asylum seekers at Christian Action, one of Chungking Mansions' NGOs. Sometimes I, or my research assistants, have engaged in formal recorded interviews with people—the personal accounts appearing throughout this book are the products of such interviews. More often, we talk with people informally and later go to a stairway or a nearby park to record all we can remember of our conversations. We tell the people we speak with that we are doing this, and none mind, provided, in some cases, that we disguise them so that they cannot be recognized. This I have done throughout this book, except when discussing a public figure, and disguise other data as well in order to protect individuals' identities.

I am diabetic, and I test my blood sugar and give myself insulin injections four or so times every day. This has occasionally been comic, as once when, after I surreptitiously (I thought) tested my blood sugar, a line formed of several South Asians and Africans who wanted their blood tested as well. More seriously, I have occasionally suffered insulin reactions whose first symptom is silence and confusion, and whose later symptoms are convulsions. Sometimes late at night in my guesthouse room I have sat for hours puzzling over who and where I am, until I finally realize that I desperately need sugar, and drink the soft drink placed next to my bed for this purpose.

Mostly these insulin reactions have not affected my human relations in Chungking Mansions, but once, spectacularly, they did. In April 2007, I collapsed into convulsions just behind Chungking Mansions and was taken to a hospital by ambulance. This had an effect on my research, because the assumption among my conservative Muslim acquaintances was that I had been drunk. I spent much time showing them my insulin and blood-sugar measuring device, trying to persuade them that I had a medical condition; eventually, they believed me.

Another point of difficulty at Chungking Mansions has concerned issues of gender. Chungking Mansions is a remarkably male-centered place. There are some female African traders of clothing and lately many more female tourists, particularly from mainland China, but up until recently, the general assumption was that young women in the building were sex workers, or in any case were seeking male attention. Many of my former graduate students, as well as reporters from mass media, are female and expressed interest to me in seeing Chungking Mansions, so I often obliged. In Hong Kong or Western countries, the fact that a man might be accompanied by a woman he is not married to might be seen as wholly unremarkable, but among some South Asians and Africans, the assumption was that I must be romantically involved with all of them.

This I learned only to my surprise, but, as in the case of so many other cultural misunderstandings, later kicked myself for my stupidity in not foreseeing. Once, a European journalist came to meet me in Chungking Mansions and despite my earlier warnings was wearing rather too few clothes. I saw her off after two hours and went back to my guesthouse room. Around midnight, there was a loud knock on my door, and a voice shouting "Police! Police!" I opened the door and found seven angry looking Muslim men outside, including one of my acquaintances. When they saw that I was alone, they sheepishly explained that they just wanted to see if my room was suitable for a guest the following day, once I left; in fact, they had been checking up on my morals.

As earlier noted, I hired assistants in the course of my research, ten in all, with five doing very extensive research over many months, and two traveling with traders they had met in Chungking Mansions: Jose Rojas to Nigeria with mobile phone traders and Maggie Lin to Kenya with female clothing traders. I chose these research assistants, all of whom were recent under-graduate or graduate students in anthropology at the Chinese University of Hong Kong, because they seemed cosmopolitan and above all because they wanted to experience Chungking Mansions—generally, they recruited me more than I recruited them. These assistants focused on areas that I my-self neglected, or that were more or less closed to me, from female African clothing traders, to the children of South Asian shopkeepers and their ad-justment to Hong Kong, to the experiences of Cantonese-speaking shop-keepers and guards, to the lives of Nepalese heroin addicts.

These research assistants did extraordinarily good work, reflected throughout this book. However, they occasionally ran into problems, partic-ularly related to gender. Most of my research assistants were female, reflect-ing the demographics of anthropology students, while the vast majority of people in Chungking Mansions are male, and it was sometimes very difficult for my assistants to avoid faulty male assumptions. One, to her shock, was kissed by a Pakistani man who took her out to lunch (an invitation she prob-ably should not have accepted); another, after unfortunately seeking to shake hands with a Pakistani man, was subject to a long string of e-mail messages proclaiming undying love. The warning that Amy Leung, in the preceding interview, offered to my research assistant, Maggie, was no hyperbole.

This is a cultural matter in large part: in some African societies sex seems more openly and forthrightly pursued than in Hong Kong, whereas in con-servative Muslim societies such as Pakistan, the very fact of a woman smil-ing at a man's words, or worse, seeking to shake his hand, may create an as-sumption of romantic interest. My female research assistants were physically safe in Chungking Mansions, but being there was at times an unnerving ex-perience for them. As one research assistant once exclaimed to me in exas-peration, "In Chungking Mansions, is sex all that anyone ever thinks about?" Eventually, I learned to be extremely careful about hiring female research as-sistants because of the potential harassment they might be subject to.

I first began publicly speaking about Chungking Mansions in March 2007 in a lecture at the Hong Kong Museum of History, which led to an ar-ticle in the Asian edition of *Time* magazine.[39] This in turn led to an upsurge of media attention, with press reporters and TV programs calling frequently for requests for interviews and tours of Chungking Mansions. These filled me with ambivalence. On the one hand, after decades of negative media at-tention directed toward Chungking Mansions, this wave of attention was positive, warming the hearts of the Incorporated Owners of Chungking Mansions, which urged me to publicize the building (Mrs. Lam told me that the *Time* magazine article, a brief two paragraphs though it was, marked one of the high points of her life). On the other hand, some of the Hong Kong and Chinese reporters were afraid to talk to the people within Chungking Mansions, preferring to focus on me, the white professor intermediary. I came to intensely dislike talking with such people. A particularly bad moment came when two very unworldly Chinese writers seeking to compile a history of Chungking Mansions, with the eager encouragement of the Owners' Association, asked me to introduce some Chungking Mansions residents to them. One African asylum seeker exploded in fury at what he perceived as my condescending efforts to start a conversation, while the writers cowered in the background: "Fuck you! You should pay us money if you want us to talk." He was right. I shouldn't have been trying to talk with him under these strained and artificial circumstances, and I later apologized to him.

With reporters I could control their access ("No, you can't use the names of any of the people I'm introducing you to; they don't want to be named," or when I was irritated or inconvenienced, "I can't introduce you to anyone; you need to go to Chungking Mansions on your own and talk to people there"), but TV crews were a potential nightmare, since faces could not easily be disguised. Anyone working illegally and seen behind a counter could conceivably be prosecuted. I consented to TV interviews because of the positive publicity it would bring to Chungking Mansions, but the encounter was sometimes traumatic. One particularly bad moment came about when an insensitive Chinese TV announcer was falsely perceived to be an undercover policeman; an African man ran away when he saw him, and real police, by coincidence some thirty yards away, followed suit, but luckily could not catch the man. Fortunately, these events apparently led to no larger repercussions, and none of my informants have been hurt by their coverage, to my knowledge. I generally stopped doing television interviews after the above incident took place, realizing that television, for all its potential positive coverage of Chungking Mansions, was too dangerous, although I have continued to talk to reporters (and some of their articles are excellent).[40]

In all this media coverage, I have assumed that the general public in Hong Kong knows full well that some people work illegally in Chungking Mansions, that copy phones are sold there, and that some people sell drugs and sex — rather than deny these matters, it seemed better to discuss them honestly in the context of a larger positive depiction of Chungking Mansions. Indeed, it is widely perceived now by people in Chungking Mansions that media perceptions of Chungking Mansions have changed for the better over the past few years. However, my worry has always been that some clueless authority would behold this newspaper or television coverage and say, "My

God! There are illegal things going on in Chungking Mansions! Let's close the place down!"

I have to some extent benefited people in Chungking Mansions, I think; my friendship is important to many, as is too my occasional infusions of cash for those without money. Still, my research benefits me more than it benefits them. I have written a book based on their lives that will help me in my career. They have told me their stories and received little or nothing in return, other than my friendship and gratitude and copies of this book. I come to Chungking Mansions on weekends and other free nights, returning at other times to my comfortable apartment on the campus of my university; they, on the other hand live in cramped and often squalid conditions. As an asylum seeker I knew well once said bemusedly to me, "Why couldn't I have lived your life instead of mine?" I couldn't answer and only squirmed.

I hope that my presence in Chungking Mansions and my research and writing of this book will help alleviate this unfairness, by getting people in Hong Kong and in the world at large to more fully appreciate Chungking Mansions and the global lives and stories of the people who pass through the building. But I don't know. Perhaps the law of unintended consequences may lead simply to a rise in property values in the building, whereby the developing world's entrepreneurs gradually leave, and the building gradually becomes like any other Hong Kong shopping mall. The evolution of Chungking Mansions will almost certainly happen due to factors far beyond any influence I might hold. Nonetheless, I remain uneasy—although not so uneasy as to have not written this book.

I seek in this book to celebrate Chungking Mansions in its extraordinary and largely harmonious cultural diversity. It is an amazing place, one that should be lauded in Hong Kong and the world over. At the same time, however, much of what goes on in Chungking Mansions is not fully legal, as we have seen and as I will further portray in the coming chapters. My assumption is that whereas the illegalities in Chungking Mansions are widely known, the wondrousness of the place is not, and that is what, in part, I attempt to convey in this book.

people

In this chapter, I discuss the different groups of people in Chung-king Mansions: traders, largely from Africa; owners, largely from China; managers, often from South Asia; and tourists, from the world over. I consider each of these groups in turn, along with the various other groups, including sex workers and heroin ad-dicts, who frequent the building.

Traders

In chapter 3, I focus on goods and those who trade in them, but let me now briefly outline who these traders are and what they do. For most of the year, traders make up the majority of the people one sees in Chungking Mansions. At their peak—during the trade fairs of October and April in Hong Kong and Guangzhou—they occupy almost every available bed in the building. Most traders at most times of year—except in January and February, the Chinese New Year season during which south China factories are closed—are from sub-Saharan Africa. Over the past decade there has been a massive increase in the num-ber of African traders traveling to south China. They buy goods in Hong Kong or in China and sell them, typically, in their home countries, dealing in a vast range of products: mobile phones and clothing are most prominent, but also watches, electronic goods, computers, TV game consoles, building materials, and used cars and car parts, among innumerable other products. A small minority trade in the other direction, bringing gemstones from their homes to Hong Kong and China to sell. Hong Kong prices are more expensive, but goods obtained in Hong Kong, especially electronic goods and mobile phones, are often perceived to be more reliable—although this has been changing bit by bit, as Chinese goods and business practices become better and more traders go to China. Almost all the goods sold in Chungking Mansions—with the exception of many of the mobile phones— are made in China, even if their labels may sometimes indicate they were made elsewhere.

These traders sometimes come to Hong Kong on business visas obtained in their home countries—necessary for those countries that have been denied visa-free access to Hong Kong—but more often they are admitted at the airport in Hong Kong. They may be admitted for fourteen-day, thirty-day, or ninety-day visa-free access, as discussed in chapter 1, depending on their country of origin and their cash on hand, as well as the extent of their previous experience in Hong Kong. Those who have previously come to Hong Kong and not overstayed the permitted limits of their stay are often treated in a more relaxed way by Immigration than are first timers. Some traders stay in Hong Kong and in Chungking Mansions for the period that their business requires—a buyer of mobile phones might hardly leave the building for a week. Other traders stay in Hong Kong only long enough to get a visa into China, after which they may take a train from directly outside Chungking Mansions to the Chinese border. Some traders come to Hong Kong or China just a few times every year or less, while others seem to be in constant motion, bouncing between Hong Kong, China, and their home countries every week or two.

The lure for the traders is China, with its cornucopia of cheap manufactured goods. These traders buy China-made goods to transport back to their home countries because their home countries do not make these goods, at least not at competitive prices. Some of the goods these traders buy, such as mobile phones, are carried back home in the trader's own luggage, often 32 kilos per bag allowed by such airlines as Ethiopian and Emirates, with extra kilos permitted if the trader belongs to a frequent flyer program, as many do. Bigger traders also pay the extra costs of air freight for additional bags. These traders are bringing back mobile phones or electronics, particularly delicate, or else clothing, particularly light, especially when vacuum packed. Other traders rent or share containers, expensive but necessary for goods such as tiles or car parts.

These traders must decide whether to venture into China, potentially lucrative but risky, or to do their business in Hong Kong, perceived to be safer and more reliable. But the entrepreneurial activities of these traders carry high risk, not only in China but throughout their global circuits. One risk is that they will get cheated in China or in Hong Kong, buying goods that have been misrepresented to them that they cannot sell back home. Alternately, they may simply miscalculate, buying goods that won't sell at home. Another risk is that the copy goods traders buy in China (many goods traders buy are genuine, but many are not) may be confiscated by authorities in China or in Hong Kong. An even greater risk is in the customs of their own countries, which may be a huge barrier, one that they can traverse through legal payments, luck, or bribery. A Nigerian trader told me that he can make 60 percent gross profit on the goods he brings back with him, but must give half of that back as bribes to various government officials. This varies from country to country, but since corruption is common and customs regulations are often unclear to traders, their transitions back into their home countries are fraught with peril.

Because many African and South Asian countries' banks do not offer letters of credit or other financial instruments accepted in Hong Kong or Chinese banks, many traders carry tens of thousands of dollars in cash—up to US$50,000 or even US$100,000. As an East African trader told me, "These traders are all carrying cash—of course! Hong Kong is the safest place in Asia to do business. I've never known a person who was robbed." Some of the African traders I have encountered hold more cash in their hands at one time than some Americans may have held in their entire lifetimes and feel secure doing so in what they perceive to be the safety of Chungking Mansions and Hong Kong (although as of 2009, more traders were wiring money or sending remittances).

It is not uncommon to see traders leave thousands of dollars in cash on a Chungking Mansions counter. Although they may get cheated in more subtle ways, their money is in this sense safe, except in unguarded moments. A popular story making the rounds in Chungking Mansions (perhaps true, although I've yet to find anyone admitting to being a victim) is of the African trader hiding US$50,000 in his underwear, who goes with a Chinese sex worker back to his room. He showers and she, finding a fortune in his drawers that might support her family for a decade, flees on the train departing every five minutes to the Chinese border. He sees his loss and follows in hot pursuit, but never sees her or his money again.

Overwhelmingly these traders are men, although there are some women dealing in garments. These traders tend to be among the wealthy in their home societies. As earlier noted, not all the entrepreneurs are African, although the large majority are. Many are Indian, often involved in the garment trade, and still others are Eastern European or Russian, often involved in mobile phones or electronics. There are also Yemenis, Filipinos, Saudis, and French—I've met people from an array of different countries involved in a mind-boggling assortment of trade. But African entrepreneurs are the most prominent in Chungking Mansions and, for that matter, in south China as well.

I occasionally have met with African traders who have come to Hong Kong for the first time. I conducted an informal evening tour of Hong Kong for two female Tanzanian traders, who expressed amazement at the tall buildings and the trains. One said, "I've never been in a train that ran through electricity before. Where I come from, trains are run by oil." She also spoke with amazement at all the "sliding stairs"—escalators—which she had seen only once before at the airport in her home country. But these traders were by no means removed from the contemporary world's technology. Throughout much of our tour, they were on their mobile phones calling their friends back in Dar es Salaam. As one of them explained to me, "Yes, I was telling my friends back home about what I was seeing, about the sliding stairs and the malls. But how can there be so many malls? Why do Hong Kong people buy so many things?"—a wise question I couldn't begin to answer, after which we had an animated discussion about the nature of capitalism.

A story I've heard from several people concerns China's National Day in Hong Kong, which features a fireworks exhibition over Hong Kong harbor to thrill the crowds of tens of thousands. Apparently a number of African traders heard the booms, saw all the people outside, and ran to the elevators for shelter, thinking that a war had started and Hong Kong was being bombed.

These African entrepreneurs have little linkage to Hong Kong, for the most part, except, perhaps, for their business forays into Sham Shui Po or other Hong Kong neighborhoods where wholesale goods are sold. Subtle racism is sometimes apparent in the 7-Eleven around the corner from Chungking Mansions. I have seen Hong Kong people enter the 7-Eleven to simply stand and stare at the Africans for thirty seconds before walking out, buying nothing. Many younger traders have tried to pick up Hong Kong women, but with little success. Some have come to know from bitter experience that, aside from simple racism, the way they are used to accosting women in Africa is considered aggressive in Hong Kong, perhaps adding to the fear with which these traders are regarded by many Hong Kong people.

All in all, it is difficult for African traders in Hong Kong. They inevitably stand out in a city that is 95 percent Chinese and are, if not necessarily victims of racial discrimination, certainly the strange and feared "other" in a Hong Kong context. This is why Africans tend to stick together in Chungking Mansions and in places like the nearby 7-Eleven. Only in these places can they gain security in numbers, and in being with people like themselves. Some of these African traders are naïve in not knowing quite what they are getting into, but all are brave in leaving their homes to seek their fortunes in a foreign land. Many will lose their shirts and never come back. Some will make tidy profits and become regular traders, passing through Chungking Mansions a half dozen or a dozen times a year. A smart, lucky few will make fortunes.

The African traders I have met in Hong Kong have global links that spread far beyond Hong Kong—these traders often follow a long and complex path, ranging from their home and neighboring countries in Africa, to Dubai, to Bangkok and other southeast Asian destinations, to Hong Kong, to south China, and back again. As discussed in the previous chapter, my research assistants and I accompanied traders on parts of their global rounds out of Chungking Mansions.

Many of the African traders staying in Chungking Mansions go to Guangdong Province, the south Chinese industrial area most immediately accessible to Hong Kong, as well as to other cities in China, such as Yiwu.[1] African traders in Guangzhou, the capital of Guangdong Province, are present in several different neighborhoods. There is the Tianxiu Building and its environs, a high rise devoted entirely to goods for sale to African and Middle Eastern merchants, an area where many Muslim traders go. There is also the Sanyuanli area, the haunt of Nigerian Igbo among others, who have regular Catholic services in Igbo at Guangzhou's Sacred Heart Cathedral. In Guangzhou, unlike Chungking Mansions, traders of different backgrounds tend to go to different areas of the city to do their business and typically sleep in apartments or hotels in the city's outskirts—there is no common place where all live and intermingle, such as Chungking Mansions. Unlike Chungking Mansions, many traders in Guangzhou do not speak English. They get by with their knowledge of a few words of Mandarin, or by hiring one of the dozens of young Chinese women—college students, I am told— offering their services as interpreters in Guangzhou trading marts (such as the one depicted on p. 62).

In Guangzhou, more than in Hong Kong, there are extremes of poverty and wealth and a division of legality and illegality, among African traders. On the one hand, there are Nigerians and other Africans living illegally who are sometimes involved in the drug trade, whether transporting drugs from Africa to China or selling in Guangzhou at street level, but this is only rarely seen in Hong Kong. Because of the sheer number of Africans in Guangzhou—20,000 is one estimate, other estimates are far higher[2]—they may remain largely unnoticed if they overstay their visas. On the other hand, there are many established and wealthy African as well as Middle Eastern entrepreneurs in Guangzhou. Some have had the capital to bypass Chungking Mansions and order directly from factories in south China with which they have established relations, typically over years. They may have long-term work visas in China.

Others are agents, or "fixers," some of whom speak fluent Mandarin, who negotiate deals for their fellow Africans. I have been in a high-end Brazilian barbeque restaurant in Guangzhou containing a hundred or more African entrepreneurs and agents in their expensive Saturday-night revels. I also stayed with a Congolese agent in his high-rise Guangzhou apartment, a place that in all its accoutrements would have been the envy of virtually all the Chinese living in the city. Some of these people have managed to legally stay in China, through favorable visas or through marriage to a Chinese woman, but their visas still may require regular renewal. They often make a regular cycle of going back and forth between Guangzhou and Chungking Mansions in order to renew their visas every thirty days. Others, especially those with less to lose, take the more risky path of overstaying their visas, enabling them to stay in Guangzhou indefinitely, but subjecting them, if caught (and if unable to pay the requisite bribe, I am told) to jail terms and deportation.

Aside from Guangzhou, many of the African traders in Chungking Mansions speak of Dubai, and particularly the Dubai neighborhood of Deira, as a place of trade. The African traders I met in Dubai in 2009 were sometimes on a circuit from East Africa to Hong Kong and China and back. As a Zambian trader told me, he often meets fellow African traders he knows from Chungking Mansions on the streets of Deira, and vice versa. Each place has its advantages and disadvantages. As a Tanzanian trader said, "Usually goods are cheaper in China, since all the China-made goods have to be shipped from China to here [Dubai]. But occasionally you find bargains here, even though the hotels are really expensive compared to Chungking Mansions." A Nigerian phone trader noted that while Dubai has many warehoused European-made phones sold at discount prices (known as fourteen-day phones), China-made phones are cheaper in Hong Kong and China.

African traders (such as the ones depicted on p. 64) choose Dubai for various reasons. Some come because of problems they encounter getting visas for China. Others are on no such global circuit, at least not yet. Hong Kong and China are places they dream of going to do business, but for now they have settled for the geographically closer and culturally more familiar world of Dubai, with its strong presence of Islam and its many Somali shopkeepers. "Yes, I want to go to China, but you can lose everything in China, I've heard," one trader told me. "You have to be very careful there."

I spent an afternoon in Dubai in an Internet café with a Zambian trader who sought to get to the Chinese source of the copy electronic goods he was buying, so that he could eliminate the middleman. He insisted that the company must have a website, but of course we only found the real European company's website, not the company manufacturing copies using the real company's name. It took me hours to convince him that a company making copy goods is unlikely to advertise itself on the Internet, and that rather than seek out this company's shadowy source, he might do better to stay and buy in Dubai (although some of his suppliers in Dubai may know exactly where these goods come from), or perhaps go to Chungking Mansions

or to Guangzhou, as close as he is ever likely to come to the source of those goods.

My research assistant, Jose Rojas, traveled to Lagos, Nigeria, to experience the daily rounds of several Nigerian traders he had met in Chungking Mansions. He found that many of the shops in Lagos are dependent upon a constant flow of new shipments from China, shipments arriving every two days, generally through Hong Kong and Chungking Mansions. These China-made goods, often copies that are disdained by well-off Nigerians who seek Japanese or European goods, are sought after by the great mass of Nigerians who can afford nothing else (see the Lagos scene on p. 65).

The traders from Hong Kong he traveled with are admired by many young people in Lagos, who suffer from an astronomically high unemployment rate. But as these traders themselves are well aware, they make only a little money, and often the money with which they buy their goods is not their own money but that of their bosses in Nigeria, Hong Kong, or China. Jose went with traders along the potholed road from Lagos to the market town of Onitsha and experienced the frequent roadblocks of soldiers seeking payoffs for allowing contraband clothing past—he himself was shaken down. With constant electrical blackouts and endemic corruption, Nigeria

cannot make its own goods, from phones to clothes to electric generators.
All must be imported from places like China, but many of these imported
goods, not least clothing, are declared illegal by the Nigerian government.

Despite this illegality, China's presence lurks everywhere. Along many of
the streets of the Lagos clothing market, goods are displayed on plastic bags
bearing Chinese characters, the bags that most Chinese factories use to wrap
their manufactured clothes. All in all, Jose found that however hard these
traders' lives may be in Hong Kong, Nigeria is harder; this is why many Nigerian young people seek to leave and try their luck, not least for the far-off
and foreign, yet also familiar, Chungking Mansions. These traders seek not
to live in Hong Kong or China—Europe or the United States is much more
the land of their dreams—but rather to see if they can make a fortune or at
least a profit at trading, which may eventually enable them to leave Nigeria
for good.

My research assistant Maggie Lin followed female Kenyan traders from
Chungking Mansions back to Mombasa and Nairobi, through Bangkok.
Some of these traders have made extensive profits from their clothing business and have started other businesses in Kenya, such as hair salons and
minibus services; they too are looked up to by many of their fellow Kenyans,

especially with an unemployment rate of some 40 percent. Some are clearly of the middle class in the country, owning cars and employing many staff, but others now only aspire to that. Maggie was told by one struggling trader in Kenya that after a few more trips to China, she hoped to build a new house on her plot of land, where she can rent out the upper floors while she and her family live on the lower floor. After she has built the new house, she hopes to have the money to finance a container filled with everything from China, from tiles to sofas, a container that she hopes will help make her wealthy (see one up-and-coming Kenyan shop on p. 67).

Maggie found souvenir t-shirts, khaki pants, and *kikoys* and *khangas*, the traditional pieces of cloth women wrap around their bodies (a popular souvenir for tourists), as the only clothing items actually produced in Kenya. Despite the tax imposed on imported products, most clothing is brought from outside the country: the "made in China" label is omnipresent from more prestigious shops to street-market stalls. For the clothing made in China, her informants told her, the design is often trendy, but due to suspicions that customers may have about quality, they need to work to convince customers that these goods are worth buying. Not all China-made products are poor quality—some are superb—but these traders are buying the very cheapest items in China, and so customers in Kenya may tend to associate Chineseness with shoddiness.

These are some of the routes and stories of the traders one encounters in Chungking Mansions, linking these traders, beyond a single Hong Kong building, to sites across the globe.

Owners and Managers

I now turn to Chinese and South Asian owners and managers in Chungking Mansions. The dominant class of owners today arrived in the 1970s and the 1980s from Shanghai or Fujian Province in mainland China, buying the cheapest property they could find—that of Chungking Mansions. Most are all but invisible in the multiethnic kaleidoscope that is Chungking Mansions; many come to the building only rarely. However, they and their children have been living out "the Hong Kong dream." Most came to Hong Kong and Chungking Mansions in more or less difficult financial straits, but through hard work over the years, they have become modestly affluent and have raised children who now have university degrees and are accountants or teachers, like Andy Mok whom we saw in chapter 1.

The children of these owners often want nothing to do with Chungking Mansions. As one university student who grew up in Chungking Mansions

told me, "If I were doing the Chungking Mansions story, I would describe how poor mainland immigrants used real estate and hard work to become wealthy over several decades. It would have little to do with Africans and South Asians. This is a classic mainland–Hong Kong success story." His emphasis is one wholly lacking in virtually all the descriptions of Chungking Mansions that one sees and hears, yet it too is clearly valid. However, this story stops with the children, who, like him or Andy Mok, leave the building that made their parents middle class. Today, many older Chinese owners are still holding on, but many eventually sell their property to the next generation of immigrants from mainland China, or to South Asians.

Many of these owners are closed off from Chungking Mansions at large, but a few have adapted remarkably well to the cultural panorama. One older man running a souvenir stand on the ground floor, carefully arranged with souvenirs for Western tourists (statues of the Buddha, jade dragons) on one side and souvenirs for Chinese (Swiss army knives, pendants) on the other, speaks six languages, all reasonably well. It is startling to be talking with him about our respective families in Japanese, then switch to Spanish to discuss his travels overseas, then watch him switch to Mandarin to deal with one set of tourists and then use French with another. Another Hong Kong Chinese man runs an upstairs travel agency and, because of his ability to speak French, has a stream of African customers seeking visas and buying whole-sale clothing from him as well. While English is Chungking Mansions' lingua franca, these merchants' going the extra mile to speak to their customers no doubt wins them additional business. I also know several Chinese store proprietors who lend money to their regular customers, not requiring full payment for traders' orders until the goods have been sold back in Africa. This is a risky practice, proprietors maintained, but does help ensure that one has regular customers.

Many business managers in Chungking Mansions are South Asians whose families have been in Hong Kong for generations, reflecting the long historical presence of South Asians in Hong Kong since the mid-nineteenth century.[3] To take just one example, a Pakistani clothing-store proprietor in his sixties was born when Pakistan was still part of India and was granted British citizenship at that time. He moved to Hong Kong in 1985 to seek his fortune. At present, all four of his daughters live in Great Britain, while his only son lives in mainland China for business. As other clothing dealers in Chungking Mansions have also said, business has become much more diffi-cult in recent years because customers can go to the mainland for goods at a lower price. At his age, he hangs on.

Many South Asian managers are fluent in Cantonese and yet feel that they are discriminated against in Hong Kong. Thus their relation to Hong Kong is distinctly ambivalent—few sense that Hong Kong, which they see as lean-ing more and more toward China, can be their home. Rather, between South Asia, an earlier homeland some now feel little attachment to, and Hong Kong, a temporary home in which to make a living for a few decades, they dream of eventual residence in the United Kingdom, Canada, or the United States. One manager told me that he does not want to be tied to Hong Kong and is thinking of moving to Canada for the sake of his children—"I still don't trust Hong Kong after the handover." A Sikh man, returning to Hong Kong and Chungking Mansions for the Diwali festival, exclaimed, "Thank God for Chris Patten [the last British governor of Hong Kong]. He enabled my family to leave Hong Kong and live in Great Britain."

This dream of leaving may be placed upon one's children. A young Indian man told me, "My father started his restaurant in Chungking Mansions twenty years ago and wants me to help him as long as I'm in Hong Kong. But he doesn't want me to stay in Hong Kong. He wants me to get an ad-vanced business degree in America or Europe and make a better life there." As an older Pakistani man said, "I manage a guesthouse in Chungking Man-sions, but my son is a doctor in London and my daughter is studying in the

United States"—making a better future for themselves not just away from Chungking Mansions but from Hong Kong.

These South Asian shopkeepers are not so different from some of their Hong Kong Chinese counterparts, up to a million or more of whom hold foreign passports as insurance for the future, keeping the option of emigration open "just in case."[4] However, unlike most Hong Kong Chinese, these South Asians may feel a distinct sense of alienation from Hong Kong because it is Chinese. In Chungking Mansions, many speak Hindi or Urdu or Nepali or Punjabi or Tamil; eat South Asian food; buy South Asian ingredients, videos, magazines, and saris for their wives and daughters; and spend their days watching the Indian, Pakistani, or Nepali TV channel and associating with their fellow South Asians. Many are devoutly Muslim: a half dozen times in the course of my research, Islamic shopkeepers have taken me aside to show me, on YouTube, videos of pilgrims circulating around the Kaaba in Mecca, accompanied by recited Qur'anic scriptures. Nonetheless, many feel that South Asia is no longer their home, a sense held all the more by their children. "I've never been to India. It's a foreign country! I'd be lost there!" said an Indian man in his twenties. "I've lived all my adult life in Hong Kong, and I will die here."

One Chungking Mansions electronics store has as its fixture a fifteen-year-old Pakistani boy (long the favorite of my research assistants Amy Fung and Ingrid Tang, from whom this description is taken) who migrated to Hong Kong with his father when he was three and who now comes to his father's shop whenever he is not in school. Raised in Hong Kong, he speaks conversational Cantonese: "All of my friends are Chinese." But he has not been taught to write and read Chinese, but only English. This reflects the peculiarities of the Hong Kong educational system vis-à-vis South Asians. Education in Hong Kong for South Asians has typically involved instruction in English, with classes in spoken Cantonese but little emphasis on written Chinese.* This boy seeks to be a medical doctor or a police officer when he grows up, but without written Chinese that future will probably be denied him in a Hong Kong context.[5]

Another store is run by a 23-year-old Hong-Kong-born Pakistani, again speaking fluent Cantonese but not reading or writing Chinese. After graduating from local schools, he started working at a car showroom but soon quit:

*In 2005, the Hong Kong government began to redirect South Asian children into Cantonese-medium schools, mainstreaming South Asians, to the consternation of some South Asian parents, who preferred English-language instruction for their children.

"I worked faster and better than the Chinese girl, but they still preferred her to me after the three-month probation." These stories reveal why so many South Asians make their home in Chungking Mansions. It is a place, unlike the rest of Hong Kong, where they can work with their fellow countrymen and not suffer discrimination for their non-Chinese ethnicity and lack of language ability (a lack that does not hinder white people in Hong Kong but that definitely hinders South Asians, given Hong Kong's ongoing racial hierarchy of "white as superior, brown as inferior"). Here are the accounts of two such South Asian men.

Johnny Singh

I started a store in Chungking Mansions in 2002; I'm now in my early forties. Business was better back then than it is now. Now you can make expenses, but you cannot save money. I have both a phone store and a watch store. My customers are African and Indian. I talk to everyone in a friendly way. If I talk to them nicely, they will buy something from me. I don't give a high price or a low price, but market price; I'm happy with that. I just came back from ten days in England and a few weeks in India to check conditions there, but business there is also not so good. It's better to do business in Hong Kong, better than India, better than the UK, better than all countries. Chungking Mansions—everybody wants to try to make money here. You can sell something because different countries' people all come here.

Before I was in Chungking, I had an office outside. I started that in 1997; I did that for five years. We sold everything. Every month I'd make HK$50,000, HK$100,000 profit. I supplied all the shopkeepers here in Chungking with what the factories made in China. At that time, Indians could not get visas to go into China, so they'd buy from me. It was very easy to make money. I had a BMW car. I had ten million dollars then! But then customers starting going to China themselves.

I bought property in my home country, a farm in north Punjab. I have lots of property there—I could retire. My mother and father tell me, "Stay in Punjab!" They didn't want me to come back to Hong Kong and said, "We are old. You stay here. We will give you a big house, a car." I said, "I cannot stay because of my son and my wife. Let me do five more years of business in Hong Kong. Then I will come." I had six stores a year ago, but now I have two. Business is down now. I've lost more than HK$2,000,000. I try my best. I have an older brother who has been working for a company in Hong Kong for over twenty-five years, but the company closed down last month; he cannot find a job now.

I was born here in Hong Kong. I am a Hong Kong person—I've been more than thirty years here in Hong Kong. When I was a child, I spent ten years in India—when I was six, I was sent back to India and came back to Hong Kong when I was seventeen. My father was Hong Kong police; he retired in 1986 and went back to India. Yes, Hong Kong is Chinese; I feel like an outsider in Hong Kong. But when I enter this building, I don't feel like I'm an outsider; I feel like I'm home. Different people come here: Indonesian, Malaysian, Indian, Sri Lankan, Bangladeshi, African, European. All countries can enter here. Outside is difficult, but Chungking Mansions is home!

I've decided that I'll bring my son back to India. He goes to English school now, but I want to teach him my mother language, Punjabi. I want him to know Indian culture. I don't want him to stay in Hong Kong. English is fine, but Cantonese? Nobody needs to learn Cantonese! My own school friends are in Punjab. They tell me that if I come back, they'll vote for me to be village president. Here in Hong Kong you can make money and live good, no problem. But I want to go back to India eventually. I'm Sikh, but I've taken off my turban and cut my hair, to be more acceptable to customers. My brother criticizes me for not wearing my turban.

There is discrimination in Hong Kong. I speak Cantonese, I grew up in Hong Kong, but I've been treated badly by suppliers who keep putting me off concerning delivery. I told them, "Look, I'm not a delivery boy driving this truck. I own these shops!" When you speak Cantonese, the Chinese get scared. If they think you don't speak Cantonese, they talk badly about you. I was in a dispute last year and was beaten. If I had been Chinese, the police would have done more to solve my case; because I'm not Chinese, they don't care. The police told me, "If you don't feel safe here, then go to the UK." They talked to me like that!

Chungking Mansions . . . after two or three years, more mainland China people will be here. They'll open up shops, and Pakistanis and Indians will all, one by one, leave Chungking. Even if there's no business, the rent will keep going up. Maybe African people will trust Chinese people more than Indians or Pakistanis, because they think they have factories. Yes, maybe the Indians and Pakistanis will vanish and only the Africans and Chinese will remain.

Fahad Ali

I've been coming to Chungking Mansions for almost twenty years because my brother has been here, but I've been working here at a phone stall only for eight months. I'm in my late twenties. I know the people here now, but also the people before them, and the people before them, and the people before them! I think that Chungking Mansions is changing very fast and in a good way. The business is not getting better—the business was better twenty years ago—but now more people are coming in; more people know about Chungking. The impression of the place is getting better. In the 1990s, people were scared to come here. At that time there were drug problems going on and gangs. Now people are more peaceful here; no one bothers anyone.

At this phone store, I sell both wholesale and retail. I don't have big African traders as customers, but my brother does. Some of the African traders place their orders, and he sends the phones back to them. Those traders are serious businessmen; they're reliable. But many store managers here have had a bad experience doing business with Africans; some guys have lost millions. When you've done business for a long time with someone, you trust him, you give him credit and say, "Next time you can pay." That's when he takes a big order without paying and never comes back—you never see him again.

Yes, mainland Chinese merchants are moving into Chungking Mansions—they try but they fail. The Indians and Pakistanis are still holding on strong. Some people say I'm stupid for saying this, but I tell people, "Don't buy Chinese phones." I can't give any guarantee for them—they can die tomorrow! These kinds of things only happen with the black guys. You give them a price and they immediately cut it in half—"HK$400," I say, and they say "HK$200." So you give them China made.*

I also work as a designer in advertising. I used to work in a big advertising company, but now the design market is not very good in Hong Kong, so I have a one-man design company in the morning and work here in the afternoons and evenings, seeing if I can do anything in the business. Trading is very good in Hong Kong; that's what I'm trying! Chungking Mansions right now, people say it's bad business, they're not making any money, but you don't see any empty shops. Chungking Mansions is making revenue for Hong Kong. Most of the shopkeepers I know here are rich!

I got married just two months ago, to a Hong Kong girl. My wife converted to Islam—she converted before we were married. But she didn't convert because of me but because of her. I can't push her to be a Muslim! If she's ready, she will do it. I've known four or five Chinese girls who have converted

---

*"China made" in this context means China-made copies of European or Korean phones.

to Islam—I'm happy for them. To my wife, I never told her to go and convert, never. It's not a matter of converting because someone wants you to, it's a matter of how you develop your own understanding.

Many of my friends are Chinese, but I don't speak Cantonese at all. I'm very bad at languages! But we are living here; Hong Kong is our home. My lack of Cantonese hasn't been a problem for me in getting jobs in Hong Kong. Yes, maybe my personality helps—I try to be friendly and good to people. There are stupid Hong Kong Chinese who practice discrimination, holding their noses when they see me, for example. But I just smile at them. There are good or bad people everywhere, in every country. Even some of my local Chinese friends are afraid to come to Chungking Mansions. They feel it's strange when they know I work here! Europeans are not afraid to come to Chungking Mansions; it's only local Chinese.

We are always hoping for a better Chungking. We want central air conditioning—when it's very hot, like today, business suffers. In many shopping centers, people come in because it's cool, but nobody will come into Chungking for that! The touts outside [handing out menus for Chungking Mansions restaurants to passersby on Nathan Road], I don't like that. They should not be there, because they're scaring customers. The management can't control them. If there are fifty Indians and Pakistanis standing outside, and they don't even know how to talk properly to people, do you think any Chinese will come in? It's a matter of this building and its reputation.

Why doesn't the management stop people from eating *paan* and spitting?* I hate it! In India, they might do that, but this is not India! You see the red on that wall? That's from spitting! No sensible person would do that. Sometimes, I get pissed off at the temporary workers, the asylum seekers, because of the way they behave. They are destroying our reputation! Business is affected because of these people! A lot of these guys, they are stealing jobs from Hong Kong residents.

The police are here for our protection, but some of them are very bad. You're a white guy here; I'm a brown guy. The police, when they're talking to you, they'll have a smile on their face, but when they're talking to me, they will have anger on their face. At that time, I really want to kick their asses. At Immigration, at the airport, I told the guy, "Just now, you had your teeth out, smiling to that white guy. But now, with me, you're angry. Why? Can you explain this to me?" He said nothing.

Paan is a betel leaf mixture commonly chewed in South Asia and sold in many stalls in Chungking Mansions.

Chungking Mansions, it's my sitting room. I come here to talk to people and meet people. In the whole of Hong Kong, this is the only place where people of all different nations can get together. Without Chungking Mansions, where would the people here go? If it was torn down, maybe we'd all go into the Holiday Inn next door and take over that place!

Temporary Workers

South Asians with Hong Kong residency can, of course, own property in Hong Kong. They often hire fellow South Asians who have no such opportunities—Indians who come to Hong Kong as tourists. These temporary workers are the backbone of the Chungking Mansions labor force. They work as clerks in stores; as touts, waiters, and dishwashers in restaurants; as touts, cleaners, and managers for guesthouses; or as goods transporters. They come to Hong Kong on a fourteen-day visa-free entry obtained upon arrival at the Hong Kong airport, twice renewable for varying numbers of days, and are permitted to stay in Hong Kong for no more than 180 days a year. These temporary workers are paid considerably less than those with Hong Kong residence and a Hong Kong identity card, typically making only HK$3,000 to HK$3,500 per month. As I have sometimes heard from temporary workers, "Why does that guy make twice as much money as me? It's only because he has a Hong Kong ID card and I don't!" As business owners have maintained to me, the potential legal risks of hiring tourist workers, including heavy fines for their employers, justifies their lower wages.

Unlike the longer-term South Asian residents of Hong Kong, who come from Punjab as well as south India, Pakistan, and Nepal, a majority of these temporary workers come from a single neighborhood, Kidderpore, a Muslim enclave in Kolkata. People from Kolkata are at Chungking Mansions in large part because the ticket fare to Hong Kong is cheaper than any other destination that can provide work, whereas from western Indian cities such as Mumbai, it is cheaper to fly to Dubai to work. As for why Kidderpore in particular is the source of so many workers in Chungking Mansions, it's difficult to conclusively say (although the fact that Chungking Mansions has many Muslims, like Kidderpore, is no doubt one factor), but it seems clear that the power of individual connections is essential: "My cousin told me he'd help me find work in Chungking Mansions, so I came here." Temporary employees such as these come to Hong Kong because jobs that pay more than a pittance are hard to find in Kolkata. Some of the young Indian men I have interviewed are married to teachers and civil servants, but make far more money in Hong Kong than their spouses back home.

These workers have a precarious position in Hong Kong, in that if they are caught working, they can be prosecuted, jailed, and barred from returning to Hong Kong.[6] However, they are extremely difficult to catch. As soon as immigration police enter Chungking Mansions, mobile phones are set to use by friends and lookouts at the front of the building, and illegal workers vanish en masse from behind their counters or sinks to mingle with the crowds of tourists and traders. Because Hong Kong Chinese still stand out in Chungking Mansions, and because undercover police are so easy to recognize, the danger tends to be minimal, although incautious or unlucky workers do occasionally get caught.

Without these illegal workers, many of Chungking Mansions' businesses could no longer afford to exist. If phone stalls, food stalls, and guesthouses hired only legal workers, labor costs would double and prices would have to be very significantly raised. Many African and South Asian entrepreneurs, who already carefully count out every dollar in considering accommodations and food, could no longer afford to come, and Chungking Mansions as it now exists would die. Illegal workers are indeed exploited. As one angrily exclaimed to me, "My boss is paying me HK$3,000 a month. Fifteen hours' work a day and only HK$3,000 a month—not good!" He has nine people in his family he must support, he said. Nonetheless, Hong Kong offers better prospects than Kolkata, which is why he returns time after time, year after year.

These temporary workers are also entrepreneurs, in a limited sense—they carry goods in their luggage when they return to India, often clothing in parcels of up to 40 kilograms, and on their return trip often carry foodstuffs, such as *dal* and Indian rice, to sell at a discount to restaurants in Chungking Mansions. They usually fly Biman Bangladesh Airways, sometimes 24 to 48 hours late departing but worthwhile because a roundtrip flight from Hong Kong to Kolkata will cost them some HK$3,000, cheaper than other airlines. At the airport in Hong Kong, these temporary workers receive vacuum-packed parcels of clothing to carry. They can pay for 50 to 80 percent of their flight between the clothing they take to India and the foodstuffs they bring back to Hong Kong. The clothes are sold throughout India, I am told.

The dream of many of these temporary workers is to go into business for themselves, but the minimum to really be able to make a start at being an entrepreneur is HK$10,000, or better HK$20,000. Given the familial obligations that many experience, this is more than most can ever scrape together. Some of these temporary employees have furtively approached me: "If you can just lend me HK$6,000, I can buy enough mobile phones to make much money for both of us. And I won't have to do this work any more." I refuse, not least because these workers generally seem to lack the business savvy to know how to proceed.

Others have approached me to ask about the pros and cons of becoming an asylum seeker, whom we will shortly discuss. Others ask, "Please tell me, is there any possible way I could get Hong Kong residency?" The answer, almost as a rule, is no, unless they can manage to find a Hong Kong girl to marry. I know of one charismatic young temporary worker who indeed had a Hong Kong girlfriend for several years, until he proposed marriage and she said, "Oh no, I like you, but I would never marry you!" With that, his chance at Hong Kong residency vanished. "She was only playing with me!" he recounts in anger.

Some of these temporary workers come to Hong Kong only once and never return, finding the pace of work too grueling or the morals of Chungking Mansions too questionable for their Islamic convictions. But most continue their migratory cycles month after month, year after year, slowly saving up the money they'll need to return home and start the business they've dreamed of during their long sojourns in Hong Kong, or else buying property at home at a rate they never could have if they had remained at home.

I had the chance to go to Kolkata for a week with a temporary worker from Chungking Mansions, to follow him on his business, meet his friends and family in Kidderpore, and better understand the thick linkages between Kidderpore and Chungking Mansions. One surprise was how hard it was for him and his fellow Chungking Mansions workers to get the parcels of clothing they carried through customs. Customs officials viewed them with disdain—as one exclaimed to me, "Indians can make clothes! We don't need clothes from China!"—and refused to deal with them except during a limited window of a few hours each afternoon, a window that evaporated if other flights' passengers came through. For three successive days, we had to take a taxi back to the airport, as my friend became progressively more despairing, seeing his slim profits vanish at our mounting expenses.

Another greater surprise was seeing how much Kidderpore, a neighborhood I had never seen before, seemed like a long-lost home: a dozen different times over the course of just a few days someone would call out, "Hello! I know you from Chungking Mansions! Remember me? Welcome to India!" It seemed that much of Chungking Mansions, on its home shift, paraded through the streets of Kidderpore—sometimes in the figure of a proud young returnee slowly riding his shiny motorcycle through the streets, followed by a retinue of a half dozen starry-eyed male teenagers.

A third surprise was how much my friend was his family's economic mainstay. His wages of HK$3,500 a month earned for just six months a year—less than a pittance by Hong Kong standards—financed his two sisters' weddings as well as his own, each attended by over a thousand people; paid for his own motorcycle, his prized possession; and would shortly fund the reconstruction of his extended family's home. Chungking Mansions really does enable him to become a "big man" back in Kolkata. He is not particularly well treated in Hong Kong—he is a restaurant tout—but he is indeed his family's hero, as was readily apparent when I talked with his elderly parents, who, beneath their modesty, were beaming at the success of their son. He provides the difference between bare subsistence and the luxuries of life for his family, such as a motorcycle, a stereo, a water purifier, and home refurbishing. Their other son went to Chungking Mansions once to work but had found it too hard. He now works at a call center in Kolkata, making good money by Indian standards and also helping out the family, but bringing in nowhere near the returns of his brother.

Here is the account of another temporary worker at Chungking Mansions.

Ahmed Aziz

I've come to Hong Kong more than one hundred times, back and forth between Hong Kong and Kolkata. I've been working in Chungking Mansions for a guesthouse owner for six years. Before that, I came to Hong Kong for trade, working with my partner. My father gave me 2 lakh (200,000) rupees (HK$40,000/US$5,100) to start the business. For two years it was very good, but then my partner stole my money. He took 5 lakh rupees from me and ran. I never saw my partner again; maybe he went to south India, to Madras, but Madras is so big. I have no relatives there; I couldn't find him. I went to the police, but my friend who is police told me I would never get my money back. So I came back to Hong Kong, this time to work.

Yes, coming back and forth as a tourist is difficult. Immigration in Hong Kong is not stupid. They know that some people come to Hong Kong for business and others for working. They give some people fourteen days, some seven days, some four days, some nothing. You can go to China and extend your stay twice, up to forty-two days, and then you must go home. I worry when I go to Immigration. You have to show money: sometimes HK$5,000, sometimes HK$10,000. I go to the boss when I need to get my stay renewed; he gives me money that I show Immigration at the China border. He trusts me—he knows I won't run away with the money he gives me! When I go back and forth between Hong Kong and India, I carry goods to help pay the expense: I carry saris from India to Hong Kong and electronic goods from Hong Kong to India. Sometimes I can make a big profit, US$400 paying for almost my whole flight, and sometimes US$250; it depends on price conditions.

I get paid HK$3,000 a month, plus lodging. My work is to bring in customers for my boss's guesthouses. The police won't bother me because my passport is legal. They just think I'm a guest. I am outside from 11 a.m. to midnight or 2 a.m. trying to bring in customers—only six to seven hours sleeping each night. Sometimes I bring in four customers a day, sometimes five, sometimes six for my boss's guesthouses. I can tell by looking at customers: Mali and Benin people might want cheaper rooms. Nigerians are very dangerous; if the room costs HK$100, he gives HK$80 saying, "I don't have money! OK, call the police!" Japanese and Koreans, they like clean rooms.

My wife is a teacher back in Kidderpore in a nursery school; my four-year-old daughter also goes there. I want to make a good life for my children! My wife makes 3,000 Indian rupees a month, about HK$600, only about a fifth of what I make in Hong Kong. I have four brothers and three sisters; I am the oldest. One brother is in California, working in water management. My second brother works in India, and another brother is in university. My brother in California makes most money, but I'm second. I give my wife HK$220 and give my father HK$2500 every month. I will work in Hong Kong only one more year and then go back to India. My father has a restaurant; he is old, and I will take over for him.

Most people in Kolkata have never been to school, but I graduated. Then I worked in a factory, but there was a lockout, a strike—India has so many political parties, so many problems. Still, I'd much rather have my family live in India than in Hong Kong. Hong Kong culture is not good. The Indonesian ladies, one boyfriend here, another there.* I like Indians: they love only one person! Yes, many sex workers are Indian, but they are sex workers; that's different. I like my country—it's great! And so I want to go back to India in one year—it's very, very nice! Now many, many companies come to India and make business—it's not so poor anymore.

Asylum Seekers

There are some 6,000 asylum seekers in Hong Kong as of 2009, mostly from South Asian and African countries; many of them congregate at Chungking

---

*He is referring to the Indonesian domestic helpers who come to Chungking Mansions on Sundays, their day off.

Mansions. We will focus on asylum seekers in chapter 4, but let me briefly discuss them here. Hong Kong, as earlier noted, is unusual among societies in the developed world in that it has a largely open border. Except for a handful of countries for which visas must be obtained in advance, arrivals from most societies are given a landing permit at Hong Kong's airport for fourteen, thirty, or ninety days. This makes Hong Kong easy to travel to as a tourist destination for people from across the globe, but this is also a major reason why Hong Kong has served as a magnet for asylum seekers. Even those who come from countries requiring visas for entry into Hong Kong have a relatively easy time getting in to Hong Kong—very few are turned away at the airport, although this of course by no means indicates that their subsequent life in Hong Kong will be easy. As one Somali man told me, shaking his head at the stupidity of my question, "Why did I come to Hong Kong? Because I knew they would let me in!"

Many asylum seekers, either at Immigration or in the days and weeks after entry into Hong Kong, turn to the UNHCR, which has an office in Hong Kong, to officially declare themselves as asylum seekers. The UNHCR may take up to three or more years to hear a case, with appeals added to this. Many asylum seekers also turn to the Hong Kong government, which is a signatory of the Convention Against Torture (CAT). However, it is not a signatory to the United Nations Convention Relating to the Status of Refugees, which is why the UNHCR is involved. These claims also may take many years to evaluate.* Only a tiny percentage of asylum seekers ever attain refugee status, enabling them to go to live in a third country, such as Canada or the United States; most asylum seekers, using one or both of these paths, indefinitely await their fates in Hong Kong.

In 2006 and 2007, asylum seekers lacked papers and could be arrested at any time by unsympathetic police, but by 2008, asylum seekers could obtain papers attesting to asylum seeker status—an asylum seeker still was jailed for several weeks, but after this was entitled to a minimal government welfare allotment of HK$1,900 payment in kind per month. It is difficult to survive on such an allotment in Hong Kong, but from a developing-world standpoint it may seem generous. I have heard that unscrupulous recruiters on the South Asian subcontinent promise job applicants well-paid positions in Hong Kong, telling them, once they arrive, to become asylum seekers.

Some asylum seekers are fleeing religious, ethnic, or political persecution or torture in their home countries; others have come to Hong Kong to seek economic opportunities. The former are commonly considered to be "real," and the latter "fake." But in fact, the line between these two types of asylum seekers is unclear—I know a number of asylum seekers who have been threatened in various ways in their home countries and who have felt compelled to flee, but who do not meet the specific criteria required in order to obtain refugee status.

It is commonly observed in Chungking Mansions that economic asylum seekers work and make money, for if they are caught and deported they have little to lose, while political asylum seekers do not work, for if they are caught and deported they face jail, torture, or death in their home countries. But this distinction too is unclear. Some economic asylum seekers choose not to work, finding it easier to live on the bare-bones assistance they can obtain and spending their time writing or simply hanging out. On the other hand, some political asylum seekers do work, despite the danger of deportation this places them in, because they feel that they must send money to their families in their home countries.

It has been surprising to me how many times an employee I come to know in Chungking Mansions admits to me, often after months of conversa-

*Lawyers tell me that only claimants to the UNHCR can be considered asylum seekers, in that they seek to be recognized as refugees and resettled elsewhere; claimants through CAT are not eligible for such resettlement. However, because asylum seekers themselves don't recognize this distinction, I use the term "asylum seekers" to refer to all such claimants.

tion, that "really, I'm an asylum seeker." Those who work engage in a variety of jobs of varying degrees of danger of being caught by Immigration. Some, especially South Asians, are employed by stalls on the ground and first floors, since by face they are indistinguishable from their somewhat more legal tourist-permit brethren, or from those fortunate South Asian employees with Hong Kong permanent residency. A number of South Asian sex workers are also asylum seekers, since this enables them to stay in Hong Kong indefinitely to work. African asylum seekers must be more careful: several I know work in guesthouses where they cannot easily be caught, since their employers can always say, "I just wanted to help a poor asylum seeker by giving him a place to sleep; I never pay him any money" (which is ironically apt, at least figuratively speaking—their pay tends to be extremely low, as little as HK$2,000 or HK$2,500 per month).

Still others pass their days working among the copy-watch and tailor salesmen outside Chungking Mansions. This is particularly dangerous, but these workers are usually experts at recognizing undercover police, fleeing before they ever approach too closely. Early in 2009, a court decision in Hong Kong gave asylum seekers the provisional right to work, leading to a marked increase in the number of asylum seekers coming to Hong Kong. Later in 2009, the law was changed, and police swooped down on Chungking Mansions, arresting a dozen illegal workers. This had the effect of emptying the ground and first floors of Chungking Mansions of illegal workers for a week or two, until they deemed it safe to resume their jobs and the situation returned to its old status quo.

Those asylum seekers who do not work tend to spend more time at Christian-based NGOs in Chungking Mansions and, sometimes, helping at other volunteer organizations in Hong Kong. All—but particularly those asylum seekers who do not work and only wait—face the agony of waiting for years with no clear future. I have taught a small class of asylum seekers at Christian Action in Chungking Mansions for the past four years, a class that is ostensibly Advanced English but is really a discussion of current events and life philosophy. I have been surprised by how famous some of my students have been in their home countries (several have prominent Internet presences and one has appeared on CNN in his earlier incarnation as a political campaign spokesman before fleeing his home country one step ahead of the police), how intelligent and assertive many are (to quote one student, "Professor, there are five things wrong with your opinion on this matter. Let me explain each of these things to you."), and how unhappy many are.

The reason for their unhappiness lies largely in the boredom and uncertainty of their present lives, entirely at the mercy of bureaucratic processes they cannot control, and also the sense that their lives are now in limbo. In one man's words, "I am in my thirties, a person of talent. I can work. But in Hong Kong, I cannot. In Hong Kong I am useless. I am only a beggar." This sense of unhappiness is also due to the sufferings and guilt they may bear from their home country: How can one overcome torture? Alternately, how can one justify leaving one's country for Hong Kong for reasons that may be murky, even to oneself? How can one justify leaving one's family behind?

The asylum seekers I know are desperate to prove that their claims are legitimate. This is most obviously the case for those who are apparently genuine, for whom their entire lives are at the mercy of the bureaucratic judgment that will decide their fate. But this is also true for those who are frankly in Hong Kong for economic reasons, who must work hard to find ways in which their cases can be rendered impervious to doubt. Veteran asylum seekers I know can recite a litany of people who have received asylum despite being "fake" ("He's just a good storyteller, that's all!") and a longer list of people who have not received asylum despite being "real" ("How could they deny him? Those UN people are crazy! They're just like the mafia!"). Their lives are staked on judgments whose validity they doubt but whose ultimate implications are absolute—they are ticket-bearers in a lottery whose prize is a new life. As with most lotteries, their chances of winning are very small indeed.

I have visited the families of several asylum seekers I have come to know well, one in East Africa and the other in South Asia. My asylum seeker friend from South Asia is a man of enormous, stubborn principle, whose reasons for doing what he did may be hard to fathom, but who has the absolute integrity of his convictions. I saw his family—his mother, father, and sisters—in the home of his relatives and brought his private letters to them. This family was very much from the country and said little, although they were clearly overjoyed to see an emissary from their son. Through an interpreter, I heard his story from his father, a man in his sixties. "My son's problem was that he refused to join the army. Lots of people did that and paid off the authorities, but he refused to pay off anyone—he was doing this out of principle. . . . I have lost several jobs because he refused to serve, but I respect what he's doing."

His son had been arrested, imprisoned, and tortured by authorities, using electric shocks and other devices. The father told me that the son's secondary school teacher said, "He is so smart. Why are they doing this to him and not to other people?" He subsequently fled, three times in all, to different nearby countries, but each time the lure of his family and friends pulled him back—

whereby he would be arrested and tortured again. Finally he fled for good and traveled overland many thousands of miles to Hong Kong. In Hong Kong, the same principles that prevented him from joining the army prevent him from working, since it is against the law, and stop him from sleeping at night, as he stews endlessly over his situation. His father died a year after I spoke with him; his son remains stuck in Hong Kong indefinitely.

I also visited an asylum seeker friend's family in East Africa. I stayed with his cousin, a young politician for the government party, who told me, "Yes, he was threatened; he was a member of the opposition. But you have to somehow cross the line to have them threaten to kill you. He must have crossed that line . . . but I don't know, because I can't really talk to him. My phone is tapped." Another relative is a prominent government minister, with whom I had a long dinner—a jovial and sensitive man who could not really voice support for the child he had raised into adulthood. It was as if my friend the asylum seeker in Hong Kong was a well-meaning eccentric who unaccountably and tragically had ventured down the wrong path in his life by opposing the government.

I later had the chance to meet his wife and children—almost unspeaking and dressed in their Sunday best—to whom I brought the array of presents my asylum-seeker friend and I had bought them. I also met his brother, who had the most telling word. I mentioned that in reading the local newspapers I saw the harsh criticisms of the government by various prominent opposition figures. Couldn't my friend have spoken out as they did and been safe, as they apparently were? He said, "They're famous. The government can't jail or kill them—they're too well known. But my brother is not famous: the police could easily kill him." Indeed, the next day, a low-level opposition figure was murdered by police, an occurrence duly covered in the newspapers. The culprits, by the time I left, had not been found. It was against this backdrop that my asylum-seeking friend wound up in Chungking Mansions.

Domestic Helpers

There are several dozen domestic helpers who work in Chungking Mansions: Filipina maids hired by families who live in Chungking Mansions or elsewhere who work in or manage guesthouses in the building. But I want to discuss more particularly the hundreds of Filipina and Indonesian domestic helpers who come to Chungking Mansions on their day off. On Sundays, tens of thousands of domestic helpers from throughout Hong Kong make their way to Central, Hong Kong's business district across the harbor, to eat, sing, relax, and congregate.[7] Some come to Chungking Mansions as well. They are drawn to Chungking Mansions by the food—the South Asian fare available is closer to their palates than the Chinese food that most must daily prepare for the families they work for—and also by shopping, since the goods in Chungking Mansions are among the cheapest in Hong Kong, especially mobile phones, electronics, and clothing. Also, some are drawn by the promise of male attention: many young women seek to be seen as feminine and desirable once a week, rather than merely as domestic helpers. Some of these women are dressed up in their slinky best; many have boyfriends among the South Asian and African men at Chungking Mansions.

One of my more memorable conversations was with three Indonesian domestic helpers one Sunday morning in Chungking Mansions, one of a number of such conversations I've had over the years. All three had male friends they were waiting for: one Saudi Arabian, another Pakistani, and the third Indian. These women gaily chatted about these "contract boyfriends"—they are together only for as long as they are both in Hong Kong. Their boyfriends pay for everything, and they themselves provide companionship and sex.

But these relationships grow. One of these girls didn't want to meet her boyfriend because she'd had a fight with him; her friends kept saying, "Get him out of your mind! Forget about him!" but she was moping, and obviously couldn't. The woman with the Indian boyfriend got a phone call from him and found out he was in jail—he was an asylum seeker detained for not yet having papers. He had been picked up the day before and asked her not to come and visit him this week on her day off.

The woman who talked to me the most told me that in Indonesia now, coming to Hong Kong has a very bad reputation: "It means you're not a good woman at all." She lives on a farm in Indonesia, and her remittance pays for fuel and other necessities back home—but she said that she could never go back to live on the farm and would start her own business instead in the city. She had a (temporary) ring in her nose and bright dyed orange hair—it did seem difficult to imagine that she could go back and live in a conservative rural community again. The other two women showed me pictures of their boyfriends and themselves on their mobile phones, but she wouldn't show me her boyfriend. It turns out that she has two—one Indian and the other Chinese—and is also married back in Indonesia. These women said that the families they worked for knew nothing about their boyfriends. I asked these women what they would do if they got pregnant. They all giggled in embarrassment, but one said, "We all know of a powerful medicine we could take."

Sex Workers

Some 85 to 90 percent of the people who work or stay in Chungking Mansions are male, and most of those are young and transient. Not surprisingly, Chungking Mansions has been a magnet for sex workers from an array of nationalities. Until recent years, an assumption often voiced within Chungking Mansions was that any young woman wearing fashionable clothes in the building was a sex worker. An attractive female student of mine did research in Chungking Mansions in the late 1990s and was, to her shock, frequently asked "How much?" by men who assumed without question her occupation. More recently, another student of mine wore a skirt to Chungking Mansions one afternoon and overheard Cantonese-speaking storekeepers (who assumed she was Filipina) saying, "Oh the girls are out early today, aren't they?"

Today, however, this assumption is no longer valid. This seems due largely to the increase in mainland Chinese tourists staying in Chungking Mansions guesthouses, many of whom are fashionably dressed young women who may know nothing about Chungking Mansions, having booked their reservations online. In order to protect these young tourists from being accosted, the guards at Chungking Mansions have become stricter, stopping women whom they recognize as sex workers at Chungking Mansions' entrance. This is particularly the case after midnight, when the front entrance to the building is partially shut, leaving only a single door. Sometimes, when I have returned late at night, a sex worker followed close behind me, trying to enter Chungking Mansions, only to be stopped by the guard, asking me, "Is she with you?"

There are indeed sex workers living in flats in Chungking Mansions—the most plausible estimates I've heard are that there are sixty to eighty in the building in all—but generally they do not approach strangers within Chungking Mansions seeking their business, as they often did in years past, except, very discreetly, around money exchange stalls. Instead, there are various stores in Chungking Mansions that as a side business dispatch sex workers to customers who seek them. My encounters with sex workers over the years have several times taken place in guesthouses, when I realized that the women staying in nearby rooms were professionals, but even in these encounters I sometimes have had no idea of this until being later informed. "Didn't you know what was going on next door?" I was asked by a guesthouse-proprietor friend of mine after my own solid night's sleep, to his great amusement.

Outside Chungking Mansions it is a different situation, with sex workers sometimes aggressively seeking customers. In front of Chungking Mansions, on Nathan Road, Chinese sex workers are sometimes found, coming
in on temporary permits from mainland China. On the corner of Nathan
and Mody Road there are often sex workers from various nationalities: I
have spoken with women who claimed to be from Indonesia, Malaysia, Thailand, and Mongolia, as well as Tanzania and Kenya. On Mody Road, near
the 7-Eleven, there are often half dozen or a dozen Indian sex workers, as
noted in chapter 1, resplendent in their bright saris. These women are often
from south India, particularly Kerala. Those I have spoken with are often
older and claim to have come to Chungking Mansions because they were
abandoned by their husbands and have children to feed. They tell their families that they are traveling to Chennai or Mumbai for secretarial work and
instead fly to Hong Kong. Hong Kong law is such that unless they overstay,
they cannot easily be apprehended by police. Nonetheless, sometimes they
are arrested anyway.

These sex workers tend not to take their customers to Chungking Mansions, but instead, more often, to the nearby Mirador Mansions, Chungking
Mansions' slightly more expensive, less crowded, and of late somewhat seed-
ier twin, where the surveillance by guards is less intense.[8] The price of these
women is generally HK$100 per hour, extending to HK$600 per night, but
it varies according to the customer, with whites apparently charged far more,
since they tend to be rich. I have heard that ordering a sex worker to one's
guesthouse room is as simple as "ordering fast food takeout." "Choices," I am
told, "range from young blonde Europeans (HK$1,000) to Chinese 'office
ladies' (HK$500); the cheapest sex workers are Filipinas and Indonesians
(HK$250 for set services)."* For a typical Indian sex worker some half of
her earnings for a transaction will go to the guesthouse and 25 percent to
the older woman watching over her, so she makes only a little herself. These
women are apparently not controlled by gangsters, who are not much to be
found in Chungking Mansions today, as discussed in chapter 1. Sex workers, as just noted, do have older women looking after them—when I have
interviewed sex workers, these older women phoned every hour, to make

---

*This price spectrum—uncomfortably reflecting the societal rankings of the
nineteenth-century anthropologists Morgan and Tylor—mirrors Hong Kong as a
whole. Sex workers from different societies are priced in a similar scale in various Hong
Kong neighborhoods, although with overall prices higher than around Chungking
Mansions.

sure that all is well—but from all I have been able to determine, this is not gang related.

It has been particularly difficult to interview sex workers around Chungking Mansions, for obvious reasons: most are to some extent ashamed of what they do and in any case see me as a potential customer. Even when I formally pay them—as I have in order to conduct interviews, as I have for no other interviews conducted in this research—it is difficult to find out much (To quote from one interview, "I am not in this business; why do you ask me these questions? . . . Yes, I like white men because they pay me more money."). This is the group in and around Chungking Mansions whom I least comprehend, but I do comprehend some fairly well. One East African woman living in Chungking Mansions has worked as a sex worker for two years, working not in Chungking Mansions but in the somewhat more up-scale bar district of Wan Chai. She carefully sends money home every month and transports clothing back in her luggage whenever she returns home to renew her visa. Her plan is to finish sex work in three years' time and start her own business back in her own country—and by that time, she should have more than enough money to do so, achieving, with pluck and luck, her aspiring middle-class dreams.

Heroin Addicts

The idea in the popular press has long been that Chungking Mansions is full of illegal drugs. Perhaps there was indeed widespread use of drugs twenty and thirty years ago, when Chungking Mansions was more of a backpacker haven, but today drug use—aside from alcohol and *paan*, the South Asian betel nut sold in food stalls—is not that frequent. Europeans and Africans occasionally smoke hashish, bought from the South Asian dealers discreetly offering their wares in various nooks of Chungking Mansions and on the streets outside, but drug use is mainly associated with Nepalese. There are some forty Nepalese heroin addicts around the building, many of whom sleep in homemade cardboard structures in the alleyways behind Chungking Mansions and shoot up in the stairwells of the building.

These men are sons of Gurkhas who served in the British Army in Hong Kong in the 1980s and 1990s and thus have Hong Kong residence rights. Many of these men—now often in their thirties or forties—have wives and children in Nepal, from marriages arranged by their parents, which they have forsaken. Apparently the expectations placed upon them when returning to Nepal after experiencing comparative wealth in Hong Kong were too great; they would rather be heroin addicts in Hong Kong, spending the welfare payments they receive from the Hong Kong government not on housing but on heroin.

Other Nepalese and South Asians in Chungking Mansions may look upon them with scorn. In one young Indian man's words, "I work many hours each day and dream of being able to live in Hong Kong. They can live in Hong Kong but they waste it. They are spoiled rich boys!" Another said, "They grew up with a sense of privilege. . . . They won't take a lot of jobs, those that are 'beneath them,' and become drug addicts." Several Christian charity organizations have been involved in attempting to rehabilitate them, but as one social worker in such an organization told me, it is a very discouraging business:

> The problem they have is that the family pressure they are under to succeed in Hong Kong is so great that they can't possibly make it. Their families are relatively well off in Nepal, but since they are in Hong Kong, they are expected to do much better here, and they can't. Their social world here is entirely the world of other addicts, and so they can never break out of it except through God. . . . Usually they relapse. All their friends are taking heroin, so that's what they always go back to.

With their Hong Kong ID cards, they can get monthly welfare from the government of HK$4,000 per month or more and use the money for drink and drugs. One Saturday afternoon in back of Chungking Mansions, I peeked into one person's makeshift cardboard shelter and saw that the book he was reading was Jared Diamond's *Guns, Germs, and Steel*, a book I had assigned that year to my graduate anthropological theory class at Chinese University.

Merchants in Chungking Mansions often complain about these addicts, especially because some of them engage in pickpocketing and petty thievery in the building. They are tolerated in part because the walkways around Chungking Mansions are public property, unlike Chungking Mansions itself. I mentioned in chapter 1 how Nepalese were driven off the roof of Chungking Mansions in 1997 by the building's security guards, but walkways, unlike the roof, do not belong to Chungking Mansions. Beyond this, there seems to be a live and let live attitude toward these people, most of who are relatively harmless and tend to commit their thievery elsewhere.

For some who live in Chungking Mansions, heroin may represent a difficult temptation to resist. I know one Hong Kong Chinese who is a recovering addict as well as a convert to Islam; he told me that there is an advantage and a disadvantage to being in Chungking Mansions. The advantage for him was that it brought him Islam and is an Islamic environment that helps his faith. The disadvantage is all the drug addicts and the overpowering temptation to return to heroin. Eventually the heroin won.

Here is the story of one of these men, as told to my research assistant, Ocean Chan.

Gurung

I was born in Hong Kong; my father was a Gurkha. I went back to Nepal from Hong Kong to study and began taking drugs like heroin—it was a good way to show off, being tough, rich, and cool. I was in prison in Nepal and in Hong Kong at different times for selling drugs. I like the prison in Nepal compared to the one in Hong Kong and sometimes I even miss that kind of life—I had good friends, good food, and even drugs every day there. But you know, I paid for it with a big price, my love, my family, even my whole life.

I've been married twice. My first wife was Nepalese, an arranged marriage. We had a big feast and wedding party, and then we went to my house and land, a good life in Nepal. But it didn't work out. I got bored and returned to drugs and was sent to jail for twenty-three months. My wife divorced me, a big disgrace for my family. I was sent by my parents to a rehab center, quit drugs, and found a job as a tourist guide because I spoke good English.

I could quit because I was in love with a beautiful girl twelve years younger than me. We got married, and my parents decided to send us back to Hong Kong to start a new life. I had a Hong Kong ID card, but I eventually realized that my wife married me only because she wanted to find a way out of Nepal. In Hong Kong I found a gardening job I liked—everything was settling down for me to start a new life. But then my wife asked me for a divorce. She had met a British guy and decided to go to England with him. I was just too naïve to think a girl would love a guy who used to be a drug addict. Oh man, it hurts so much. I started to take drugs right away with my friends. Maybe I still loved her; maybe that was an excuse, but the drug really eased my pain. Maybe it was my karma; I must have done something wrong in a past life.... My parents asked me to go back to Nepal to start over again. But most of my friends were in Hong Kong. In the back alley here we are all from Nepal. It's tough to live here, especially when it's raining and water keeps dripping down, but I can live here for free.

I took up drugs again, but I got weak and lost my job. Eventually I found another job as a guard at a night club, but I needed more money. I began to steal electrical supplies from construction sites—see, I have a scar on my foot from a dog bite. I started to sell hashish, marijuana, and cocaine to European and African customers. I've been sent to a rehab center twice, but as soon as I get out, I return to Chungking Mansions. There's no choice for me anymore; I have nowhere to go, and I can't work anymore after taking drugs for so many years.

I feel happy in Chungking Mansions; I have shelter and also can get free meals [from a Christian NGO], and I can talk to people in my own language. I feel at home. I tell young people to quit, because they still have a chance to start over, but not me. You know, I'm quite satisfied with my life now. I once went to the church because the missionaries who feed us for free had been asking us to go. The minister started to talk about quality of life: being simple and of course loving God. Our life is quite simple; we just sleep, get high, share hash, and sleep. I think I love God too. Yes, we are living a simple life; whenever we take drugs, we forget about pain, we feel contented. These are similar feelings of love, aren't they?

There's another reason I like Chungking Mansions: I can make friends with people from different countries. You know, there's no nationality when we smoke hash together. I just made a European friend a few days ago, a tourist. The guy came from Holland; it's legal to smoke hash in his country. I took him to the park to hang out and smoke hash together. It was nice.

Tourists

In the midst of all this—the bustle of entrepreneurs seeking deals, the harangues of touts seeking customers, the enticements of sex workers, and the whispered offerings of hashish sellers—is one more group, the tourists, one of the largest in Chungking Mansions. They come primarily because it is so cheap. Chungking Mansions remains a backpacker haven, although less so than thirty years ago, as opposed, for example, to the Holiday Inn immediately next door, whose rooms are ten to twenty times more expensive. They also come for the adventurousness of the place, especially Japanese and Europeans, who may have long known about Chungking Mansions from their earlier backpacking days and from such book series as the *Lonely Planet* guides, in English, and *Chikyū no arukikata* ['how to walk the world'], in Japanese.

Today, the Internet directs many prospective tourists to Chungking Mansions (perhaps the largest website on Chungking Mansions is in Japanese, chock full of good advice for Japanese visitors, although there are comparatively few Japanese visitors staying in Chungking Mansions these days).[9]

These tourists include both those who seek out the cheapest rooms in Hong Kong and those who seek adventure of a particular kind (as one British man in his thirties told me, "The websites all warned me that I should never stay in Chungking Mansions, so I knew that I had to come here"). On the other hand, South Asians living in China and elsewhere come to Chungking Mansions for a taste of home—the television, the restaurants, and the video and magazine stalls offer them the sense of being back in India or Pakistan, as nowhere else in East Asia does.

Tourists are a less obvious part of Chungking Mansions than the groups we have already discussed, simply in that unlike workers or entrepreneurs, most do not remain in the building but depart in the morning and return at night. Nonetheless they play a pivotal role in occupying the majority of guesthouse beds on some nights, particularly during mainland holidays such as May Day and National Day (October 1). The number of tourists has been steadily increasing in the last several years, due to increasing numbers of tourists booking rooms on the Internet. I have given Argentines advice as to where to meet Hong Kong girls, commiserated with Americans over the follies of George W. Bush, discussed with Egyptian tourists the nature of Islam, talked with Bhutanese about their society's "gross national happiness," considered with Japanese whether they should leave their country and move overseas, talked with Englishmen about the glories and woes of their national rugby team, and commiserated with tourists from the Maldive Islands as to their worries over whether global warming would submerge their country forever. Of the 129 different nationalities I have found in guesthouse logs in Chungking Mansions, the majority are tourists, arriving from everywhere on the planet.

Those tourists who choose their lodgings through the Internet sometimes experience a rude shock. One mainland Chinese tourist said to me in Cantonese, "I didn't know there would be so many Africans here. It's horrible!" She had found her guesthouse on the Internet and had been attracted by its low prices, but the Internet page made no mention of the particular building her lodgings were in, which to her was beyond belief in its ethnic diversity and "otherness." Another mainland Chinese tourist said plaintively to me, "I want to eat Chinese food, but there are no Chinese restaurants here.* Why not? Isn't Hong Kong part of China?" To which I answered that Hong Kong is part of China, but Chungking Mansions is not part of Hong Kong

---

*There is in fact one Chinese restaurant on the first floor of Chungking Mansions.

but rather an island of the developing world in Hong Kong's heart. Why else would its prices be so cheap? She looked puzzled and asked me if there were any "disco bars" near Chungking Mansions to which she might go.

This bewilderment is by no means confined to mainland Chinese. I met a young Colombian woman who approached me at the door of the guesthouse where we were both staying, as if she were a little afraid to venture outside, to ask, "Is this place always like this?" I told her that it was, but that it was also perfectly safe to wander through; she seemed less than fully convinced. This fear seems partly gender specific: these young women may be stared at by many in the overwhelmingly male population of the building in a way that makes them uncomfortable. As one American woman fumed to me, "I've never been eyed like that in my whole life!"—although beyond the overly direct male gaze, young women are generally safe from male predation. I spoke with a couple of male Malaysian tourists, coming to Hong Kong for several days, shocked by what they beheld after expecting only a nondescript cheap hotel. I asked one of them what he would say about Chungking Mansions once he returned to Malaysia, and he said, "It's good, but I'd never, ever bring my girlfriend here. . . . For Muslim women, this would be a terrible place to be!"

Among the shell-shocked tourists I have met, mainland Chinese and Americans stand out. However, of late, more sophisticated Chinese tourists have been coming, seeking adventure like some of their European, American, and Japanese counterparts. A couple from Shanghai with whom I spoke was disappointed that they saw no "rats falling from the ceiling," as their guide-book had promised them. I explained that I myself have never beheld a rat inside Chungking Mansions (although I've seen a number in the alleys outside the building) and that unless they got very lucky, they might never see such a sight.

Let me describe a few of the more memorable tourists I've met. One Japanese man, utterly enthralled by what he called the "ethnic chaos" of Chungking Mansions, worked for a well-known brokerage in Tokyo and was in Hong Kong partly for vacation and partly for investment. In Japan, if one invests in hedge funds, the government charges 20 percent in taxes, but not in Hong Kong, he said, where there is no tax at all on these investments. He comes to Hong Kong early Friday afternoon and goes to a large Hong Kong bank and invests his money; then he spends two days immersed in the world of Chungking Mansions. "It costs me 60,000 yen to fly from Tokyo to Hong Kong and back, so if I have a million yen to invest, it's well worth doing this. Plus I get to spend my weekend in this amazing place."

He, just like the Indian temporary workers described earlier although on a far larger financial scale, is a beneficiary of Hong Kong's laissez-faire governmental system and free economy. He is by no means the only entrepreneur tourist I have met. I know of Indonesians who visit Hong Kong for pleasure but take back made-in-China Islamic prayer shawls to finance their trip, just as I know Indian and Latin American tourists who do the same with electronic goods such as mobile phones. Twenty China-made iPhones surreptitiously carried home in one's luggage and sold to friends and acquaintances can make one's trip a very profitable journey.

There are also spiritual tourists. I have met several Europeans immediately after they had attended a ten-day Vipassana retreat in the country area of northern Hong Kong, which required them to be silent for ten days. The final day of the course extolled the spirituality of India, perhaps (along with their limited finances) leading these people to wind up in Chungking Mansions after the course ended. One concluded our conversation by folding his palms together and uttering *namaste*, a South Asian term quite out of place in the Islamic atmosphere of Chungking Mansions. Another spoke of the spiritual benefits of his silence and simply smiled in wonder at all he saw in Chungking Mansions—its bustle seeming to overwhelm him after so many days of silent contemplation.

There are also dreamers, who have wound up at Chungking Mansions because it is one of the cheapest places in the developed world in which to live, but who imagine a success that has yet eluded them. An elderly Algerian-Canadian writer sends me unreadable chapters of his spy novel to which I don't know how to respond, e-mails me intricate questions of English grammar, and occasionally borrows a few hundred Hong Kong dollars from me, sometimes to pay it back. He dreams of making millions from his spy novel; I can only tell him that because I don't read spy novels, I just don't know. Meanwhile, with his Hong Kong residence permission easily renewable every ninety days on his Canadian passport, he can make Hong Kong his home.

A New Zealander apparently in his sixties told me that he has been in Hong Kong a month and will stay a few weeks more. A good friend of his, he claimed, was the Philippine ambassador to China and in several days someone from the US Federal Reserve was coming to talk to him about how to raise funds—he is a financier, he said, staying, just for fun, in Chungking Mansions. He was ashamed of where his life has brought him, it seems, judging from his transparently tall tales.

A middle-aged Turkish man, looking like a Western hippie from the 1960s, described to me his travels across Asia and his plan of writing a book about Islam, while the staff of the food stall we were sitting in scoffed in Urdu, "Why is the professor talking to an idiot?" He was not an idiot but a dreamer, as are so many in Chungking Mansions. Young people, like the scuffling entrepreneurs or temporary workers or asylum seekers, can hold these dreams more plausibly. Who, at present, can altogether dismiss their dreams? But older people have a harder time, since their dreams appear increasingly elusive. This is all the more true at Chungking Mansions, which, because it is so cheap, may be the last refuge for not a few international dreamers. They stay there for their remaining days because their remaining dollars will go farthest there.

Dreamers and last-chancers are of course not only tourists. I have sipped whiskey behind Chungking Mansions with a Tanzanian who told me that he had been fired from several jobs in Dar es Salaam for drunkenness. His affluent family, as a last resort, sent him to Hong Kong to see if he could succeed in trade despite his addiction. And I have met an ethnic Indian restaurant owner from Singapore, who had fled thinking that he had killed a fellow Indian in a brawl. He came to Hong Kong with much cash on hand and a dream of fleeing to Canada, but also a murder charge potentially hanging over his head. Both these men I met only once. They too and their ilk are part of Chungking Mansions' cavalcade.

How These Different Groups Interact

We have briefly examined all of the different groups in Chungking Mansions. A key to understanding Chungking Mansions is to understand how these different groups, of different pursuits and ethnicities, interact.

Much of the occupational interaction is a matter of the roles people play. The restaurant tout flashes menus and makes his pitch to bring in customers. The mobile phone store salesman discusses the merits of different phones. The guesthouse proprietor shows rooms and bargains over prices. As we've seen, the majority of entrepreneurs and businesspeople coming to Chungking Mansions are African; the majority of tourists are mainland Chinese and European, along with Japanese and Australians and people from all over the world; and, with a number of exceptions, the shopkeepers and guesthouse and restaurant managers are either South Asian or Chinese, with a smattering of Filipinos. Thus, interactions between these different groups frequenting Chungking Mansions are almost inevitably a matter of interethnic interaction.

It is not impossible for a member of a given ethnic, linguistic, or national group to deal only with members of his or her own group. There are a few Chinese proprietors in their isolated shops dealing largely only with Chinese customers, some African traders who deal primarily only with their fel-

low countrymen, and some South Asian temporary workers who wash pots or pack phones or clean rooms who may lead their daily lives largely cut off from interethnic interaction. There are many tourists who, apart from a few words with the clerk in the guesthouse they stay in, may never be involved in Chungking Mansions' ethnic swirl. But these, other than perhaps the tourists, are the exceptions: interactions between different occupational and ethnic groups are more typical.

Much interethnic interaction is purely practical, consisting, for example, of Africans in the South Asian ground-floor food stalls attempting to order food that suits their palates. As noted in chapter 1, there are only a few African restaurants in Chungking Mansions. Thus, many Africans find themselves having to eat South Asian food, which they may find unpalatable unless they can make it clear that they desire no spiciness in their food. Many times I have seen Africans first question the proprietor whether or not a South Asian food stall really is *halal*, as its sign claims, and then ask which, of all dishes proffered, they can actually eat. A food stall on the ground or first floor of Chungking Mansions, with nine chairs and four tables, may have patrons of five different nationalities seated by one another, not because they know each other, but because there is no room and because people have to eat. Conversations sometimes start, leading to friends being made or arguments breaking out.

Beyond this is the negotiation between South Asian/Chinese proprietors and African wholesale customers on the ground and first floors. I will describe these complex negotiations at length in chapter 3, but suffice it to say that fortunes may be made or lost on the basis of these negotiations. If an African does not appear to have much knowledge about mobile phones, he will sometimes be cheated; a Pakistani proprietor cackled to me, "That guy is so stupid! I sold him some fourteen-day phones* as if they were new and made HK$4,000 just like that!" The calculating African phone buyer will carefully plan how to show himself as knowledgeable and sophisticated before the Pakistani or Indian or Chinese phone dealer, so that he can get the best possible deal, knowing when to wheedle, when to joke, when to get angry, and when to compromise, as well as when, precisely, to insist on "Lowest! Lowest!"—the absolute lowest possible price the dealer can offer. The savvy African entrepreneur knows exactly the rules of self-presentation before the foreign phone dealer he is faced with—he'd better know these rules if he wants to avoid losing his money.[10]

These interactions are generally in English, the lingua franca of Chungking Mansions. Language usage is fascinatingly nested in Chungking Mansions, with different speakers finding the closest and most intimate language in which they can speak. Speakers of African ethnic languages delight when they find one another, as I have seen, for example, with two speakers of Hausa or of Luo. They speak a language that their fellow Africans cannot understand, just as speakers of Punjabi and Bengali communicate while to some extent ignoring their fellow South Asians. At a more generalized level, speakers of Hindi-Urdu can communicate with their fellows from across the South Asian subcontinent, as speakers of Swahili or of French can communicate with some of their fellow East or West Africans. At a general level above this is English. Those Africans who don't speak English tend to congregate not at Chungking Mansions, but in Guangzhou's Tianxiu Building, among other areas, where French as well as Mandarin prevail.

Occasionally other common languages emerge in Chungking Mansions. I had dinner one night in a food stall at which a Bangladeshi, a Cameroonian, and I all wound up conversing in Japanese. The Bangladeshi lives in Japan and goes to university there, and the Cameroonian sitting next to us,

---

*"Fourteen-day phones" are warehoused European models returned by their original buyers, typically selling for 50 to 60 percent of the price of new phones.

who had spent several years in Japan, joined in. We drew quite a crowd, the Bangladeshi, Cameroonian, and American animatedly conversing in a language none of our onlookers could make any sense of. I also once spoke with two businesspeople, one from Somalia, the other from Iraq, who, once they found out they both had lived in Sweden for the past ten years, began conversing with one another in Swedish, ignoring me.

I have also seen Japanese tourists communicating with Chinese merchants and guesthouse proprietors by writing in the Chinese characters that they share. And there are the various business proprietors, such as the souvenir-stand operator described above, who operate in multiple languages. French is especially useful for several Chinese and Pakistani proprietors I know who are able to negotiate with West and Central African customers in their own language. Nonetheless, despite the use of these occasional alternative languages, English is the common language of Chungking Mansions—coupled with price negotiations taking place through the ubiquitous calculator.

I have seen or heard of, over the years, some remarkable interethnic interactions in Chungking Mansions. A West African prospective phone buyer once fled wide-eyed and in terror when a Pakistani phone dealer introduced himself as "Hussein"; he apparently mistook the dealer for the former Iraqi dictator or his ghost. A Muslim phone store manager said to an African Christian customer: "My friend, you are a Christian, and yet you are causing me all this trouble; I must rewrite all the invoices. Why do you do this to me if we are both men of God?" The Christian held his tongue, but told me later, "His God is not my God."

I have seen a dozen Africans from different countries transfixed before a televised Manchester United soccer match, bursting into delirium before the stoic indifference of the Indian shopkeeper when an African scored the winning goal. I have seen a Hong Kong Chinese phone dealer bullied by Nepalese heroin addicts into giving them "beer money": they approached him with smiles but also with a degree of menace, whether heroin fueled or feigned, knowing that he was an easy mark. He is an alcoholic and was quite drunk by this late in the evening, but not so drunk as to have lost his instinct for self-preservation. He gave them HK$10 each and later told me, "They are my friends, so of course I give them money."

One way in which ethnic relations can readily be apprehended is in employment patterns. Often managers hire primarily people of their own ethnicity or nationality: a Nepalese guesthouse owner I know, for example, hires only Nepalese. As his employee told me, "My boss used to hire Indians, but the Indians cheated him." I asked, "Don't Nepalis ever cheat your boss?" "Oh no, we would never do that!" he exclaimed, with what seemed to be horror.

Other managers hire across national bounds: Indians are commonly hired by Pakistanis and vice versa, a simple matter since Hindi and Urdu are virtually the same spoken language, even though members of the two societies often disdain each other. Still other managers hire on the basis of religion. An African restaurant proprietor I know makes a point of hiring Indian Muslims as his staff, since they and he share their Islamic faith, the most important basis of commonality, he maintained. Often hiring is dictated less by ethnicity than by practical circumstance: as earlier noted, a number of South Asian asylum seekers are employed in stalls on the ground and first floors, since South Asians are less likely to be stopped by police and asked for ID. Chinese-run guesthouses, on the other hand, may hire African asylum seekers to work for them at low wages, simply because the police can't easily catch them, and they may bring in African customers. This has nothing to do with interethnic sympathy and everything to do with business practicality.

Long-term interethnic interactions take place typically between merchant and customer or between managers of neighboring or nearby stalls. Many of the Pakistani phone dealers, for example, have several dozen African clients whom they may see six or more times a year, selling them hundreds of phones at a time. These clients and dealers rarely know each other beyond business dealings, but they have developed a relation of trust, essential for their business—although as we saw in Fahad Ali's account, this does not rule out the possibility of being cheated.

As for the relation of neighboring stalls, a Chinese electronics stall owner may be next to an Indian grocery or a Pakistani phone dealer, and interaction is inevitable. When these stalls are in direct competition, serious tension may develop, but mutual interrelations may develop as well. I know of one South Asian wholesale clothing merchant who goes to the nearby Kowloon Mosque five times a day to pray—whenever he goes, he does not shut his store but asks the Chinese wholesale clothing merchant across the corridor to keep an eye out on his shop, and she obligingly does so. He repays in kind when she takes leave of her shop. On the other hand, I know of a long-standing simmering quarrel between an Indian Sikh phone dealer and his Pakistani Muslim rival in a stall just eight feet away that may be due more to business competition than to ethnic rivalry, but that will never overcome its undertones of ethnic disdain: "You worship a God with eight arms!" the Muslim is reported to have (inaccurately) sneered.

Sometimes, interethnic interactions can lead to love. I asked an asylum seeker from West Africa married to a Hong Kong Chinese woman how he met her. He told me that in Africa he had become a believer in the Japanese religion Sōka Gakkai. In Hong Kong, he went to a Sōka Gakkai temple, met a fellow believer, and married her—a Japanese religion, scorned by many in Japan, enabling a West African to capture the holy grail of asylum seekers, marrying a local Hong Konger. I have heard many variations of this kind of story. In what passes for a lobby in a small Chungking Mansions guesthouse, I met a young woman from Japan and her prospective husband from Kenya. Her family was waiting at the expensive Peninsula Hotel to meet him (he could not obtain a visa to enter Japan), and the couple was nervously pacing back and forth before their agreed-upon meeting time. If the family approved, they would marry. (They did, and the couple subsequently married; a year later, she left him and returned to Japan.)

Interethnic interactions span the life course. My research assistant Maggie Lin saw an African woman enter a clothing store with her seven-month-old daughter in tow and leave her daughter with the Hong Kong Chinese proprietor for a few minutes. An array of nearby shopkeepers stopped by to play with her and cuddle her—they all knew her by name. The Chinese proprietor, knowing that the girl's mother had spent all of her money shipping goods back to Africa, prepared a plastic bag full of clothes for the little girl as a gift, since the weather was turning cold. My research assistant Jose Rojas observed two South Asian children playing in the back walkways surrounding Chungking Mansions, one with a scooter and the other one with a little bicycle. An African man, drinking at the whiskey stand, saw the scooter left unattended and as a joke hid it. The little boy looked puzzled, and the African man came from behind, lifted the child up in his arms, and took him to his scooter. They had never met before and did not exchange a word but laughed with each other for a long time before the children went back and continued their play.

More tragically, I myself went to the hospital with Ghanaian friends to visit a gravely ill Indonesian domestic helper in her twenties. The Ghanaians expressed puzzlement at what was wrong with her—she was paralyzed on one side of her body and blind—but since her Ghanaian boyfriend in Chungking Mansions had died of AIDS, the diagnosis seemed clear enough, although the Hong Kong Chinese doctor wouldn't confirm it when I tried to worm the information out of him. They visited her every day for several weeks until, medically stabilized, she was sent back to Indonesia to die. They did this partly because they knew her as an old friend ("She used to be so beautiful!") and partly from guilt: she had AIDS and a Ghanaian had infected her, they eventually could not help but realize.

These examples all depict warm human feeling across ethnic bounds. However, more often interethnic interactions may lead to disdain. We have seen how both Johnny Singh and Fahad Ali bristle at the racism they occasionally encounter from Hong Kong Chinese. Indeed, I know several Hong Kong Chinese shopkeepers in Chungking Mansions whose largely unwitting racial prejudice makes me cringe. In a broader sense, most people in Chungking Mansions engage in ethnic stereotyping. Africans, South Asians tell me, are "of low intelligence" and "naïve." South Asians, Africans tell me, "only scheme and think about business." Pakistanis, Indians say, "always want to fight," while Nigerians, East Africans say, are never to be trusted: "If you ever find that a Nigerian is staying in the room next to yours, change rooms. Otherwise the Nigerian will use witchcraft on you."

Stereotypes based on business experience might perhaps be slightly more accurate. A Pakistani phone dealer said, "People from Mali are easy to cheat. But Nigerians—they are really clever. You'll lose money on them." The Chinese wife of a business owner said, "Americans, Canadians, and Europeans are polite, but not Indians and Africans!" A Hong Kong proprietor of a store said to me, "I don't like dealing with Africans because they are so aggressive and demanding, though some are cheerful. I don't like Indians because they want to bargain down my price. I like Europeans and Japanese because they will pay the price I ask for." A West African trader with long experience in Chungking Mansions said, "Hong Kong people don't like Africans. I don't know what Hong Kong people are thinking. Maybe it's always about money. Africans help each other, but we don't talk much to Indians. They only think about business. Indian people are scared of black people. . . . I'm Christian. We are scared of Muslims because they are so quick to fight. Their thinking is very strict."

Stereotypes are sometimes punctured. An African Muslim asylum seeker told me that a Pakistani Muslim had scolded him at the mosque: "You don't know anything about Islam! You go to the mosque just for the free meal!"* The African Muslim then recited various Qur'anic verses to the Pakistani: he clearly knew more about Islam than the Pakistani did, to the latter's consternation. I had dinner with four Africans at an upper-floor Indian restaurant in Chungking Mansions, and when the owner gave out cards for his restaurant, they were given to me but not to the Africans, who very quickly and vociferously complained, until they too received cards—the owner will presumably never again make this mistake.

A mainland Chinese guesthouse keeper surprised me and, it seemed, herself when she said, "My favorite guests are West African Muslims. They're so

---

*During the month of Ramadan, the Kowloon Mosque, like many mosques, provides a free meal at its sundown service for those who are ending their daytime fast.

honest—they'll never cheat you—and so nice! And Japanese too. But I really dislike some Chinese, so pushy!" Another mainland Chinese guesthouse owner spoke of how African traders keep the room clean but mainland Chinese with children were the worst in her experience, since they spoiled their children and let them do what they liked. Stereotypes, although widely held, do give way before experience in at least some cases.

Chungking Mansions' interpersonal relations, if not always overtly friendly, are generally peaceful. People from more or less warring societies the world over come to Chungking Mansions (India versus Pakistan particularly come to mind) with competing creeds (Muslims and Christians are both richly represented in Chungking Mansions, as are Hindus and Sikhs). But they do not fight with each other, as they might in their home countries—or at least if they do occasionally quarrel, the quarrels are soon enough set aside in Chungking Mansions' universal striving to make money. As a Pakistani said to me vis-à-vis Indians, "I do not like them; they are not my friends. But I am here to make money, as they are here to make money. We cannot afford to fight."

Chungking Mansions is no utopia, and fights do break out from time to time—between Sikhs and Muslims, between Muslims and Christians, between Pakistanis and Africans, between Pakistanis and Indians, and between Nigerians and East Africans, among other groups—but these fights are comparatively infrequent. All in all, compared to many of the societies from which its traders and workers come, Chungking Mansions is remarkably peaceful. The general attitude of Chungking Mansions is, as shown in the quotation above, that the pursuit of profit makes ethnic and religious discord no more than an unwelcome distraction.[11] One story I have occasionally heard in Chungking Mansions is of how an Indian and an African got in a fight on the way up the elevator, but by the time they came back down, they had their arms around one another as newfound friends. This may or may not have happened, but it seems at least plausible.

Just as interethnic tension is comparatively muted in Chungking Mansions, so too is class tension, the tension between rich and poor. The gap between the rich and the poor—between owners and temporary workers, between the large entrepreneurs and the small traders—is enormous in Chungking Mansions, but most view it as a fact of life rather than an injustice. One young illegal worker bitterly complained to me about his boss, the restaurant owner: "I make just HK$3,000 a month working from 7 a.m. to 2 a.m. every day. He makes tens of thousands of dollars [actually, around HK$40,000 a month], and he only comes here when he wants to." But his dream, he told me, was to go into business and own a restaurant, just like his boss, exploiting future versions of his young self.

An asylum seeker I know illegally works for his relative in a phone stall, earning HK$2,300 a month in a stall that nets HK$100,000 a month, almost all going to his relative. His dream is to break free of this relative and cut his own deals, becoming a business magnate himself. "I know an asylum seeker who made HK$100,000 last month on a big phone sale," he told me. "That's what I want to do!"

The system itself, in all its inequalities, is thus not questioned, but only one's place in the system vis-à-vis certain others. Why is this? One reason is that those who have come to Chungking Mansions, even if they have been persecuted and have fled in the case of asylum seekers, nonetheless have enough money to fly to Hong Kong, something that the vast majority of their compatriots cannot ever do. This reveals that they are among the elite of their home societies. Chungking Mansions is basically a "club of the third-world successful," including even those at its lowest stations, despite the downtrodden status they may suffer in Hong Kong.

The poor in Chungking Mansions are highly unlikely to become rich, the illegal workers will probably never gain Hong Kong residency or enough capital to become entrepreneurs, and the asylum seekers will probably be rejected in their claims, as are well over 90 percent of asylum seekers in Hong

Kong. But, again, the poor and the rich alike buy into the basic assumptions of Chungking Mansions, those of capitalism. In this sense, Chungking Mansions is really no different from anywhere else in Hong Kong or in China or throughout most of the capitalist world today—it features the same vast gaps of rich and poor as elsewhere. It differs only in that it is more visible: instead of the exploitation of faceless corporations, Chungking Mansions enables exploitation by individual entrepreneurs whose faces those they exploit know very well. But the exploited seek, in general, not to rebel against their oppressors but to emulate them.

This, then, is the panorama of people in Chungking Mansions in their interactions. I examined in the first two chapters of this book Chungking Mansions as a place and the different groups of people within the building. In the following two chapters, I consider, in greater depth the goods that pass through Chungking Mansions and the webs of laws that constrain Chungking Mansions before turning, in this book's last chapter, to the larger meanings of the building and the people within it.

goods

THREE

The Passage of Goods in Chungking Mansions

Chungking Mansions would not exist as a center of low-end globalization were it not for the passage of goods through its corridors; it functions today to enable the trading and transferring of goods from China to the developing world of Africa and South Asia and elsewhere. How do these goods circulate? Who are the merchants and traders who sell and buy these goods, and how do they do business?

The traders in Chungking Mansions embody low-end globalization, as we discussed in chapter 1, globalization that takes place not through the dealings of large corporations, but rather through individuals dealing with one another largely on the basis of trust and working with a high degree of risk, often carrying their goods themselves across the globe. This form of business migration is neither new nor unprecedented—consider, for example, the "informal commercial importers" in Haiti and elsewhere in the Caribbean and the street entrepreneurs in Ciudad del Este in Paraguay, as well as the Congolese traders in Paris and African street vendors in New York.[1] But what may be unprecedented is the sheer scale of their activity in such a concentrated place.

It is impossible to know for certain the scale of trade in Chungking Mansions. My rough estimate is that some 20 percent of the mobile phones recently in use in sub-Saharan Africa have been sold in Chungking Mansions, judging from sales in 2007 and 2008. Phone stalls sold an average of 15,000 to 20,000 phones a month, I am told, averaging out the wide variations from month to month over the year, with established phone stalls selling 20,000 to 30,000 a month and smaller stalls selling 5,000 to 10,000 per month. These are whispered figures given to me by store employees—sales figures are secret information, given the intense competition between phone stalls in Chungking Mansions—but seem reasonable. There were approximately ninety phone stores in Chungking Mansions in 2007 to 2008. If we assume 18,000 to be an average sales figure, then 1,620,000 phones were sold per month, or 19.4 million phone sales per year, in Chungking Mansions. There were 126 million mobile phone subscriptions in sub-Saharan Africa in 2007, with many individuals having multiple subscriptions.[2] This makes the assumption of 20 percent seem broadly plausible.

Phone traders have told me that, if anything, this percentage is too low. Beyond this, there is a stream of phones that transit through Chungking Mansions, on the path from south China to Africa and elsewhere, and are stored in warehouses in and around Chungking Mansions while traders organize transport. If we include these phones as well, then the number of phones bound for sub-Saharan Africa that pass through Chungking Mansions would be much higher. All in all, the phone trade through Chungking Mansions is a significant chunk of the global economy of mobile phones in the developing world.*

For other goods, such as clothing and watches, the percentage of goods passing directly through Chungking Mansions is no doubt smaller, although by no means insignificant. However, sales information for clothing, watches, and electronic goods seems to be even harder to acquire than that for mobile phones. Given the variety of sources for these goods, including small south China factories with highly hidden records, there is simply no way this information can be known. Chungking Mansions is a significant node in the developing world economy, but exactly how much of a node is anyone's guess.

Throughout the world, the passage of goods takes place to an extraordinary degree beyond governmental control; less than five percent of the goods passing through the world's ports are ever inspected.[3] In the developing world, this lack of government control over the passage of goods happens because governments lack the capability to fully control the economy. The state seeks to exert control but cannot—its reach exceeds its grasp, because its citizens can easily evade it. In Hong Kong, this happens in part not simply because the state can't control it, but because it won't.

Hong Kong has consistently been rated as the world's freest economy, the economy most unbound by the strictures of state bureaucracy, by the Heritage Foundation and the *Wall Street Journal*.[4] The freedom of the Hong Kong economy is to some extent mythical: property developers and other magnates in fact have inordinate influence on government policy.[5] Nonetheless, economic freedom has long been the dominant ideology of Hong Kong.[6] While the state does in part control the economy in many areas—for example, in its regulation of street hawkers[7] as well as its clampdown on large-scale production of copy goods—it is fair to say that by and large the

---

*Because of the dire state of landlines in most of sub-Saharan Africa, phone cards don't tend to be used with landlines but with mobile phones instead. Many Africans still go to local phone stalls when they need to use the telephone, but these places' high rates makes owning a mobile phone far more economical in the long run, which is one reason why mobile phones are so keenly desired in Africa. In 2009, due to the global economic downturn, the figure I've given for monthly sales in Chungking Mansions phone stalls is substantially lower. I have heard that in late 2009 the average phone stall sold under 10,000 phones per month.

Hong Kong government is the embodiment of laissez-faire and of neoliberalism, the doctrine that the government should get out of the way and let the market have free rein.

To use an earlier era's parlance, Hong Kong is a first-world island between two third-world economic blocks: China, which is rapidly developing but still lacks full rule of law in its economic activities, and Africa. Chungking Mansions, in turn, embodies a third-world informal economy that is made possible by the first-world neoliberalism of the society in which it is located.

Selling Goods

In chapter 1, I discussed how businesses such as guesthouses and restaurants are run in Chungking Mansions; let me in this section specifically consider businesses selling goods. The shops in Chungking Mansions sell many different kinds of goods, and each has its own particular way of doing business. The souvenir shop on the ground floor must sell goods every few minutes or hours, as is also true for retail electronics shops and luggage shops—they depend on a steady flow of customers. The wholesale phone and clothing stores, on the other hand, depend on far fewer customers—a dozen customers each buying a few hundred suits or phones each week may be more than enough to pay the rent and make a profit—but if those customers don't show up for a few weeks, it may mean ruin. As one wholesale phone-stall proprietor told me, "I might get 25 or 30 customers a day coming in to ask about prices and models, but if I can make just one sale a day, I'll do well." I focus here on stores selling goods wholesale, because this is Chungking Mansions' major significance as a node of developing-world trade.

Why do these proprietors set up stores in Chungking Mansions? For some, particularly South Asians, as discussed in chapter 2, Chungking Mansions may seem to be one of the few places in Hong Kong where they can comfortably live and work. A Pakistani with Hong Kong residence rights can set up a phone stall on the first floor of Chungking Mansions and feel at home with his fellow Pakistanis, who are competitors but also may be friends or acquaintances, as he could not feel at home in any other business environment in Hong Kong. Pakistanis, partly for this reason, overwhelmingly dominate the trade in mobile phones, managing, as of 2008, some 80 percent of phone stalls in Chungking Mansions—although this percentage has been declining somewhat in subsequent years, with the influx of mainland Chinese.

Others wind up in Chungking Mansions because it makes sense given their business interests. Some mainland clothing shop proprietors own clothing factories in China, while others have familial links to mainland factories making the kind of low-end clothing that African buyers prefer: relatively cheap products that are not popular in the Euro-American market. These merchants came to Chungking Mansions because of the higher degree of status and trust that buyers may give to shops in Hong Kong, as opposed to those on the mainland, and the stream of developing-world potential customers passing through the building, as nowhere else in Hong Kong.

Still others wind up in Chungking Mansions simply because rents are cheap, as compared to elsewhere in Hong Kong. In some cases, these businesses have little to do with the dominant business current of Chungking Mansions. I interviewed an opal dealer whose office is in the upper floors of Chungking Mansions. He receives opals from Australia, which are then sent to Shenzhen, China, where they are ground and placed in various settings. They are then sent back to Hong Kong, to his office, and shipped to Australia to be bought by tourists. These tourists, most typically mainland Chinese, come to Australia and want to buy finished opals, since opals are Australian. However, since Australian labor costs are high and Chinese labor costs are low, these tourists, ironically, buy Chinese-processed opals in Australia, courtesy of this man's business (and the businesses of many others like him, at least a few of which are also in Chungking Mansions). He has been in Chungking Mansions twenty four years in all; his business could be located anywhere in Hong Kong, except for his consideration of rental prices. His Australian wholesale buyers may have no idea what Chungking Mansions represents, and he sends an employee to their nearby fancy hotels to guide them through the throngs to his Chungking Mansions office.

Stores selling different types of wholesale goods have different business models. There are some fifteen watch stores selling distinctly low-end watches, often running as little as one US dollar each when bought wholesale. There are many watch sellers outside Chungking Mansions murmuring "Copy watch?" particularly to white passersby, who are seen as the most likely customers—copies of Rolexes, for example, at a small fraction of the price of an original, for sale at HK$400 to HK$800. But these sellers are not linked to Chungking Mansions, but instead to relatively secluded shops in nearby buildings; in Chungking Mansions, the bulk of business is in low-end wholesale watches, sold by the hundreds or thousands.

There are also some thirty clothing stores. As noted above, many of these stores have close links to mainland factories. This is also often true for watches and mobile phones, but seems particularly true for clothing. For clothing dealers, those who deal in brand-name goods tend to sell factory

rejects, with bad stitching or other defects, or warehoused clothes of earlier seasons, or else samples, leftovers, or items that didn't pass other countries' importing regulations. Sometimes the path of these goods is extraordinary. An item of clothing, for example, may begin with an order placed by a large American or British department store. The fabric and material come from countries such as Bangladesh and the item is manufactured in China or Malaysia. The finished product is shipped to the United States or Great Britain where it is then rejected or remaindered only to be sold back to Hong Kong where it is then bought by African traders.

The biggest problem that Hong Kong clothing sellers have is their competition over the border in south China. Unlike electronics and phones, the general perception in Chungking Mansions is that clothing made on the mainland can be trusted, as long as the buyer looks closely at how the goods are packed. Competition also comes from the working-class Hong Kong neighborhood of Sham Shui Po, some two miles north of Chungking Mansions, an area specializing in wholesale goods, where many clothes dealers with warehouses offer clothes specifically suited for the African market. Many of these are outlets for Chinese factories just over the border. The deals there are often better than those that can be obtained at Chungking Mansions, African entrepreneurs tell me—they stay in Chungking Mansions, but no longer buy much there. Clothing merchants at Chungking

Mansions whom I know are sometimes filled with gloom over the difficulty of making money in such a difficult environment.

The most common stores in Chungking Mansions are mobile phone stores, with some hundred in all at present, and these are also the most complicated in terms of the different types of merchandise they sell. Shops often have their particular specialties: China-made branded phones such as G-Tide or Orion; China-made no-brand phones; China-made knock-off phones such as "Sory-Ericssen"; China-made copies of European, Korean, or American brands exactly like the original*; fourteen-day phones, which are European-brand phones that have been returned by their original owners and have been warehoused and eventually sent to Hong Kong and Chungking Mansions to be sold to developing-world buyers; or used phones.†

Any given shop may have a diversity of phones. A ground-floor shop may typically have used phones at the very bottom of its glass case—phones with no original packaging—and fourteen-day phones, which could pass for new to the undiscerning buyer, a bit higher up and better presented in the glass cases. At its top display, it may have China-made new phones as well as China-made copies of European or Korean phones. All these different kinds of phones may be available within the store, but as we will shortly discuss, the buyer had better know exactly what he wants if he is to avoid getting taken advantage of.

All in all, what we see in Chungking Mansions are the castoffs or copies of developed-world prosperity sold to the developing world. The ultimate significance of this we will discuss later; for now, let me just indicate that wholesale sellers of goods in Chungking Mansions overwhelmingly maintained to me that they saw their role as providing what their customers wanted, no more and no less. If their customers wanted flashy goods that looked new, they would provide them; if their customers wanted copies, they would provide them; if their customers wanted cheap, shoddy goods,

---

*Most commentators use the terms "copy" and "knock-off" as synonyms. In this book, I differentiate between these terms: a copy, in my usage, is manufactured to seem indistinguishable from the original, whereas a knock-off, in the effort to obtain a degree of legal protection, has small differentiations, such as a change of one letter in the brand name, to make it not exactly the same as the original.

†Why are these fourteen-day phones sent all the way to Hong Kong, rather than shipped directly to Africa, to be sold wholesale? I do not fully know; however, because many traders combine different kinds of phones in their purchases, mixing fourteen-day phones with China-made copies and China-made branded phones, Hong Kong remains an optimal place to buy phones for African traders.

they would provide them. They sought to satisfy the wholesale buyers who made their businesses possible, while charging them enough to make a tidy profit, and asked no larger questions, for they had enough to worry about in being able to keep up within the fast-changing market of Chungking Mansions. How many traders are buying phones in order to launder money made from the sale of drugs or weapons? This no doubt exists, to an extent, but the merchants I know don't ask, they simply sell. If "dirty money" is defined very broadly as money "generated outside of the formal economy," then much of the money changing hands in Chungking Mansions is "dirty," although buyers and sellers certainly do not see it as "dirty."[8]

These merchants are at the mercy of distinctly local forces—if a new stall opens next door that has a warehouse and a particularly good set of wholesalers, then one's stall may rapidly be driven out of business. These merchants are also at the mercy of global forces. If China tightens its entry policies toward certain African nations, it may lead to a flourishing of the market in Hong Kong, with some Chungking Mansions stalls making windfall profits, since if China is off-limits, entrepreneurs must buy in Hong Kong. If, on the other hand, Hong Kong tightens its entry policies, the reverse may happen. If exchange rates shift, as happened in 2008 when the yuan, which earlier was at 106 yuan per 100 Hong Kong dollars, sank to 96, this too may have a large effect. If US dollars stop flowing so readily through African countries, as happened in 2008 and 2009, then many traders may simply stay home, with local businesses shutting down. The fall of oil prices in 2008 greatly affected the Nigerian foreign hard currency flow and caused the national currency, the naira, to change in value from 118 per US dollar to 168 per US dollar in a single month. Nigerian traders stopped coming, and some Chungking Mansions merchants suffered greatly. In Chungking Mansions, the local is distinctly global, with distant events sometimes powerfully affecting business one way or another, at the same time that the global is distinctly local.

Taking Advantage of Buyers

For the stores selling goods wholesale in Chungking Mansions, there are always competing impulses at work. To develop its customer base, a stall must be more or less honest in its dealings—a customer who knows that he has been taken advantage of will never come back. On the other hand, a particularly ignorant customer may be easy to cheat for a large profit, making the temptation irresistible. As an African buyer of phones told me,

The phones for sale in Chungking Mansions: the outsides look good, Sony and other brands, but the inside of many of them is rubbish. . . . You learn what the good stores and bad stores are—the bad stores, after you buy from them, your customers, after five or six months when their phones are broken, they come back to complain. . . . I think 80 percent of the mobile phone stores in Chungking Mansions cheat customers sometimes.

Several phone-stall proprietors vociferously refuted this comment when I showed it to them (this chapter has been read by several Chungking Mansions merchants for their critiques). In one's words,

Phone-sellers can't cheat customers; these traders know what they are buying. Nobody's cheating anyone! Africans are not stupid! If a trader buys 500 phones from me here in Hong Kong, we give guarantees—we will be responsible for the 500 phones. I will ask the trader to check each phone one by one. If there's any problem, we'll take it back.

These merchants suggested that the trader quoted above was naïve and perhaps lazy, in not adequately checking the phones he had bought.

Still, phone stalls do tend to be sly in various ways. As one Pakistani merchant told me in 2007, "We change the phone's housing. We refab it. Then we sell it to you as if it were a brand-new phone. You don't know this. But we know."* How often are buyers cheated? In retail sales of phones in Chungking Mansions I am told that "probably 50 percent of sales involve deceiving the buyer by charging a higher price, but in wholesale, no more than 5 percent. They're smart. They know!" This phone dealer continued, "It depends on the country. Tanzanian people, for example, are still far behind, but Nigerian people are far ahead. We sell camera phones that we get for HK$30 to Tanzanians for HK$300. They don't know the technology that Nigerian people know." He is saying that the more technologically sophisticated a country's customers are, the less likely the entrepreneur will be cheated, for he will carry that sophistication to Hong Kong.

*By 2008, refabbing—changing the fourteen-day phone's housing and beyond this, rewiring the phone's motherboard—had become more sophisticated, and so the cheating that this merchant described had become less egregious. More broadly, the phone market has been evolving with such rapidity that a strategy used by merchants in Chungking Mansions in one period may be entirely abandoned a year later; my discussion in these pages is thus necessarily dated.

When the proprietor owns the store, or rents the store from an absentee landlord, the motive for cheating may be clear, since the money earned will go directly into the proprietor's pocket, but cheating may also take place when only a clerk is present to mind the store. One young Pakistani man working in a store selling China-made new and copy phones told me that his boss had given him a list of phones with the minimum price they can be sold for. Anything above that price he pockets, and no one asks any questions. He said to me, "Look, I'm Muslim. I don't want to cheat anybody, because I am before God"; but still, he said that he would regularly charge customers a slightly higher price, so that he could pocket the extra profit.

He also noted that if he makes the price too high, the customers will all go to another shop instead. His moral from this was that "you can make money by cheating people, but you can only cheat people a little bit. If you charge too much, you'll have no customers." In the world of Chungking Mansions, mobile phones—unlike, for example, the stores in the building selling computers—bear no price stickers. This, I am told, is because the market is always changing. Also, no doubt, it is because this unmarked price enables prices to vary in accordance with the knowledge of the buyer.

Copy Goods

The "cheating" discussed above is generally a matter of misrepresenting the price or the quality of goods, rather than of claiming that copy goods are genuine, but copies of many kinds of goods are widely available in the stalls of Chungking Mansions. To turn first to watches, there are original watches, copy watches, and knock-off watches—for example, the HK$10 knock-off "Seciko" watch I bought at Chungking Mansions is some fifty times cheaper than the Seiko watch it was emulating. As a business columnist in East Africa wrote a decade ago, "How, for heaven's sake, can one distinguish a 'Citizien' watch from the high quality Citizen; 'Smatch' from the Swiss Swatch; and "Sekico" from Seiko?"[9]

Several African traders told me that for close relatives, as well as for customs officials, they buy original watches. For their customers, however, it would make no sense to buy original watches, since almost none of their customers have remotely enough money to buy original brands such as Seiko or Citizen. All maintained that they do not represent these watches as original, but since their customers tend to have no idea of the distinction between original and copy goods, the argument is moot. Their customers may have never heard of the brands these copies are copying—they simply want cheap watches, and sellers sell these watches cheaply.

Clothing is a separate matter. I am told that any trader in Chungking Mansions can easily enough get copy clothes made. As one trader said, "If you want a thousand copies of an Armani jacket, they can provide it with no problem; they'll just get on the phone to their Chinese factory." Typically, the labels are copied but not the design and workmanship. Since the goods these stores sell are manifestly different from the goods sold by high-end brands even though their labels may be the same, the proprietors of these stores tend not to worry about prosecution. Despite this, many stores refuse to sell to white people, who are reputed to be particularly concerned about issues of intellectual property. Several West African traders I've met regularly wear the striking clothing designed by their Chinese clothing outlets as advertisements. The designs they wear may well be copies of other African clothing in the market, but not of global brands, and so the copying goes unprosecuted.

Copies are a more pivotal issue in the phone market. As with watches and clothing, it is almost never the case that a shopkeeper sells a trader copy phones claimed to be real. In discussions between a phone seller and a wholesale buyer, phones are never spoken of as "fake," and generally not even as "copies" when sold wholesale, but generally as "China-made"; when the phones in question are Nokia or Samsung or Sony-Ericsson, the connotation is obvious.* Over and over again, I have heard phone dealers offer a model wholesale for a higher price, for example HK$500 apiece, and then, when the buyer expresses no interest, say, "How about HK$200 apiece?" This sudden downward leap reflects the shift between real and copy—buyer and seller generally say nothing explicit, but both know that with the drastic drop in price, this line has been crossed.

These copy phones are not necessarily garbage—some work for years and may possibly even last as long as the original phone, if they are A-grade counterfeits rather than B- or C-grade counterfeits, all of which may be sold by phone stalls. Phone stalls are well aware that when receipts are written for phone sales, they must avoid writing the brand name of the phone, so that these particular copy phones cannot be traced back to their stall.

I have occasionally heard from stall keepers comments such as, "Oh no, my store would never sell copy phones. But that store over there—all they sell are copies!" However, in 2007, despite the fact that the display windows of many stores showed new China-made phones, many phones sold were

*Ironically, Nokia, among other brands, manufactures phones in China. But in Chungking Mansions, "China-made Nokias" means copies.

Nokia, Samsung, and iPhone copies. One store clerk told me that his boss warned him not to sell to Chinese people, and some stores do not sell to white people either, unless they are obviously from Russia or Ukraine or other poorer countries on the market for copy mobile phones, for fear of undercover police (Hong Kong police are overwhelmingly of Chinese ethnicity, with a smattering of South Asians and British). "No one is directly afraid of police, because they don't come around much, but you still have to be careful," I was told.

In 2009, the Customs and Excise Police handed notes to many phone stalls in Chungking Mansions saying, in so many word, "Please don't sell copy goods." Whether this was prelude to an eventual large-scale police raid, or simply a gentle reminder, was unclear to the phone-stall proprietors (as I write these words, a year later, the latter seems to have been the case). Police and the courts have prosecuted at least two stalls selling primarily copy phones; the word in Chungking Mansions is that you can have copy phones on display and a few hundred in stock or otherwise available, but not so many as to be conspicuous. In late 2009, agents from Nokia began legal proceedings against twenty-one phone stalls in Chungking Mansions found by their undercover investigators to have been selling copy Nokia phones, but the word from several Chungking Mansions phone stalls was that their evidence was weak, since most phone stalls were suspicious of these investigators in their inquiries and told them little.

Some phones are knock-offs (in my usage of the term), bearing slightly different names from the original, such as "Nokla" or "Sory-Ericssen," providing a degree of protection from prosecution. As a phone-stall operator told me, "Yes, there is a Nokla N-95, made in China to avoid copyright issues. But that Nokla is an exact copy of Nokia N-95. Only the alphabet has changed." Others are copies in alphabet as well, and in name and appearance are all but indistinguishable from the original, except to the trained eye. A phone trader told me that he was never fooled:

> You can see if a phone is a copy by its housing, its box, its accessories. If you show me a mobile, I can tell you within a microsecond whether or not it's a copy. You can tell by weight—copies are lighter than the originals. And the housing, the accessories, the manual—there's a certain amount of difference. The original, in the manual, provides a website to register; the copy phone doesn't do that. Original phones may have the website listed right on the box, but not copies. There's also the ID numbers. Copy phones may provide this too, but the number will be fake, as you can tell by dialing the manufacturer's number to check.

As the above indicates, one very easy way to tell the difference between real and copy is by weight—a copy Nokia, for example, has generally been 40 percent lighter than a real Nokia because of the materials used in its Chinese production. However, by 2009, some Chinese phone manufacturers were getting more sophisticated—now some make heavier phones, and in this sense these phones are indistinguishable from the European originals. Beyond weight, one can examine, above the SIM card, the company code and can generally tell whether the phone is a copy or not by the quality of the lettering. Beyond lettering, one can tell what is China-made and what is not by opening up the phone and looking at the motherboard, which shows distinctly different characteristics if it is China-made.

One cannot distinguish genuine from copy phones simply on the basis of price. It is not the case, for example, that HK$2,000 phones are genuine and HK$500 phones are copies, or HK$450 phones are real and HK$150 phones are copies; rather, there is a whole range of prices. Basically, China-made copy phones are far cheaper than European- or Korean- or Japanese-made phones, but there are genuine phones, very old models, that might go for as little as HK$150, and there are copy phones that may go for a far higher price—it all depends on the model that is being copied, as well as the quality of the copy. Only to focus on genuine phones and copies is a bit distorting. Typically, phone stalls deal with a complex array of different kinds of phones, as we have seen.

By 2008, China-made phones under their own brand names were becoming more prominent—the market in copy phones, or in used phones, was diminishing compared to the market in China-branded phones, new phones made in China, which were increasing in quality. However, by 2009, another shift had taken place: China-brand new phones had to an extent given way to fourteen-day phones, due to ongoing problems in China-made phones' durability, particularly in terms of their batteries. Merchants estimated to me in fall 2009 that 60 percent of the phones sold in Chungking Mansions were now fourteen-day phones, with most of the rest China-brand new phones. This has had the effect of making phone sellers more and more "legal," as the demand for copies goes down.*

*The only components of phones in which copies remain rampant are batteries; because the original batteries are so expensive, many phone stalls replace the batteries in fourteen-day phones with China-made copy batteries and sell the originals separately. With older models of phones, customers may never know, since the copy batteries may work as well as the original batteries, but with newer models of phones, with more demanding functions, the difference is apparent, I'm told.

Manufacturers and Middlemen

The wholesale shops in Chungking Mansions are under the threat of being supplanted by manufacturers from China, who are coming in to Chungking Mansions to start their own stores, or of being forsaken by customers, who go into China themselves to buy goods at a cheaper price. Goods in China are reputed to be of low quality—particularly phones and electronics. But Chinese phones are getting better, as are too the facilities available on the mainland for traders. All in all, for stores in Chungking Mansions, China is both the source of goods and a distinct threat. Chungking Mansions' wholesalers represent nodes in between—most of what they sell is made in China and fans out across the globe. Chungking Mansions thus plays the same role that Hong Kong itself has long played—it is an entrepôt between China and the world—but many merchants have been complaining that business is becoming more and more difficult.

Merchants love to complain, but it seems that many of the stores selling wholesale goods in Chungking Mansions are indeed facing trying times because of the pressure of China. As one Hong Kong Chinese businesswoman in Chungking Mansions said, "There is no future for the small or middle-size export companies which only aim to earn the tiny price differences of goods between mainland China and the rest of the world. Only large companies will survive." The room for Chungking Mansions to be the middleman between mainland China and foreign businessmen is shrinking rapidly, she believed, just as would be the case for Hong Kong as a whole in coming years.

A Hong Kong Chinese clothing merchant said, "Because China has developed so much, there's almost no room for Hong Kong in the clothing industry any more. China's garment industry is already world-class." A Pakistani phone-stall proprietor, reflecting the view of Johnny Singh in chapter 2, suggested that Chungking Mansions itself would become more and more Chinese, because, with new visa regulations, Chinese who start businesses could remain in Hong Kong: "The Chinese can get phones directly from their factories and can sell more cheaply than we can. There will be no need for the Pakistani [middleman]."

On the other hand, other merchants in Chungking Mansions complain vociferously about mainland Chinese business practices and say that they will not succeed in Chungking Mansions. In one phone-stall proprietor's words, a man who had lived four years in China:

> The problem with the Chinese is that they will agree to anything until they get your deposit. But once they have your money, they will deliver whatever

they want. You have a contract, but for them it has no meaning at all. It's like
a piece of toilet tissue. . . . I moved to Hong Kong to get away from all the
headaches in China. It's dangerous to do business in a country where you can't
have any arbitration, any rule of law.

A shoe merchant in Chungking Mansions had a similar complaint. "The
Chinese make small shoes and the Africans want big ones. The Africans
make an order for large shoes, and the Chinese say yes, but then their actual
shipment to Africa might have many shoes that are much smaller, not suiting
the African market." From Hong Kong, he now has shoes made in factories
run by Hong Kong entrepreneurs in Guangdong Province, so he can largely
trust the sizes to be delivered to his African customers.

When one goes into Guangzhou, there are places remarkably like Chungking Mansions, such as the Tianxiu Building and the Canaan Export Clothes
Wholesale Trading Centre. These places are often far more bustling with African traders than Chungking Mansions. The number of Africans based in
Guangzhou, after a downturn in 2008 and 2009 due to the visa crackdown
around the time of the Olympics, has shot up again. At the time of this
writing, many more African entrepreneurs are in Guangzhou than in Hong
Kong. If this remains the case, then Chungking Mansions' future as a center
of low-end globalization may indeed be limited.

On the other hand, if some Chinese business practices continue to be as
slipshod as Hong Kong merchants have described to me, then Chungking
Mansions' role as a site for the business of low-end globalization will continue. As I review this chapter in May 2010, it appears that the number of
African traders, and particularly phone buyers, in Chungking Mansions has
gone down somewhat as compared to two years earlier—the traders are now
more likely to be in China, although many have also been kept at home in
Africa by the world economic downturn. As one phone-stall merchant told
me, "Yes, a lot of Africans have moved to China—they want to establish
themselves there. But most of them are there because they cannot get a visa
in Hong Kong.* If they can, they'll come back to Hong Kong, because they
can trust the phones here."

---

*I heard this statement from a number of Chungking Mansions' merchants and
traders in late 2009—the word on the ground is that China is allowing in African traders and hampering them from entering Hong Kong, as is Hong Kong immigration itself in its greater degree of restrictiveness.

Tricks and Travails of a Phone Stall

I spent many hours in a phone stall over a year-long period in 2007, at the end of which Mahmood, my prime informant, returned to Pakistan. Six months thereafter, the stall went out of business. The stall was the size of a bathroom, with two seats edged next to the glass counter. During the time I was there, four people were working at the shop: Mahmood's relative, the boss, who spent his working time scouting for sources for his wholesale phones; Mahmood, who managed the stall on a day-to-day basis; and two temporary workers from India, who spent their time unlocking the codes of foreign mobile phones as well as packing phones that had been sold. The two Indians were required to go back to Kolkata once every forty-two days. A job of these tourist-permit employees was bringing in copy phones from China. One told me that he tried to look very confident, and the customs people at the Hong Kong-China border never confiscated the goods he carried.

Some 90 percent of the customers in this stall were African, with another 10 percent from Europe, the Middle East, or India and Pakistan. The Europeans often sought very particular models, those models desired back in their home countries' specialty niches. Indians and Pakistanis were Mahmood's most difficult customers, he said: "If they know I buy a phone for HK$250, they will seek a price of HK$249." He said that consumers in Nigeria, as well as India and Pakistan, want the latest model—they might buy China-made phones, genuine or copy, that have all the latest accoutrements to impress their friends with. On the other hand, consumers from other African countries more often wanted anything that works—this is what their customers seek. All in all, Africans are easier to deal with than South Asians, Mahmood maintained; many are naïve, but some of them are "crazy," he said. Once, an African entrepreneur walked in while I was talking to Mahmood and typed into the calculator a model of Nokia he wanted that didn't exist. Mahmood said that the man was simply playing with him.

Let me describe some of the negotiations between Mahmood and his customers, first, some retail transactions. A potential customer, a West African woman, came in seeking a personal phone. Mahmood showed her first a HK$450 phone, a fourteen-day Nokia model; then, when she said it was too expensive, he showed her a HK$90 copy phone and then a HK$190 phone, which was real but French in language and thus cheap. The potential customer was unable, both because of language and ignorance of the phone market, to say what she wanted, so Mahmood offered various choices: "Here is this phone for this price and that phone for that price. What do you want?"

In another transaction, a Frenchman asked for three Siemens C62 phones. Mahmood immediately asked him about a different and comparable phone. The customer indicated he hadn't heard of it, and, as a result, Mahmood immediately knew that he didn't know much about phones and could charge accordingly. The customer bought the three phones without knowing that he had been taken for a price 30 percent higher than he otherwise would have paid.

In still another transaction, Mahmood offered an East African buyer a phone at HK$280; the buyer wanted six pieces. The man said, "No, no, it should be HK$200!" Mahmood said, "No, I bought it for HK$249." The potential buyer was disgusted and left. Mahmood then said, "Actually I bought them for HK$140. He'll be back tomorrow! It's all just the beginning of the game. Eventually I'll sell it to him for around HK$180. But this guy just got off the plane from Africa today, so why not?" Mahmood said that if a buyer was very smart, his stall might be able to make only HK$10 per phone in profit; if the buyer was ignorant, HK$70 or HK$80.

Wholesale trade involving far more money is more complex, but more elusive. I watched Mahmood at work trying to sell 3,000 phones to a Cameroonian buyer, from which his store could potentially make a profit of HK$60,000, in a deal that eventually fell through. Just a few of these deals a month would bring his stall huge returns, but for every one deal that came through, a hundred more were never consummated.

The phone business is remarkably changeable, and Mahmood was continuously worried about catching the latest trend, and convincing his relative to follow that trend, or else his stall might go out of business. Mahmood told me in mid-2007 that the new trend was refab phones reworked in China (see footnote, p. 113). It is difficult to recognize these phones, but one way to check is to examine the phone's screws to see if they have been loosened; however, this is an imperfect means of detection. Mahmood told me that an old Nokia model might sell for HK$150 as a fourteen-day but HK$100 refab; thus the dealer can make considerable profit by selling these refabs as fourteen-day phones.

If a buyer did not know what refab phones were, then Mahmood felt free to mix them in with fourteen-day phones. He gave the example of putting water into milk. "If you mix two glasses of water into one glass of milk, it will be apparent, but if you put 20 percent water into milk, then most people won't know." Ethically, he said this is reasonable, since his stall too was sold many phones that, despite claims otherwise, were not fourteen-day but refab phones. Mahmood said that even very smart African traders sometimes could not recognize refab phones. One trader was fooled by Mah-

mood, in that Mahmood told the refab people to tighten the phone screws to an unusual degree, so that it would appear that the phones had never been opened. The buyer was Nigerian, where all the phones go into a big open market, according to Mahmood—thus, this buyer would suffer no negative consequences if, after several months, many of his phones stopped working. No one would complain, or know, he said.

Mahmood also worried greatly about the weekly and monthly flow of customers. January and February 2007 were slow months, because Chinese factories were closed for the Chinese New Year, as is the case every year. While the stall sold just 2,200 phones in February, in March it rapidly picked up, with 6,000 phones sold in the first ten days of March. One day in early March, a big customer stopped by, a Kenyan woman who regularly buys 1,500 to 2,000 units each month; one of the workers in the store was sent especially to China to pick up her order of China-made parts. On the other hand, a businessman from Ghana could not come to Hong Kong because of visa restrictions; the store had an order of 7,000 phones for him, representing HK$175,000 in potential profits that they lost.

By mid-June, there was another downturn; Mahmood believed that it was because the store should be dealing primarily in China-made copy phones, but was not—not because of any fears of breaking the law, but because it was too much work for his relative to implement, and his relative, Mahmood told me, was too busy staying out all night with his mistresses to do proper work for the phone stall he owned. Mahmood became despondent because his relative had begun frequently shouting at him for being "lazy." In the summer of 2007, instead of shifting to China-made phones, the stall shifted more to used phones, to meet customers' demands. The used phones simply functioned as phones, but they tended to last longer than the China-made phones. In July, the stall sold 16,000 phones, selling to a few big customers but still making relatively low profits compared to many other phone stalls in Chungking Mansions.

By autumn, a new shift was beginning, one that would pick up steam over the next year. New China-made phones were becoming cheaper, and also better, so that a wholesaler could get a new China phone with a color screen for HK$60 to HK$70. This was bringing unease to many of the Pakistani-run phone stalls, not just Mahmood's—the Pakistanis have had a monopoly on fourteen-day-phones in Chungking Mansions, but Chinese company representatives might begin to come in, selling their own new phones, offering better prices for buyers. But the question about these phones was this: How long would they last? After six months, will these new Chinese phones still be working? If so, then the business for which Mahmood worked, unless it rapidly changed course, would be severely jeopardized.

As it happened, however, Mahmood's father suddenly became severely ill in Pakistan and then died, necessitating his return to the country, along with the not inconsiderable amount of money he'd saved while in Hong Kong. The stall he worked for, as earlier mentioned, did not long survive his departure.

Varieties of Traders

I have met an extraordinary array of traders at Chungking Mansions. Here are some entries from my own and my research assistants' notes from 2006 through 2009:

> A phone trader from Tanzania comes to China once a month between May and December, the peak buying months in Africa, buying phones in Guangzhou and bringing them by train to Hong Kong and then by plane to Tanzania as extra luggage. He can pack in seven phones per kilogram, he said, carrying back an average of 700 phones per trip, by paying for an extra weight allowance. He can make an average profit, after flight, luggage, and accommodation costs, of US$500 per trip, he claimed.

A Senegalese trader buys gems in the Congo, goes to Germany to sell them, then Bangkok and Hong Kong; he has been doing this for five years. He showed me photos on his cell phone of Goma, in the Congo, where he said it was incredibly dangerous—"you can get killed any time"—and said he'd been robbed at gunpoint there.

An Indian trader from Bangalore is in the business of buying classic Leica cameras and parts from various Indian cities and bringing them to camera dealers in Hong Kong. He tried to sell me a Leica M-6, "used but 99 percent perfect," for HK$25,000; a dealer would have sold it for HK$39,000, he said.

A trader from East Africa deals in knock-off Jacuzzi baths made in south China. He sells to business owners and also to government ministers, he said—people with enough money to buy Jacuzzi-like baths with televisions and CD players installed.

A Kenyan trader of garments now living in China comes to Hong Kong to renew her China visa every 30 days and also to buy single items of clothing that she thinks will sell well in East Africa. She then commissions a factory in south China to make up to 10,000 copies for her under her own label, which she hires fellow Kenyans to take back to East Africa.

A Ghanian trader has visited Hong Kong five times since 2004. His business is selling hip-hop clothes. He's been visiting different places to buy goods— Dubai and Vietnam—but has found that made-in-China clothes sold by Hong Kong agents are of better quality. He has opened three retail shops in Accra on the basis of his earnings from his travels.

A trader from the Maldive Islands imports DVD players. There are 300,000 people there, so he knows pretty much everybody on the islands, he said. There is a flat tax of 5 percent on all imports; he sends his goods air freight and charges 60 percent markup on the goods he brings back home.

Two female traders from Kenya travel from Bangkok to Hong Kong to south China to Dubai to Nairobi, spending two to three days in each location. They go to specific shops to place orders, get the goods, and then leave for the next country. They're in the garment business, they say, because "women have an eye for clothes." Hong Kong and China are best for suits, India for leather bags, and Dubai for shoes, although these shoes are made in China. They've been in this trade since 1997.

A trader from Jamaica: I didn't believe him at first, thinking that he was a Hong Kong asylum seeker telling me a story, but indeed he seems to be a trader. It's a simple flight—Hong Kong to London, London to Kingston. He gets electronics, mobile phones, and other goods from China and sells them not just in Jamaica but in Guatemala, Nicaragua, and other Central American countries (he speaks a little Spanish, but not much, as I found from questioning him). He said that Mexico used to be a prime source of these products, but no more: China has become the provider of choice.

An Arab-Indonesian trader—his father is Yemeni and his mother is Indonesian—originally tried to send mobile phones back to Indonesia by ship. He says that 15 percent of the phones weren't working by the time they arrived, because of the sea air; now he uses air freight. Among his other business activities, he imports American Verizon phones into Chungking Mansion—he gets the phones from the US and all the accessories from China and sends it all back to Indonesia.

A Frenchman is in Hong Kong for the trade fair. He buys MP4 players—if he wants to make a big order, he'll go into China to buy them. He said quality wasn't an issue—people in France buy all kinds of Chinese goods. "China is taking over the world. In twenty years, we'll all be speaking Chinese!"

A trader from Gambia buys wholesale cloth in south China. He shook his head in disgust when asked about his business: "They're bloodsuckers in Guangzhou, but it's better than working as a farmer in Gambia." He asked if I could help get him cheaper accommodations so that he could stay longer in Hong Kong—HK$150 a night was too much for him.

A trader friend from Tanzania and another person from Congo Kinshasa began talking business—doing it in English as well as Swahili, for my benefit. The Tanzanian buys used cars in Hong Kong and sends them to Dar es Salaam; he suggested that the Congolese trader can then send the cars from Dar es Salaam to Matadi, around the Cape of Good Hope, to sell in the Congo. From Matadi, on the Atlantic Coast, they can be transported by road to Kinshasa—the only usable stretch of highway in the Congo. "I have three cars here that we can ship tomorrow, if you're ready." He said that including airfare and all expenses, he could guarantee a profit margin of 300 percent.

A trader from Zimbabwe once imported clothes but now imports tires from used Hong Kong vehicles. He trades in US dollars, and the Mugabe government is desperate for US dollars. They harass him in customs; he works through the UK since he has relatives there. Given the ridiculous Zimbabwe inflation rates, he must call Zimbabwe every morning to find out the exchange rate and reworks prices accordingly. But the container will take weeks to get to Zimbabwe, so renegotiations are always required. He carefully stays out of politics—"if you support one party and then another comes to power, you're dead!" He is in his thirties and supports eight people in his family.

These are only a few of hundreds of stories my research assistants and I have heard. These traders are distinguished by their different countries of origin and goods they deal in, and also by the direction in which their goods flow. The broadest pattern of this trade, followed by well over 90 percent of traders, is that of traders from poorer countries going to Hong Kong or China to bring back goods to their own countries. This is what we see in the traders of mobile phones, clothing, building tiles, furniture, and the whole panoply of goods traveling by luggage, air freight, or container to Africa and an array of other societies. But there are also traders going in the opposite direction. Gem traders and traders of gold from Africa fit this pattern—taking not finished goods from China back to Africa but rather raw materials from Africa into Hong Kong and China for finishing.

This fits dependency theory: raw materials coming from the extreme periphery, and finished goods being exported to that periphery, in the classic pattern of wealthier countries exploiting poorer ones.[10] Other traders, especially from India, do not quite fit this pattern—the trader in Leica cameras, for example, uses the fact that India is less developed technologically to exploit the fact that India may have older cameras that contemporary camera enthusiasts from the West or China may avidly seek out. The importer of Verizon phones too reveals the complexity of interactions: the designations of developed and developing world are more complex than is typically assumed. In any case, Chungking Mansions clearly serves as a clearing house for goods and information, just as does Hong Kong as a whole.

I've heard stories about Colombian drug dealers who have set up stock in Chungking Mansions in their efforts to move in on the Chinese cocaine trade. Chungking Mansions, the tale goes, is the only place in the Chinese-speaking world where, as white and brown people, they can blend in undetected to go about their business. Possibly the story is true, although I doubt it. I've also heard stories of arms dealers, in AK 47s, land mines, and other such goods, although I've seen little indication that these may be true. In 2008 Hong Kong police arrested an American staying in Chungking Mansions on suspicion of terrorism; eventually he was jailed as an errant hobby-ist for his transgressions in owning several police batons and stun guns.[11]

Then there is the remarkable story of the Ghanaian gold trader told to me by my asylum-seeker friend. My friend relates, and swears as to the truth of this story, that he met a man at the entrance to Chungking Mansions who had a mouthful of gold teeth; the man wanted to eat, and so my friend led him to a Ghanaian restaurant in Chungking Mansions' unlicensed upper floors. My friend met him a day later and saw to his amazement that the man now had a set of ordinary white teeth.

My friend asked him how that could be, and after much hesitation, the trader told his story:

> I smuggle gold from my country. I am the last born in a family of ten. Both my parents died when I was young. We grew up in poverty and then one day my brother suggested that we start a gold business. We began by buying gold from poor illegal miners and selling it to middlemen. Soon we realized that we were struggling for nothing, only making these middlemen richer. My brother told me that we would make more money if I would travel to Hong Kong and sell our gold there; he knew a customer who buys for a good price. . . . My brother told me that the only way to be rich is for me to lose my teeth. I went to a clinic where my teeth were removed; after one month I was fitted with the teeth you see here. That is how it started. Usually my brother and his friend craft gold teeth into my mouth, one by one up to thirty-two. I then come straight to Chungking Mansions. I get my room first, and then I call my customer in mainland China. It takes him less than two hours to get here. We go and get my teeth all taken out. . . . You know, brother, we Africans must do everything to fight poverty; if not, we will die of hunger.

This is an extraordinary story, one of many swirling around Chungking Mansions. One reason why this trader might have felt compelled to replace his teeth with gold was that it is illegal in Hong Kong to deal in gold without going through licensed dealers. Customs in Hong Kong might have investigated if he had had gold ingots, but not if the gold was locked away in his mouth.

But let us now move back from these stories to ask, who, generally speaking, are these traders? One point to remember is that despite the occasional accounts of shady goings-on such as the stories related above, most of this trade is largely legal. This is why these traders are so accessible. Over the years I have approached countless strangers in Chungking Mansions at food stalls and in corridors to ask, "Where are you from? What business do you do?" Only a very few times have they not been willing to answer (or more frequently, cannot answer because of language difficulties). Far more often, they talk for minutes or sometimes hours about their work and travels—the problems they encounter, the pleasures and perils of their work, and the profits they can make. The popular imagination in Hong Kong, and perhaps in the Western world as a whole, is that these developing-world traders are surreptitious and in the shadows, but this is not generally the case in Chungking Mansions. Most are quite open about what they do and proud of what they do.

The Generation Gap among Traders

All the traders in Chungking Mansions are more or less wealthy by the standards of their home countries, if not of Hong Kong. This is easy to lose sight of in Chungking Mansions, where one often sees Africans haggling over food and room prices—even Chungking Mansions, in all its cheapness, represents developed-world prices for these developing-world travelers. Some older African traders and merchants I have spoken with bemoan how uncouth younger African traders are, but in fact, these younger traders represent the upper classes in their countries in being able to buy a plane ticket to Hong Kong, something most of their compatriots could not dream of.

One Tanzanian trader told me, "It's hard for an ordinary person in my country to buy a ticket to Hong Kong—US$1,300. For many of these Africans, especially those from West Africa—in one way or another, they'll tell you, 'My uncle is the governor,' 'my nephew is a colonel in the army'—it's connections." As two young Central African traders related to me:

> Trader 1: I first came to HK in 2004.
> Trader 2: I first came in 2003.
> Trader 1: My uncle owns the company I work for.
> Trader 2: My father owns the company I work for. Of course they taught us what to do.
> Trader 1: My father was asking me what I would like to do with my life. He said, "I'll give you money, but what's your plan?" My friend suggested that we go to Hong Kong and China. He said, "If you give me money, I can show you the business. If you have US$10,000, you can go to Dubai, then to Hong Kong and buy mobile phones."
> Trader 2: If there is a problem in my home country, all I have to do is call my father, who will get on the phone to someone else—everything is done through connections.

Indeed, I have met a number of traders who tell me, for example, that their uncle was Idi Amin's Agricultural Minister, or the Ghanaian Commissioner of Prisons; some of these traders are no doubt embellishing their connections but some probably are not. Many of these traders are the scions of the African upper and upper-middle class, with the capital and the connections to put them on the path to Hong Kong. But this does not mean that they necessarily make money—often they fail.

Many of my interviews with traders have been conducted with men in their thirties, forties, and fifties who have been in the trading business for decades, although all only came to Hong Kong and China in recent years; they have, in large part, mastered the business of customs and other uncertainties. These people often have extended China connections and seem to know exactly what they are doing. They also tend to be largely legal in their dealings with customs in China and in their home countries, often eschewing bribes for more methodical procedures, if they are able. Several have told me that the key is to not seek windfall profits, but rather a relatively small but steady gain trip after trip. Many of these traders have made a hundred or more trips between Hong Kong and their home countries.

Elder, experienced African traders often feel scorn for younger traders, who they see as generally incompetent; there is a distinct generation gap among traders. For young Ghanaian traders, coming to Hong Kong has served as a rite of passage, a way of gaining status at home.[12] Among Igbo traders from Nigeria, a young man who has come to Hong Kong and succeeded has in a way "graduated" by becoming, in some senses if not others, a full-fledged entrepreneur, able to make a profit not just at home but in the world at large.[13] "Now that I have made some money in China, people look at me differently back home," a Nigerian trader told me. "They respect me; they look up to me." A young Tanzanian trader said to me, "I must succeed here. My family is totally depending on me. To be a man, I cannot fail."

It seems clear that there is a considerable price to pay for failure, as Christian Lo has outlined in his discussion of unsuccessful Ghanaian traders who stay in Hong Kong to work illegally.[14] A Tanzanian trader in his thirties whom I interviewed discussed young traders at length:

Why do these small traders even come to Hong Kong? This is a question that for a long time I've been asking myself. Most of them, you'll see them today and then you'll never see them again. They don't last for more than six months; some only come once. It's like a style: 'Business is in Hong Kong; someone's going to Hong Kong. So the day I get money, I'll travel to Hong Kong.' If their families sell property in one of Dar es Salaam's up-and-coming neighborhoods, they may get US$15,000, US$20,000, and they come to Hong Kong. They really think they can get rich. I know two of these traders who have each lost US$15,000. They got this money from family inheritance, family donations—it's given to them with all the family hopes. They go home only with a few hundred dollars. What are they going to say?

They sometimes come to me for advice. I tell them, 'Don't go to China. Just buy in Chungking Mansions and go straight back home.' They don't know what a copy is—that if you buy an Armani suit in China, it's not original. Hong Kong customs officers won't allow that. Some African traders really don't know this.

Another older Nigerian trader remarked to me, "Some of these young traders are so ignorant. I remember one guy who got into Guangzhou telling me he wanted to take the metro to Japan. Did he think it was the next street over? They're just desperate to get out of Nigeria but don't know what they're getting into. If you fail to make money overseas, it's very, very shameful." These older traders often tend to see themselves as having learned the ropes on their own; in one's words, "Even from the start, when I came to Hong Kong, I knew what I was doing." But their juniors may well be wiped out before ever gaining such experience, they are saying.

The young traders I have spoken with seem unwittingly to confirm this view. A Kenyan trader in his early twenties insisted to me that he would have no problem getting his 600 copy Boss suits over the border between China and Hong Kong because "Hong Kong is now part of China. China is the parent and Hong Kong is the child. The child will never hurt the parent. So Hong Kong must let all copies through customs; otherwise, it will hurt the Chinese economy." I suggested to him that he had been lucky so far in getting through Hong Kong customs without having his goods confiscated, but he didn't believe me.*

Some, perhaps most, of these younger traders will be wiped out—I've heard one estimate that only 40 percent of first-time African traders make it back a second time—but others will no doubt eventually be successful, succeeding their elders. Several times I have met elder African fathers and their young adult sons—and once, a mother and her son—in Chungking Man-

---

*He is partially correct in his analysis: only a very small percentage of copy goods are confiscated at the border. However, this has less to do with Hong Kong's fealty to China than with its own neoliberalism, as well as the fact that the Hong Kong-China border crossings at Lo Wu and Lok Ma Chau are among the busiest in the world and most goods pass unimpeded.

sions, the former teaching the latter the tricks of their trade before handing over their business and retiring.

Techniques of Traders

It is remarkable how easily and quickly deals can be accomplished in Chungking Mansions. I once met an Indian man coming to Hong Kong to trade for the first time. I chanced upon him as soon as he entered Chungking Mansions and joined him once he had found a room and returned to the ground floor of the building for business.

The first thing he did was to look around in Chungking Mansions at all the things that are sold—particularly mobile phones and electronics—and then immediately called his financial backers in India to find out the latest comparative prices on a range of goods. He then talked to the Chungking Mansions sellers he found most suitable about where they got their goods and found out where in China the goods came from. These sellers served as outlets for Chinese factories, so they had no compunction about providing him with this information. He then scheduled a visit to Shenzhen, in southern China, to a factory making the goods he sought to buy. The day after that, he returned to India.

Because he could use his mobile phone, in the visit I witnessed he could get started remarkably easily—he came to Chungking Mansions knowing no one and was able to set up business in just a few hours' time. Indeed, although the possibility of getting cheated certainly exists, this is a primer in how to do business—fly in and immediately start checking prices at Chungking Mansions; immediately phone back to one's home country and work out the comparative prices; and then make the factory connections where the price differential is greatest. This would have been difficult twenty years ago, but it's perfectly plausible now: cheap mobile phone communication, along with cheap intercontinental transportation, is what makes Chungking Mansions' low-end globalization possible.

There are wide variations in how traders work, so let me provide just a few typical patterns, first for mobile phones and then for clothing. A small trader in phones will typically buy a few hundred or thousand phones at different stalls in Chungking Mansions, depending on the orders of buyers or anticipated desires of customers back home. Typically it will be a mix of different kinds of phones, some fourteen-day, some used, and some China-made new phones, knock-offs, refabs, or copies, although some traders specialize in one particular type among these phones.

All traders say they check very carefully; as a Ghanaian phone trader explained to me, "I check all the phones, every phone. I open up to check the battery and the model. No, I don't look deeper, to check the wiring—we can't get to that." He, like other phone buyers, will return every phone he is not satisfied with—when he returns phones, the phone stalls, as a rule, tell him that they themselves were misled, cheated by their wholesalers. He is given a ninety-day guarantee on phones by his Chungking Mansions dealer, a standard guarantee, but he must check closely anyway, because he does not know for certain that he will be able to return to Chungking Mansions over the next several months.

After this examination, he, like other traders, has his phones packed and wrapped in a particular fashion so that the baggage screening machines will not pick up the fact that the phones have batteries in them, which is against some airlines' rules. Traders generally calculate that they can carry seven to eight mobile phones per kilogram, or ten to eleven if they are carrying China-made phones. Thus, they can carry some 250 to 300 phones within their weight allowance—often thirty kilograms with a degree of flexibility allowed for a few extra kilograms—400 to 500 more within the additional allowance they must pay for, and as many hundreds more as they can pay extra air freight or bargain for from the unused baggage quotas of their fellow traders.

These traders get to the airport by taking one of the regular buses ferry-ing passengers to the airport, which stops just across the street from Chung-king Mansions. But the drivers of these buses often refuse to allow traders who are carrying excess luggage to board. Traders with excess luggage may instead use one of the array of South Asian–run vans parked in the lane just behind Chungking Mansions, which charge less than do taxis and which, as a bonus, help traders transport their boxes from the upper or lower floors of Chungking Mansions.

This depiction does not, of course, hold true for those who buy their phones in south China—in Shenzhen, Guangzhou, or any number of Chi-nese cities and towns within two hours of Hong Kong. That, by most ac-counts is riskier business, both because phones in China, especially copy phones, are less trustworthy and also because customs at the China–Hong Kong border can always confiscate fake goods. This only very rarely happens, particularly if goods are brought into Hong Kong in individuals' personal baggage. But it can happen, and the potential of it happening always casts a shadow. Hong Kong customs does not examine goods leaving the territory by airplane, so a trader leaving Hong Kong with mobile phones in his lug-gage generally need not worry, at least until he reaches customs in his own country.

Only a minority of the clothing traders staying in Chungking Mansions actually buy their clothing in the building. More typically, they go to Sham Shui Po, as earlier mentioned, where there are a number of clothing wholesalers devoted to the African market. The reason why many of them prefer to buy goods in Sham Shui Po is that many wholesalers do not just sell clothes—in some stores, a trader cannot simply buy goods and take them away. Rather, everything is made after it is ordered; the Sham Shui Po wholesaler hears the African trader's requests and calls the factories in China immediately to confirm the design and estimate the costs.

In effect, these African traders are not simply buyers, but designers: they come to Sham Shui Po with a particular idea and they choose materials, prints, buttons, and any other details to ensure that what they buy is suited to the tastes of their end customers. Their orders, once samples are approved, generally take no more than a few days to fill. Those traders with particularly large orders may go into China themselves to buy, while those seeking only a few dozen or hundred items may stick to Sham Shui Po.

A notable technique of many traders in clothing is to find original clothes that grab one's eye and then get exact copies made. Others may change minor details, to Africanize the item to suit ever-changing local fashion trends. Some traders search for good designs in Hong Kong, or in other countries such as Malaysia, and then order the clothes they want and give sizes to the wholesale shop in Chungking Mansions. The shop then contacts a garment factory in mainland China, which sends the goods to Nigeria, Kenya, or wherever the trader is working from.

How much profit do traders typically make? The profits that several small traders have reported to me range from US$400 to US$1,300 per trip, including the extra frequent-flyer mileage they can obtain. Other traders, those with their own companies, may make substantially more. These traders report a profit margin all over the map: anywhere from 20 percent to 100 percent or more.

Given the great expenses of travel—for traders from East Africa, a minimum of US$1,000 per trip is required, and for those from West Africa, substantially more—one may ask why these traders bother to come to Hong Kong. Couldn't they simply phone in their orders? A number of traders do indeed place their orders before they come to Hong Kong, so that they are ready once the trader arrives. Others, particularly those who have trusted, long-term relationships with their suppliers, stay back in their home countries, placing their orders with those who do come to Hong Kong. But overwhelmingly I am told that one must be there—in the informal economy, one cannot trust merchants that one cannot see face-to-face and cannot trust merchandise that one can't personally inspect piece by piece.

The Lure of China

Most traders find Hong Kong an easier place to do business in than China, in large part because of the language issue: "Here in Chungking Mansions I can talk and people understand me.... I can negotiate prices. It's much harder to do these things in China," a Kenyan buyer of electronic goods told me, in a comment echoed by many others.

At the same time, however, there is the sense that to seek a really big profit, China is the place to go: "The big fish go to China. We little fish stay in Hong Kong. China is there for large scale, for the big fish, not the small fish. The small fish will stay in Hong Kong; they need Hong Kong," a Tanzanian clothing buyer said. A Nigerian businessman based in China echoed the marine metaphor: "China and the merchants who do business there represent the ocean, while Hong Kong is just a pond.... But those in the pond still can catch benefits from the ocean."

Many traders I have spoken with tell of difficulties in China in terms echoing those of the merchants earlier discussed. As a West African trader of phones told me,

> I bought two hundred mobile phones in China, but one hundred weren't good. I went back to China and told them. They said they'd check and then told me they'd give me my money back in six months. Eventually they only paid me for fifty of the phones. I don't do business with that company any more. After that, I never buy mobiles in China; I'd prefer to buy them in Hong Kong. In Hong Kong, if a mobile is not good, I bring back that mobile and it's instantly changed, but not in China.

Smart traders are well aware of these problems and have ways of dealing with them. One East African merchant dealing in office supplies told me that the company he does business with in China shows him every step of the production process. When the goods are being packed in the container, he takes photographs, and the owner of the Chinese company—a young woman—makes a CD, giving one copy to him and keeping a copy, so that both sides have an exact record of what was packed. Another trader found out recently that the Chinese factory he buys from was giving him a foreigner's price, charging him more than they would an ethnic Chinese. He learned of this practice from a Singapore man on a flight in China. Rather than getting angry at the Chinese, he simply hired the Singapore man and gave him a commission for getting the business himself as a Mandarin speaker and ethnic Chinese.

The most successful traders I have interviewed are those traders in south China who speak Mandarin and intimately know Chinese society and culture, frequently as a result of having studied in China and lived there for a decade or more. Often they are not primarily traders, although they certainly engage in that, but also middlemen between Chinese manufacturers and African traders who come to them in search of connections. A problem is that in an African cultural context the broker cannot easily ask for payment for his services directly from the trader, especially if the trader is a friend of a family member. If there are commissions from Chinese factories for his services, as there generally are, and if the order is big enough, he will profit handsomely—although he also may bear responsibility for the goods shipped from the factories he recommends to the buyers back in Africa.

The visa situation for Africans in China has long been tenuous. I came to meet a number of long-term residents of China in Chungking Mansions, since they had to come to Hong Kong to renew their China visas. In summer 2008, in the run-up to the Beijing Olympics, the situation in China became more precarious, and many Africans who had previously been able to obtain long-term visas in China were now given only a few days, or even shut out of the country altogether. Although the situation improved for many after the Olympics ended, some Africans remained shut out of their adopted country.

The most poignant case of this was that of a Kenyan man in his sixties who was a trader in agricultural machines between China and his home country. When I spoke with him in fall 2008, he had not returned to his apartment in Guangzhou for three months because he could not get a visa, and he did not have the money to return to Kenya, where, in any case, he had no home, his children having taken over his properties. He spent his days and months waiting in a tiny guesthouse room in Chungking Mansions, until either the Chinese immigration authorities relented or his friends in Kenya came through with an investment they had promised him. One day I went to visit him, and he was no longer there; I could not reach him in China. What happened to him I will probably never know.

One large pattern in trade is the competition between African traders and Chinese corporations—the latter have more capital and may squeeze the former, shaping traders' strategies. A gem trader from Madagascar said that he first dealt in clothing and then in seafood before turning to gems. He began with clothing because there was a high demand and little supply in Madagascar, but then Chinese clothes merchants migrated to Madagascar and forced many locals out of the industry by offering cheaper prices and larger quantities of lower-quality merchandise.

He then turned, at a customer's suggestion, to dried seafood (apparently shark's fin, considered an aphrodisiac) and was temporarily successful. However, as soon as the Chinese realized that locals had a taste for such products, they began to import them, and once again he had to find another product to trade. One of his friends introduced him to the stone business, sapphires brought from Africa to China, a market that the Chinese have yet to penetrate although sooner or later they probably will.

Another African trader told me, "The Chinese are very clever. If you send goods to some African address two or three times, they'll take note and send a Chinese company agent there who will sell their goods there more cheaply than you can." Ultimately the African traders in Chungking Mansions are in competition with Chinese merchants and companies; the Chinese will eventually win, but this hasn't happened yet.

The Perils of Customs

A major problem faced by these traders once they return to their home, and the biggest barrier many traders face in their pursuit of profit, is that of customs officials in their home countries.[15]

Some bigger traders—those who deal with single types of goods whose value is officially given in the consignment paperwork—can pass through customs of various countries more or less legally, without paying bribes. But even these traders must sometimes take extraordinary measures, by developed-world standards. As one Tanzanian trader in machine products told me, "It would be absolutely insane to leave the container open for a night, because you'll never see anything again. I try to arrange everything in one day, even paying the customs officers overtime. I just have to stand there until they're finally done. And they take their time." He pays a standard 12 percent duty on his goods.

Other traders, especially if they are dealing in an array of different goods, say they have no choice but to bribe. As a trader from West Africa said,

> If I pay customs, I may lose everything. I can't pay it all. If you buy a hundred mobile phones, you must pay fifty as tax. It's better to give the customs person two mobile phones as a present instead. You have to be illegal; you have no choice. It's the only possible way. I have a friend, his father is a minister in the government. Everything he buys he pays no taxes. He can do that because his father works in the government. When someone is a minister's son, nobody can touch him. . . . Sometimes customs comes to my shop and says, "Oh, how much did this phone cost?" because they want money. You cannot stop them. If you don't give them money, they bother you. So you pay them off. The customs in Africa is not like Hong Kong or the US. When you come back, they want to check everything. They always want money. Better to give them a present.

He showed me the array of wallets and purses and mobile phones he had bought as gifts—some for his sisters, others for customs officials. This is the way everything works in his country, he said.

He indicated that corruption and connections worked hand-in-hand, in the sense that the better connected a trader was, the less he would be harassed by customs. If someone is seeking excess money from him in customs, he will go to his higher-up connection to alleviate it, he said. Another trader, from East Africa, spoke of how he must carry back in his own consignment of goods fifty kilos of gifts, because so many government ministers and officials want something from him. He brings back many suits—he took one look at me and told me my waist size; he was right.

There are different ways in which bribes are paid. In some places, like the Congo (Kinshasa), the trader simply forks over the money and goods, whether intended as customs payment or as bribes. In other places, it is subtler. In Nigeria, it is common for the officials at the airport to signal the trader to leave their bribe at a designated place where they can easily retrieve it after the trader has left, so that it does not seem too suspicious. As law enforcement has been tightening, it is safer to proceed in this less direct way because it is less incriminating.

In some countries, including a number in Africa, traders are viewed simply as an easy source of gifts and cash with which to line one's pockets. The idea is that aside from the formal payments of customs, which go into the national tax coffers, the trader also owes the customs officials something more personal, a private gift for expediting customs. In other countries, traders may be treated badly for more nationalistic reasons: they are seen as bringing in goods that undermine the industries of their home countries.

This is the case in India and, at least rhetorically, in Nigeria. The temporary workers with whom I traveled back to India carry in their luggage China-made clothing and seem despised by customs. Customs in Kolkata only allows these traders to have their goods processed between two and five in the afternoon, with arriving passengers taking first priority. As I discussed in chapter 2, sometimes the traders must make their way back and forth between their homes and the airport day after day, waiting for the customs officials to finally deign to deal with them: they are at bureaucracy's mercy. This is true not just for clothing; an Indian trader of electronic goods said, "Anything electronic you bring in, they'll try and tax you on it, even though India doesn't really have an electronics industry to speak of. It's a hangover from the socialist, protectionist government of decades past."

The Nigerian government has banned all clothing imports in order to encourage the local production of clothing, but the effect is simply that clothing in Nigeria is smuggled in, rendering all traders illegal. This is the argument over free trade versus protectionism that can be heard in countries across the globe and often decried in the pages of journals such as the *Economist*, advocating open markets above all else. In this case, this argument directly affects these small traders in their pursuit of a living.

Once traders arrive back in their home countries, there are a variety of different paths their goods take. It is hard to know these in detail, since the basis of my research has been people more than goods, and the people I know are often no more than one link on a complicated distribution chain. To my regret, I have never been able to follow an item from its manufacture in south China to its final destination in a consumer's home in Africa or South Asia. Many of the traders I know have no idea where their goods ultimately go. The Indian traders discussed above simply hand their parcels of clothing to waiting wholesalers in the Kolkata airport and receive their payments: "The clothes are sold in markets all over India," is as much as I have been able to find out. Nigerian phone dealers often sell their consignment to wholesalers in the central phone market in Lagos; more often than not, they never see the retail buyers of their phones, and inferior phones cannot be traced directly back to them. Many traders I know belong to larger entities, either informal groupings of traders, in which they buy goods for "the boss," or more formal companies. In these cases they are more or less protected from direct individual risk.

On the other hand, some traders are directly involved in the sale of their goods to retail customers. I have spoken with a clothing dealer from Zambia who packed his clothes in several bags and took a bus off to villages to sell them. As he said, "The timing has to be right—it has to be after the harvest, when people have money." Sometimes he traded in kind, clothing for whatever foodstuffs he could obtain from their harvests. But now he has a store in Lusaka, so the wholesalers from the villagers come to him to buy clothing.

Indeed, many traders I have spoken with have stores in urban areas, in cities such as Nairobi, Accra, Dar es Salaam, or Kampala, and buy to stock their stores. The owner of an electronics store in Mauritius said that his customers all know full well when he makes his runs overseas to replenish his merchandise; they want his newest goods and so await his return. He told me that he had called his wife back in Mauritius the day before we spoke, and she had said, "Customers want to see you back here. Why don't you change your flight? Don't come back Thursday, come back tomorrow."

The general rule is that the more individual and the smaller the volume of trade, the greater the risk. This is both because customs in particular can more easily exploit those who lack connections and because the vicissitudes of an unpredictable global market at home and abroad can so easily destroy those traders who lack the backing of companies or patrons. I met a Nigerian trader who was blindsided by a fire on December 20, 2007, perhaps set by real-estate speculators, in which the largest clothing market in Lagos burned to the ground. Because his buyers were based in this market and lost most of their money as well as stock, he suddenly found that he had no customers for the clothing he had bought in Hong Kong and lost his shirt. I have mentioned traders blindsided by the Beijing Olympics, or by exchange-rate fluctuations in the wake of the economic downturn of late 2008. Their difficulties might have happened to the entrepreneurs of high-end globalization as well, but the risk is far higher for these vulnerable foot soldiers of low-end globalization.

Here are the accounts of several traders I've met in Chungking Mansions.

James Frimpong

I used to be engaged in importing mobile phones, but I stopped because the market was so crowded. Now I deal with electronic goods and particularly with computer accessories, things like hard drives and connecting cables. I'm Ghanaian. I had a large shoe factory in Ghana, but I got away from that. My wife is Ghanaian German and has been living in Germany for the past seventeen years. I wonder, still, if I should go to live in Germany; I've already begun to scout out opportunities.

I've been to Hong Kong four or five times; I've only been coming to Hong Kong for a year. I've long been a businessman—I was dealing in coffee and living in Nigeria for a few years, as well as dealing in the shoe business. As a businessman, there's always risk, but I can calculate it. I keep changing what I buy and sell based on the price. The last trip I made, I bought headkerchiefs for women, especially Muslims. The average price was 9 rmb [*renminbi*, the currency in mainland China], a little over one US dollar. I was able to sell them in my country for about five US dollars; there's a huge difference. In Ghana, I had gone around the market, asking for prices of certain goods, and saw that there was a huge demand for headkerchiefs and for scarves to tie around the waist. That's why I don't depend on one item only but keep changing, depending on where I see the demand. I don't sell to the market people; I sell directly to the consumer. This makes my goods go very, very fast. I have lost money on trips. On one trip, I found that they were doing a bonanza sale on some of the kinds of goods I bought; I was forced to sell at their price.

No, I don't know, usually, whether what I'm bringing in is copy or not, but I can tell by the price whether or not it's a copy. As for customs, the young traders often don't know the rules, they don't know how to play the game, and that's what gets them into trouble. You can go to the consular officer in any place that Ghana has a consulate and look up the trade rules, what you get charged for in terms of imports and how much. But a lot of the young guys don't do that—they simply carry it back, without thinking through what they're going to have to pay. This is where problems come in—these guys then may offer bribes, or do various things to overcome the duties they're asked to pay. With me, it's clear: because I've got a clear list of what I'm carrying, and because I've checked the rules in advance, I know how much it's going to cost me.

When I come to Hong Kong I want to stay in Chungking Mansions, an area with lots of Africans. This is the heart of Hong Kong; this is where the action is. Here you meet people who are your type, and you can get lots of information. If you deal with the Chinese, you can get ripped off. But here they can give you a note of caution: "Hey, watch out. . . ." China is worse than Hong Kong for racism. There are damned silly people there—I mean it! You sit on a bus, and no one will sit next to you sometimes. That happens a little in Hong Kong, but in China, it's like a vacuum. They have no regard for you there. But it's not a problem for me: I just do business and leave. I don't allow certain things to weigh me down.

My mother had nine kids, and my father had three from another marriage. Now there are two in Italy, one in South Africa, three in the US, and three in Ghana—yes, we're scattered all over the world. I don't see them very much, but we talk all the time on the phone. They're in the US legitimately—they have their green cards. One used to work for an oil company in New Jersey and has a degree in mechanical engineering—now he's a big person in Ghana. One of my brothers is trying to set up a radio station in Italy. We all manage. Yes, anywhere can be home, if we can make money there! My father lived in London in the late 1940s and 1950s. We inherited a taste for adventure from him! I left Ghana much later than anyone else. My grandfather was the first person to introduce modern shoe technology into Ghana. My grandfather helped my father to win a scholarship to learn leathery and tannery, and that's what I wound up doing.

Life changes like the shoreline of the sea. You could be up today and down tomorrow. I was exporting raw coffee to Europe—I was in big-time business. I took out a huge loan to expand the business, but that year we had the shock of our lives—coffee prices collapsed. That ended my reign. It took me four years to pay off the money; the bank wanted to auction off my holdings. I've led a very good life, and the credit goes to my father. In Ghana, I'm not particularly rich. There are people streets ahead of me. But I'm making a living. Business is a risk, just like life. All life is risk, but you have to do your homework too, investigate everything.

Ernest Msika

I'm from Tanzania and have been coming to Hong Kong and to China for the past five years. I trade in building materials—there's been a boom in my country in construction. The government in Tanzania had mismanaged factories; goods had less quality, and prices were high. Our economy started opening up in 1995 to 1996: that's when the government decided to let people do business. Roofing materials, cement for plastering walls, ceramic and porcelain tiles, gypsum board—I import all these from China.

In Tanzania, no, I don't really meet customs agents who ask for money under the table. There is an inspection company that I use, owned by the Swiss; before I ship my goods from China, I invite one of their agents in China to inspect them and indicate the real value. The customs office in Dar es Salaam accepts this; the inspection company has proved the value, so there's no problem. Most of the time, it's traders who start the problem— they start cheating. If you cheat, and the customs officer finds out, he'll use that as an advantage to get some money from you. But if you declare your goods—3,000 square feet of tiles, and they look and see 3,000 square feet of tiles—it's clear, there's no problem about it.

In East Africa now—Kenya, Tanzania, Uganda—you can calculate the taxes from the goods in advance. But my friends in West Africa always tell me that they can't do that there—they can't calculate in advance. Last week, my friend was telling me that he went to Kinshasa, in the Congo and didn't pay any duties—he landed in the airport and there was no customs officer. On another occasion, though, he paid US$4,000 in taxes for goods worth US$2,000, so he can't ever calculate.

But you know, most traders in this world, they don't like to pay duties. They think it's their right to make more profit. Most traders who are complaining are small scale—they mix goods, maybe fifty mobile phones, twenty pairs of jeans. It's hard to calculate duties for them; it's a headache for the customs officer—he has to calculate each and every item. Most of the small-scale traders don't take the time to do research. It's like they are trading based on sheer luck: "If I can pass through customs, thank God! If I get stuck, it's a bad day." They don't know how much they're supposed to pay. There is much corruption going on between customs officers and these small-scale traders.

These small African traders now, the number is being reduced because the bigger traders control the market more and more. The big traders see this as a way to speculate: they don't have to worry about whether they can sell three or four phones. The bigger scale you are, the less you have to worry about fixed costs, like transportation. Also, these big guys are the ones who can evade taxes more than anybody else. They can, for example, get a container and buy a used car, cut out the petrol tank, and fill it with mobile phones; no one inspects it. What the customs officer sees is the car. A small trader has to carry his phones on the flight: the customs officer at the airport can easily see that. Yes, everything I do is legal. That's why I'm not scared to talk to you. Yesterday after we were talking, someone came up to me and said, "Do you know that guy? He was asking you lots of questions."

There is a language barrier in China. I took a two-month course in Chinese; I do speak Mandarin Chinese. I decided that China is going to be my second home in business for the coming ten to fifteen years. Still, I feel very strongly that Tanzania is my real home. I want to contribute something to the society, change it. People worked hard in Hong Kong and look at what it is now! I'm always telling my fellow Africans, "If you run away from home, then who's going to build Africa?" They're always complaining. That's our problem. We complain a lot, but we don't contribute anything to build our home. I have friends in Great Britain and America—I tell them, "If we got together, we could create some changes. We could do something!" Yes, governments may be bad, but the governments are run by people.

In customs in Hong Kong, they keep taking Africans out of line and searching them. This happened to me last time I came to Hong Kong. I said to the customs officer, "Do you think I'm stupid? If I wanted to smuggle drugs, I wouldn't have them in my luggage. I'd just get a Chinese girl to take them in."

Kofi Nyame

I'm from Ghana; I've been to Hong Kong four times. Sometimes I can make as much as fifty percent profit, other times, no. I've always at least recovered my costs. But sometimes you can get bogged down in the harbor or the airport in Ghana waiting—your goods may lose value. Some people want to cheat the customs. If you want to cheat them, and you are caught, that's a problem. But if you go the legal way, the charges on the goods as customs fees are sometimes higher.

If I have my way, I would rather cheat them. Sometimes it's difficult, because there's not just one person—there may be two or three or four people there, so it's not easy paying them off. But sometimes it's possible. The laws are strict in Ghana, but there are some people who are willing to take bribes. If you have a container, it's very difficult to bypass customs. You can underdeclare the value of the goods, but you can't dodge the whole container!

I deal with electrical items, fluorescent tubes and fittings. I don't necessarily have to come back to Hong Kong and China—I can hire an agent who can pay the balance. Yes, I can trust the agent—he's Chinese, but he works with Africans. Of course he's still an agent—if they want to manipulate you, they can! If I have liquid money, I buy mobile phones; they're quick, and in two or three weeks, they're sold and finished, so I can do other things. I sometimes sell to established stores, but also to small businesspeople selling in street markets. I'm trying to make a living, and I must look around to know what can help me to do that. I'm exploring all the avenues.

I completed school in 1994 and then went to Israel to do manual jobs and lived there for a number of years. But I didn't want to stay there—they are not my people. I didn't like to stay in somebody else's country. Salaries were much higher in Israel—there I do a manual job and get my dollars, but in Ghana I do a decent job and don't get dollars. So I closed my eyes and worked in Israel. In Ghana, I could have had a much better job, but at that time, we were under military rule and there was such hardship—it's better now. I only travel now so that I can make money.

Yes, in Hong Kong I stay in Chungking Mansions. Guesthouses are very expensive—I must pay HK$100 to HK$120 per night, apart from food. So I spend five days, one week, and I have to go back. I see Hong Kong as a cosmopolitan area with many people from many places. But in Chungking Mansions, African people go to certain places, certain guesthouses, and Indian people go to other places—that's the situation.

Every time I come here, there's money on me. Typically, an African trader might carry from US$5,000 to US$20,000. But there are also very big businesspeople, people who send lots of containers back—they pay through the bank. Sometimes people get a room in the guesthouse with two beds, for two people. But I don't like it—I get a room with one bed. If there are two people, you don't know if you can trust them. I've never had money stolen. They say in China, they snatch your bags on a motorbike—you're warned about that. I've heard that many times about China, but not about Hong Kong.

I've built a house in Ghana—I have two kids in school. Yes, Ghana is my home; there's no place like home. Being an African is like being a Jew—no matter where I am, I'm still an African. First I am a Ghanaian; secondly, I'm Ashanti. I see the Ashanti as my brother, but outside of Ghana I am Ghanaian, just like Scotch people outside of the United Kingdom. I'm proud that I am Ghanaian. If you come to Africa, Ghana is the first. Other Africans see us as a pacesetter. We Africans have to concentrate on developing our continent. There are so many stigmas, so many difficulties. Only we can do it. That's why, even though I've traveled so far, I want to go back. I'm proud of myself, my culture, and my country, as an African and a Ghanaian.

Abraham Idowu

I'm Nigerian; I spend half of my time in Guangzhou, half in Lagos, and come to Hong Kong for visa purposes. I've been to places all over the world, but there's no building like Chungking Mansions. It's such a mixture. Chungking Mansions is for everyone. When I first came to Chungking Mansions, my Hong Kong business connections said, "What are you doing in that place? That's a slum."

I first left Nigeria for trade in China in 2004. After I got my master's degree, I worked with a bank for eight months in Nigeria, but I was restless and didn't like doing the same thing every day. When I went to China, my folks, my friends said, "China? What are you going to do there?" I had information about cheap products; I went with my friend, who had more experience. Once I arrived, before I knew it, I fell in love with China; since then, I've never looked back. Because of the language, it was very difficult at first. I had an interpreter. The people I was buying from in China told me that I didn't need to use an interpreter; she was getting extra money. Now I have translation software I use—that's all I need. They laugh at me for the little Chinese I know, but that's enough.

I supply computers to the Nigerian government. As for accessories, yes of course, I get copies made. But the main business—computers—I don't compromise. If the computers don't work, if there's down time, they're going to get mad! That wouldn't be good for the business. I'm not the main provider of computers—I'm very small. Typically, in Nigeria, a big man gets the contract, and he sells small portions of it to other people—you've got to do it well so that he'll give you more next time. Am I doing well for someone my age? I'm trying my best. I was fortunate—I got some right information at the start. But if I got in trouble, I could make calls. The connection could even be someone you've never met, a friend's uncle, for example. Because your friend knows you, he can stand for you. Tribe helps too—it helps everywhere.

The new government in Nigeria is trying to end corruption. Instead of bribing someone, why not pay the right fees and give back to society? But corruption is inevitable. I send computers back to Nigeria for the government; for these, I pay 5 percent duties. But I can't take just one thing in the consignment; those other things will not be declared. What you declare you pay to the government. But what customs sees that you don't declare—that's where the corruption comes in. It might be stuff for my friends—people at customs might see my shirt, my suit and say, "I'd like three of those." If you declared this, it would be considered contraband; you couldn't get it in the country, so you've got to hide it in your consignment.

Customs is the hardest part of my business. Some customs guys will take US$50, others US$200, others US$1,000; some need a suit, others shoes, to get the job done. They'll say, "I really like that wristwatch," or "I don't have a belt"—you know what they want. It's PR; it makes them know your name—when the government is clamping down, you can call them and they will help you. I call them in advance: "I'm going to be coming in this Saturday." If there's trouble, they'll say, "Don't fly this time." Yes, this is corruption, but they don't call it corruption—it's like you're returning a favor. Of thirty dollars, the government gets ten dollars of tax; the officials get ten dollars for themselves, lining their own pockets, and I get ten dollars profit.

China has caused factories to close all over the world, because goods are made so cheaply there. To make goods in Nigeria is going to cost more than importing. In Nigeria, you have to buy diesel generators. The costs are so high—why waste your time and money? It's easier to go overseas; in China they can make your order in weeks. It's crazy to have to do this, but it's cheaper.

I'm not married yet. Maybe next year, I don't know who. But Chinese girls are too emotional—they don't trust their guys. If I get married, I have to marry a traveler. She doesn't have to be Nigerian—it could be anyone. I love my country. I want things to get better, the government to be responsible. But I call myself a black Chinese—I wouldn't mind living in China twenty years from now. I could adjust to anywhere!

In China, I'm always busy. All these phone calls of people who want something done. In Africa, we're family inclined. If someone wants something done, they get to you through someone you know: they come to you through your sister, or mother, or brother, or father. You have to do it. I really like Hong Kong because I don't have to deal with the people who call me in China; I tell them, "Sorry, I'm in Hong Kong. I really can't help you now." In Nigeria, there's so much to do—rushing around getting papers from different offices and so on. What takes the most time is traffic. I get so tired. It's only in Hong Kong that I don't get tired.

The Significance of Goods and Traders

These traders exist because it is cheaper to buy goods such as building supplies, furniture, and clothing, as well as electrical goods and mobile phones, halfway around the world in China than in traders' own countries, even after adding in plane fare, shipping costs, and customs expenses. The traders I spoke with, such as Abraham Idowu, said that because electrical power was so unreliable, because taxation rates were so high in their home countries, and because "no one trusts things made in Africa, they have to be from overseas," it makes perfect sense for them to be able to do what they were doing. The comfortable livings they are often able to make, at least in their home countries, attest to this.

However, some of the traders I interviewed used this question to bemoan the state of Africa. As another Nigerian trader told me, "Why can't my country make anything for its own people? Why is the electricity so unreliable? Why is my country so poor even though it has so many natural resources?

What's wrong with Africa?" he asked, with considerable anguish. His answer was colonialism's legacy, although he acknowledged that ended fifty years ago: "Why are our leaders so bad today? Why is there so much corruption?" He could not answer these questions.

I often asked African traders as well as officials whether the traders' role is positive or negative for their customers and their countries. Are they simply buying shoddy goods with which to cheat their customers? Some traders acknowledge exploitation: "I get good mobile phones for my family and friends in the city, but cheap copies for villagers. They don't know any better," one West African trader told me. An African business official said bluntly, "These traders are criminal. They're not helping the African people they sell goods to; basically they're cheating customers. All the hard currency goes out, to buy these products, and the products are of low quality." An East African legislator, knowledgeable about trade, spoke to me as follows:

> My conservative estimate is that 65 percent of traders coming from China cheat. They are always trying to beat the system by avoiding customs, which is a major issue to the community. When they reach the market, they play on the ignorance of clients by not telling them that these are counterfeit goods, or used goods; they still try to sell them at the price of the original. A conscious consumer will know that a given Nokia phone is not original, but an ignorant consumer will go ahead and buy it. After two weeks the ear piece is dead, and you fix it for US$5; after another two weeks, the mouthpiece is dead, and that costs you another US$10; a month later, the battery is worn out, and so you must pay US$15. . . . In essence, you've bought the phone twice, which equals the cost of the original, good phone.

This is no doubt often true, but may be only one side of the story. Many traders indicated that whatever they themselves were doing to make money was dwarfed by the monumental corruption of the governments in their home countries. The products they brought home, even if copies, are not necessarily of low quality, although often they are. Most copy goods are functional for at least a while—definitely clothing and most mobile phones and electronic goods as well—and high-quality copies are often practically as good as the original at a fraction of the price.* The prices charged to their

---

*How do original manufacturers view copies? A Nokia employee once told me strictly off the record that Nokia may not much object to copies of their mobile phones. Since their buyers are those who cannot now afford the real model but aspire to it, their purchase of copies may lead to their eventual purchase of the genuine article if their

fellow countrymen for these goods reflect the costs incurred by these traders' global routes as well as their desire for profits, but the sheer number of traders means that competition keeps their prices down, at least in many areas.

Most traders I spoke with maintained that the role they played was a fundamentally positive one. This is hardly surprising, given the fact that they are defending their livelihoods, but their reasoning is nonetheless worth noting. A Ghanaian mobile phone trader said, "Of course we're helping our country in our trading. Before, only a very tiny number of Ghanaians had mobile phones, but now almost everyone does. That's because we bring them the phones." An intellectual Congolese trader said that traders like him are "expanding the imaginations" of the poor, by showing them what high-quality goods are like—giving them the chance to see good things will cause them to no longer take for granted that everything around them must be broken and shabby, he claimed. A reflective Kenyan trader told me, "Nobody in my country can buy an original brand of suit, or an original phone by a famous company. It's too expensive. But these copies can show them good things. The traders are bringing the world to Africa. They are bringing home goodness!"

It is indeed these traders and the goods they carry that bring, through China and Hong Kong, the world to Africa, for better or for worse. Chinese goods, according to these traders, however much disdained by some traders and customers, have an extraordinary impact. For all the shoddiness of many Chinese goods, they do bring to poor African societies a taste of the world beyond Africa. Even if this taste is copied, flawed, or used, it is nonetheless a real taste of the world beyond. This is the ultimate significance of these traders: they bring at least a facsimile of global goodness to the world's poorest continent.

---

incomes can ever match their aspirations. This is a complex matter. If copy phones are sold as originals, then companies such as Nokia and Samsung have every reason to object, since the copies downgrade the image of the originals. However, if copies are sold as copies, then there is less reason to object. Jose Rojas spoke to a genuine Nokia dealer in Lagos, Nigeria, asking him about the copies sold throughout the city; he was told that customers knew very clearly what they were buying and that copy phones were almost never confused with genuine phones. On the other hand, I myself spoke with a Nokia dealer in an East African city who was incensed at the number of customers who brought their copy phones to his shop for repair—they had no idea of the difference between copy phones and real phones, he said. In 2007, and more aggressively in 2009, Nokia initiated legal action against Chungking Mansions stores selling copy Nokia phones, indicating that at least officially, the company was unwilling to look the other way in the copying of its goods.

These traders may have a limited future. Chinese companies are moving into many African countries, as I've discussed, and may increasingly replace these traders over the next decade or two. Scholars have written extensively about China's growing trade and political relations with Africa.[16] This is increasingly becoming not just a matter of government or large corporate entities but of smaller Chinese companies and independent entrepreneurs as well. China's movement into Africa represents a shift of global significance, as China increasingly replaces the West, and particularly Africa's earlier European colonial masters, as sub-Saharan Africa's major trading partner and patron.

From a more particular standpoint, it seems likely that Chinese in Africa will increasingly be replacing the Africans who come to China, since they have money and the economics of scale on their side. Eventually, to the extent that Africa is able to fully enter the globalized world, African traders' migrations between Africa and China may no longer be necessary. For now, though, these traders, like the camel caravans or merchant ships of yore (but far more quickly) are bringing the goods of China back to their homes. They are, in a sense, the Marco Polos of developing-world globalization.

laws

FOUR

The Omnipresent Shadow of the Law

Chungking Mansions would not exist as it is today if not for the flow of goods in and out its doors, as we have just seen. But these goods are traded against the backdrop of a matrix of laws, laws that can be transgressed only by taking a degree of risk. The backdrop of law is the case not just for traders. Whether it is the restaurant owner concerned about Chungking Mansions' lawless image, the temporary worker seeking to be seen only as a tourist, the trader with copy goods that just might get confiscated, the traveler concerned about the safety of his cash, or, a major focus of this chapter, the asylum seeker dreaming of a home in a new country, the law, as embodied by the police in Chungking Mansions, is ever present and inescapable.

Most people in Chungking Mansions need to worry about the law in at least some aspects of their livelihood. Many storekeepers understate sales on their annual income taxes (as is true throughout Hong Kong). Many stores sell copy goods that can always, at least in theory, be confiscated. Many businesses hire illegal workers, which, if found out, could subject them to severe legal penalties, and these workers themselves live an existence that is legally precarious—their lives could be completely disrupted at any time by the police.

All these people are by and large safe from prosecution: all this is more or less tolerated. Drug dealers are often prosecuted; overt thieves are prosecuted; visa overstayers may be caught and jailed; and copy-watch sellers hawking their goods on the sidewalk in front of Chungking Mansions are occasionally prosecuted, as are sex workers. But all in all, Hong Kong is a relatively safe place for these businesses and workers to do what they do outside the letter of the law. For most low-end traders, complete adherence to the law in all its different manifestations across the globe is economically suicidal—the law limits traders at every step of their journeys. But for traders in Chungking Mansions, as with every other occupational group in the building, the law can be at least partially ignored.

One example taught me how much Chungking Mansions is outside the law. Early in my research, I was contacted by a newspaper reporter who sought to interview some of the people who worked in Chungking Mansions. After a half hour of talk, I trusted her and sought to help, but then I realized that none of the dozen people I knew best at Chungking Mansions would be available for her to interview, at least not with their names made public. Several were asylum seekers, whose names and identities cannot be publicized. Several others were temporary workers. Others were restaurant or guesthouse managers who either employed illegal workers or operated premises that were unlicensed or that had sundry other violations that might come to light and thus sought to remain unnamed and unquoted. No one wanted to talk on record, perhaps confirming this reporter's sense that Chungking Mansions is indeed a den of iniquity.

Chungking Mansions is not a den of iniquity, as should be clear by now; the legal violations of my informants were generally less matters of morality than of legal technicality. There is great exploitation of poor, low-level workers by rich owners and managers, but this is a feature not of Chungking Mansions alone, but of Hong Kong and the capitalistic world as a whole.

There are gross injustices taking place in the corners of Chungking Mansions—I have seen, before I could understand what was going on, an Indonesian maid who had lost her job being raffled off to the highest bidder for sex. I have spoken briefly, before being hustled away, to a Pakistani asylum seeker forced to work as a slave for his employer, on pain of being turned in to police and deported if he spoke up. I have seen an African, passed out from drink, repeatedly kicked in the head by Nepalese who felt he had insulted them. But these are exceptions: Chungking Mansions is by and large a civil, peaceful, and even a moral place.

I believe that this is the case because of Islam, with its stern moral codes governing some half of the people in Chungking Mansions, coupled with Hong Kong's own tolerance toward human diversity, preventing the intolerance toward non-believers sometimes apparent in places like Pakistan from being imported into Chungking Mansions. I also believe that this is the case because of the Hong Kong government's neoliberalism—its emphasis on business over all else—which I view as having a largely positive effect on the building. The illegalities my informants were engaged in were, again, technical more than moral matters. But these illegalities form a pervasive background to their day-to-day lives, marking what they need to look out for. They cannot forget the law, in all its potential intrusions into their lives.

Conflicts Within and Beyond the Law

One of the more interesting aspects of life in Chungking Mansions is the lack of overt police interference in most areas of business. In fact, the police are almost always somewhere around Chungking Mansions. In cases of overt robbery or violence, they very rapidly show up. But in many of the conflicts I have seen in Chungking Mansions, the police are kept distinctly out, or are in any case ineffective.

Indeed, the law is not often invoked by those who have grievances. I know of several cases where owners of property in Chungking Mansions took their dispute to small claims court, but this is unusual. Except for the owners of Chungking Mansions property, few people in Chungking Mansions ever seek judgment from the courts. One reason for this is that both the seller and the buyer of goods may not be Hong Kong residents. Another reason is that business dealings in Chungking Mansions sometimes leave no paper trail.

A salesman of Indian background, a long-term Hong Kong resident, told me that he was having a difficult time because he had borrowed money from his Hong Kong Chinese friend to invest with an East African businessman in years past. The African absconded with his money; he has the phone number in Africa, but when he calls, he's told "I'm sorry, he's not home," and lately, "He's gone. I don't know where he is." When he sees his Hong Kong Chinese friend during the Chinese New Year, a time when debts are traditionally repaid, he feels particularly bad, being reminded of the money he owes but cannot return. He said to me, "I've learned my lesson. When I was young, I was a nice guy, but I've learned not to be a nice guy anymore."

Given the fact that so many Chungking Mansions' traders come once or twice or a half dozen times and then never appear again, there are no doubt many debts left unpaid. Like Ahmed in chapter 2, who had lost all his money

to a business associate who absconded, there is nothing this man can do—
legal and police safeguards will not help him regain his lost money.

I had dinner with the Pakistani owner of a Chungking Mansions food
stall who told me a convoluted story about how in 2005 he had invested
HK$1.2 million with another Pakistani shopkeeper in Chungking Man-
sions. The shopkeeper paid him back HK$50,000 and then, in the next
meeting, gave him a check for HK$1.2 million that bounced. The debtor
fled, and the owner never saw him again. As he told me, he first went to the
Hong Kong police, and they said, "We can't intervene: this is a civil matter."
He then went to a lawyer, who said, "You'll have to pay HK$100,000 up
front, and then you might not win the case."

He said that several people he knew had offered to kill the debtor in Pakistan. He knows where the man is: he discovered that the debtor's father had
disowned his son, so that he would not be liable for his son's huge debt. "I
do not want to kill him but only kidnap him and get my money back. After
that I'll figure out what to do with him," he said. He went to Pakistan for
three months looking for this man, but could not find him. His restaurant
in Chungking Mansions lost HK$400,000 during that period, he said. His
blood pressure soared and he had a stroke. His doctor told him, "You must
stop thinking so much about this! It's not good for you!" He is still consumed
by this anger, but he told me that he will not go so far as to commit murder.
"If I hire someone to kill him and his father, I can't get my money back, even
though I could do that easily. I want my money back!"

Another incident, more harmonious in its eventual outcome, I learned
of when I found my favorite Pakistani-run food stall temporarily closed.
Several Pakistani men had entered a few days earlier, ordered food, and
hadn't paid. The Hong Kong police were called and threatened to arrest the
culprits, so they finally did pay, but several hours later they returned, ate,
and again refused to pay, and when my friend, the cook, complained, they
smashed a beer bottle over his head and also assaulted a restaurant tout. My
friend refused to involve the police because he was worried that the police
would discover that his tout was working illegally; instead, he chose a route
based on kinship. He discovered that his acquaintance was the uncle of one
of the men who had assaulted him; they subsequently returned to the restaurant in the company of their uncle and told my friend that they would never
again bother him. This solution, he felt, was far more secure than legal rem-
edies, and, indeed, those men did not bother him after that. (A few months
later, however, the restaurant was bought out by an adjacent restaurant, after
which I never saw him again.)

Another friend of mine, a Punjabi Indian Sikh, related a story concerning the competing phone stall just across the corridor from his own stall that was run by Pakistani Muslims. They were regularly calling customers from his shop, saying, "Come here! We can give you a better deal!" In response to this, he lowered his prices—on a HK$500 wholesale phone, he began to charge just HK$510, he told me. Then they threatened him and also threatened his wife, a Christian, who also worked in his stall; they conspicuously came close to her, taking her photograph. He then challenged them to a knife fight, he told me, and they called the police, who questioned him. He knew that the Pakistani shop had illegal workers, and he told the police about them, but those illegal workers were not in the shop when the police came; the Pakistanis knew that he might retaliate in this way and let their workers have the day off.

A few months later, the Pakistani shop owner brought him some sweets, apparently wanting to make peace, but he refused to eat them—"I didn't know what was in them. Maybe they were trying to poison me!" This Sikh man finally told his competitors ten feet from him, "Don't call the police; let's do this religiously. We'll go to your temple of Islam and my Sikh temple, and we'll talk to authorities there and get their judgment; that's the way we can solve this problem. You can take my young son, and I'll take your young son, and we'll go to each others' temples." This proposal, although never taken up, largely defused the situation. How much of this tension is religious and how much is business using religion as an excuse is an open question (I suspect the latter). In any case, religion rather than police or courts was seen as the key to resolving this problem.

When the law is actually invoked, it may be ineffective toward those who seek its help. One South Asian shopkeeper I know was set upon in an alley behind Chungking Mansions by several South Asian men wielding field hockey sticks, who beat him badly enough to require hospitalization. He sought for the police to arrest the men who had beaten him, and the police detained them, but because he had no evidence other than his own word and because witnesses refused to speak up, the police released these assailants. He was incensed:

How could they let those people go? They tried to kill me! They might come back! The law in Hong Kong isn't effective. The police said that they couldn't use my testimony: "We need camera evidence, CCTV evidence." Someone's guilty of a crime. I can point out the people who beat me—I know who they are. But the police won't help me.

In a personal sense he was quite right to be upset, but in a legal sense he had no evidence beyond his own words and wounds, so the police could do nothing in bringing his case to court. The mastermind of the assault against him was eventually deported to Nepal, I have heard, but this man remained deeply unhappy about the fact that the law could not punish all those who had assaulted him.

Among traders, I know of almost no cases of seeking to involve the law in business dealings. This is partly because these traders are often in Hong Kong so briefly that going to court is impossible. Beyond this, these traders are already in a shady area of legality if they are buying copies. Furthermore, traders can sometimes pass on shoddy goods they have bought to their customers with minimal consequence, so even if they are cheated, they can themselves avoid the economic consequences. Finally, many of these traders don't know that they have been cheated.

All in all, unless cash has literally been stolen, the police will not be called. One trader told me that he lost a large amount of money because of his order of six hundred phones, he rejected three hundred and put them in a separate pile, a few feet away from the pile of phones he had accepted; somehow the store workers managed to slip sixty defective phones back in his pile. These phones, he discovered after paying, were unworkable. But there is absolutely nothing he can do—he cannot even be sure that he was cheated, since he himself might have been careless.

There are times, however, when even traders may become involved with the police. Nigerian traders rely upon an informal system of money transferring, whereby designated people bring hundreds of thousands of US dollars in cash into Hong Kong from Nigerian merchants and then redistribute the money to its Hong Kong recipients for a fee. A person nicknamed "Dollar Man" has been the boss of this system; in 2008, his office in Hong Kong was robbed by two African men wearing hoods, to cover their faces, and carrying toy guns. A group of Nigerian traders in Hong Kong formed a posse to look for the culprits immediately after the event, because they were worried that it would damage the Nigerian image in Hong Kong, resulting in tighter visa regulations. Within a few days, they had located the stolen money and returned it to the offices of Dollar Man so that it could be distributed to its rightful recipients and had brought the culprits to the police. In this case, in order to salvage the lawless reputation of Nigerians in Hong Kong, these people cooperated with the Hong Kong police—although I also later heard from a policeman that the men who brought the culprits to the police were in fact seeking immunity for their own violations.

I discussed in chapter 3 how the biggest legal challenges facing many traders concern their transporting copy goods in China and Hong Kong and their fraught passage through customs in their own countries. Except for the bigger entrepreneurs—who claim to be fully legal, but who in many cases no doubt simply engage in a higher level of corruption—this always shadows the traders I know. They can lose their goods or profits in an instant because of the law or officials, corrupt or otherwise. This, again, is the omnipresent shadow of the law, never far from most traders' minds, although a shadow that is largely absent from traders' concerns within Chungking Mansions itself.

I close this section by relating two more incidents in which the law is invoked or evaded, both involving heroin. An African interpreter for Hong Kong Immigration told me, in the 7-Eleven near Chungking Mansions, how he was called to the airport to interpret for an East African woman caught bringing heroin into Hong Kong through a swallowed condom in her stomach. This is a normal part of his work, but in this case he found that it was a woman with whom he had been casually chatting over beer in this very same 7-Eleven just two months earlier. He counseled her surreptitiously as best he could before formally interpreting for her; she eventually received sixteen years in jail.

A Pakistani friend of mine working illegally in Chungking Mansions called me frantically one afternoon, saying that the police had caught him. I was in the building and reached him five minutes after his call to find twenty or so people lined up before the police, who had found a packet of heroin dropped on the ground and had rounded up everyone nearby. My friend, upon seeing me, slipped HK$12,000 into my pocket, fortunately unseen by the police. His fear was that the police would search him and find that he had money that he shouldn't have had, as an illegal worker, and confiscate it. My fear was that if his act was seen by the police, my picture would appear in all the local mass media: "Professor Arrested in Heroin Bust." After the police left, I shouted at him for a minute and gave him his money back; then we both laughed in relief for several minutes more. He was illegally working but had nothing at all to do with heroin, I know with certainty. However, as these cases both reveal, the lure of quick money through heroin or other forms of criminal activity always lurks around the edges of Chungking Mansions.

The Role of Police

There are two levels of authority in Chungking Mansions, the building guards and the police. Chungking Mansions has its own force of guards,

stationed at a post near the building's entrance; at the elevators at crowded times, to maintain order in the long queues; and walking around the building. These guards carry no weapons, and their role is more to maintain order at the elevators and to stroll around the building making sure that nothing is amiss. Occasionally they do thwart crime (a guard won a commendation in 2007 for stopping a would-be burglar from cutting the cable of the CCTV system so that he could avoid being filmed; the guard did this without calling the police), but almost always, whenever anything serious happens, they summon police.

One function of these guards is to maintain the security room, with its large bank of CCTV screens, whereby the corridors and stairways of Chungking Mansions are monitored. The footage of these cameras is available in case crimes take place, and often victims or police seek such footage to review; I have been told that police pay four or five visits to the security room each month, to investigate crimes or potential crimes, and so too do some residents of Chungking Mansions. This seems reminiscent of Michel Foucault in his description of the Panopticon, the constant surveillance of prisoners in a structure imagined by Jeremy Bentham, in which "all is observed."[1]

However, I myself am surprised by how little seems to be acted upon. The cameras bring a degree of order to Chungking Mansions, since footage of burglary or violent crime can be retrieved—most merchants in the building seem grateful for their presence—but mostly the cameras are ignored. Sometimes I have passed heroin addicts shooting up in the stairways and elsewhere, oblivious to the cameras that may be filming them, which have no effect upon their lives.

More directly involved in carrying out the law are the police. Police too, perhaps surprisingly, are respected by most of the people in Chungking Mansions. This is partly because of the police's professional behavior. When an asylum seeker I know claimed to have been beaten by the police for no reason, other asylum seekers guffawed and refused to believe him: "Hong Kong police don't do that. You must have hit the policeman first." This is also because of the contrast between police in Hong Kong as compared to traders' or merchants' home countries, where bribery of police may be an everyday affair. A Congolese trader, fresh in Hong Kong, initially refused to believe me when I told him that he couldn't bribe Hong Kong police if ever he found himself in trouble; bribery was second nature to him.

Underlying this is the apparent fact that the police do not want to get involved in Chungking Mansions' matters, as Andy Mok maintained in his interview in chapter 1. To find out more about this, I interviewed a policeman in 2007 for several hours. Here is what he told me:

Billy Tsang

For a long time, police had a bad image of Chungking Mansions because so many complaints came in as compared to other places. In fact, it's gotten a lot better over the past few years. But many younger police still think Chungking Mansions is dangerous, because it's the senior police who do the training, and they stick to the old image. The biggest problem in Chungking Mansions for police is visa overstayers, people whose visas have expired.*

---

*The overstayers Billy Tsang is speaking of are mostly asylum seekers. At the time of this interview in 2007, asylum seekers were not given legal protection, as they were just a year later through laminated documents issued to each individual attesting to his or her legitimate status as an asylum seeker. At present, while there continue to be overstayers in Chungking Mansions, the many hundreds of asylum seekers in the building, whom I shortly discuss, are not among them—they are legally in Hong Kong, although they are not allowed to work.

But it's not simply because they're overstayers—bad guys use them for prostitution and drugs. It's much easier to get an overstayer to do these things because they're already outside the law; they're not going to go to the police.

Yes, some of the people who sell drugs are Nepalese, but very often they recruit overstayers. A Nepalese with a Hong Kong ID might recruit sex workers from among overstayers—it's easier to find sex workers among those people. The issue, for heroin addicts such as the Nepalese is not simply drugs themselves. If these guys get HK$4,000 a month in welfare benefits, it's not enough to support their addiction, so they do anything to get more money. One day last month, there were four robberies committed in Chungking Mansions by these addicts.

As for sex work, one basic fact is that police in Hong Kong can't arrest someone for simply standing around. You can only do that on the basis of complaints. But even on the basis of a complaint, all the police can do is check IDs and see if these women are legally here in Hong Kong. The same is true for counterfeit goods: the Customs and Excise Department won't act unless there is a complaint. As long as deception takes place only in Africa and not in Chungking Mansions, then the police may not act—there are more pressing issues to worry about.

The group involved in fighting, more than any other, is the Nepalese. The reason is that in Nepalese society, fighting is the way you show that you're really a man. A lot of the disturbances in Chungking Mansions seem to involve Nepalese, far beyond their numbers. Pakistanis also fight, but they fight less out of honor than out of self-interest.

There used to be Pakistani gangs in Chungking Mansions, led by a guy who linked his gang to the Chinese triads for a number of years. Several years ago, he was arrested for blackmail and repatriated to Pakistan—he's gone now, and there are no gangs. Because of the Chungking Mansions security apparatus now in place, no one can jump up and say "I'm the boss of Chungking Mansions," as was the case a few years ago. Even then, they didn't usually seek protection money but made their money in other ways, like drugs.

Yes, the younger police bring in people like asylum seekers; older policeman say, "Why are you causing these problems for us?" Many young policemen want to follow the book. Older policemen say that the primary offenses are things like murder, rape, and robbery: real offenses to public order. Things like overstaying, that's a much lower priority, because it's not really an offense to public order.

The head of the ownership committee at Chungking Mansions, Mrs. Lam, has done a very good job, partly because she's so well connected to the larger neighborhood community outside Chungking Mansions. She's been a big help in getting messages out through leaflets in all the different languages that are necessary—Urdu, Hindi, French, Nepali—telling people, "You're part of Hong Kong too. So if any crimes happen, please report them." There is a Crime Information Form, a CIF, available at the guard's booth that can be filled out anonymously. If, for example, an overstayer is raped by her employer, she can turn in this report; she may not want to give her name, but the information will still go to the police. The police can't act, because it's anonymous, but the police will have this on record. She can file this form—mail it in anonymously—without being in danger herself.

The police get fifteen or so calls a week concerning Chungking Mansions. Most are minor—complaints about too much noise—but also there are complaints about overstayers: "This restaurant has someone washing dishes who's definitely an overstayer!" A lot of those calls are bogus—some customer feels he's been treated badly, or there's a dispute about a bill—at least 50 percent are fake. There are also occasional calls about robbery and also about fighting, one or two a week.

If an asylum seeker or anyone else runs when they see police, they have to be caught. Never run! If you just stay calm, the police probably won't ask you for any papers. Another matter is that the touts in front of Chungking Mansions who hand out leaflets for Chungking Mansions restaurants need to learn to behave in a Hong Kong style rather then an Indian style. If you hand out leaflets, the legality is murky, and for the most part police overlook it. But if you are aggressive, grabbing people's clothing, that's a problem.

The rule about the police only acting on the basis of complaints does not apply to drug dealers—the police don't need complaints to investigate them. Many drug dealers get caught because they're in competition—a drug dealer in a different neighborhood anonymously reports on a drug dealer working around Chungking Mansions to get rid of his competition. But at other times, undercover police will also come in to catch them.

The police really do want to establish relations with the nonethnic Chinese. For all these people, the key message is don't be afraid of the police. Fill out the CIF form—the police won't just put the form away; they'll act.

After this interview, I was immediately confronted with the practical reality of Billy Tsang's words. As I reported earlier, the Pakistani cook at a restaurant, along with his temporary employee, was assaulted. I brought him a CIF from the guard post, but because it asked for name and address, he refused to use it. He said that he tried to call the police three times during the assault, but the police never showed up; the Chungking Mansions guards didn't help either. He was deeply skeptical about going to the police, because it would endanger his employee (and, I might add, he as employer as well), who might be sent to jail for working illegally.

I called Billy Tsang thereafter, and he reluctantly said that the police couldn't help under these circumstances. Despite his idealism, when this small Pakistani restaurant was threatened with hoodlums, the Hong Kong police were useless. This is why this Pakistani cook decided to use not police but rather kinship and friendship—the fact that his friend was the uncle of one of his assailants—to solve the problem, as we saw.

There are different types of police coming to Chungking Mansions. There are the regular police, with billed caps, who generally don't care much about illegal immigrants, being more concerned with crimes such as robbery and assault, and with maintaining public order; Billy Tsang is among them. Then there are the police specifically charged with finding immigration violators, among other duties, who wear blue berets and who are more likely to arouse fear and wariness in Chungking Mansions. There also are the undercover police, the CID, who are primarily seeking drug dealers, but also occasionally arrest copy-watch salesmen plying their trade on Nathan Road, as well as illegal workers.

My friends who sell copy watches have shown me how to recognize undercover police; several have also told me that they know the undercover police in the area by their faces. Through their tutelage, I myself came to recognize undercover police rather easily; more than once, I have greeted them, after which they smile sheepishly. Clearly, these undercover police are not trying particularly hard to be undercover, which is probably for the best, given the nature of Chungking Mansions.*

There are different views of police and of illegality held by different businesses in Chungking Mansions, based on the position of the business vis-à-vis the illegal labor market. Many of the half dozen upscale (by Chungking Mansions standards) Indian restaurants upstairs have a largely local Hong Kong Chinese clientele. Their business depends very much on whether Chungking Mansions is seen by locals as a dangerous building to enter, or rather as a place that is "appealingly exotic."

Some of these restaurants hire temporary workers or asylum seekers as touts, dishwashers, or waiters, even though their managers generally deny

---

*In November 2009, two asylum-seeker employees were arrested for working illegally at a first-floor restaurant. I was told that two undercover police ate meals at the restaurant on three successive days before making the arrests, revealing how labor intensive it is to gather sufficient legal evidence for such arrests.

it. In one restaurateur's words, "We don't hire anyone on tourist visas. If you're caught, it's a HK$200,000 fine and six months in jail for the business owners. That's too much of a risk. We only hire local Hong Kong people." This restaurant does indeed hire illegal workers, despite this person's words. Nonetheless, restaurateurs such as him see the police presence as highly beneficial to business. As another restaurant manager told me, "I see the police as my friend. They are helping the image of this building. We need to attract the local market, and the local market is scared of Chungking Mansions. It's good what the police are doing."

Guesthouse owners and managers may have a somewhat different view. They too—particularly in the more expensive places that depend upon the tourist trade from China, Japan, and Europe more than on African businesspeople for their customer base—see it as essential to their business that Chungking Mansions be regarded as safe, clean, and appealing in its multicultural mix. But their business does not come from Hong Kong, and so they need to be less concerned with the still largely negative local perceptions of Chungking Mansions.

Beyond this, many guesthouses have something to hide from the police. A number of guesthouses have unlicensed blocks of rooms where they can take guests when their primary guesthouse is full. Some are managed by Filipinas hired as "domestic helpers" and thus technically not allowed to work beyond the home (which may be a flat on the same block in Chungking Mansions, owned by their Hong Kong Chinese employer). And a number of guesthouses—particularly those seeking African customers—hire African asylum seekers as helpers or managers to draw in those customers. These guesthouse owners and managers welcome the presence of police in keeping Chungking Mansions more orderly, but they also are quite nervous about the appearance of the police at their own guesthouses.

The police raid Chungking Mansions every few weeks or months, going to the upper floors to ask for ID cards or passports; occasionally they go to every flat in the building, not just the licensed guesthouses. There are sometimes particular reasons for this. Once it was apparently because—so I gathered from the word on the street—a number of Pakistanis were engaged in human trafficking, bringing women across borders, particularly from Mongolia, for sex work, which had come to the attention of the local mass media. Another time it was because a female Canadian tourist had vanished, with her last known place of residence being a guesthouse in Chungking Mansions.[2] More often, police raids are simply one of the police's regular activities in search of overstayers.

Guesthouse owners and managers may grumble about the inconvenience these raids create for their guests, but more obviously they are concerned with the fate of their own illegal employees (who most often are not those with expired visas, but rather asylum seekers or temporary workers with papers giving them the right to be in Hong Kong but not to work). Word, however, travels fast in Chungking Mansions. As one guesthouse manager told me,

> If we have a Filipina maid working for us, no one calls us to tell us that the immigration police are raiding Chungking Mansions. But since we're on an upper floor, we know long before the police get here, since they go up floor by floor. The police can't arrest a Filipina in the guesthouse—you can always say, "she's been here just ten minutes"—but it will cause trouble.

As for hiring an asylum seeker, a guesthouse manager said, "If they are sleeping in the front of the guesthouse and police come, the manager can just say, 'They needed a place to sleep and couldn't pay for a room, so we let them sleep in front.' There's no way that Immigration can prove otherwise." When I asked why these guesthouses hired illegal workers, I was told very frankly, "Our business couldn't survive if we didn't hire them." Whether it is a matter of bankruptcy or simply diminished profits were they to vanish, it seems clear that many of the Chungking Mansions guesthouses do indeed depend upon these workers.

It is occasionally expressed in Chungking Mansions that Hong Kong police are racist, favoring Chinese, as in Johnny Singh's and Fahad Ali's accounts in chapter 2. As I heard from one ground-floor shopkeeper, "The Chinese guy who runs the outside newsstand beat a Nepali with an iron rod a few days ago. The police didn't do anything to this Chinese guy. He was taken into the station and then released two hours later and was back at work. That's not right!" Others said that the police were almost never racist in their behavior, despite language barriers. But this charge of racism is the single most consistent criticism made of police in Chungking Mansions.

Those working illegally in Chungking Mansions face severe sanctions if caught; the copy-watch salesmen on the lookout for undercover police mentioned above have very good reason to be vigilant, for if they are arrested they face a fine, a potential jail sentence, and deportation and confiscation of their passports. But most workers have a relatively relaxed view of this possibility. An illegal worker at a guesthouse went downstairs to the Chungking Mansions entrance at around midnight one night to search for customers; I asked him how he could do this, and he smiled and said that although he was illegally working, he would never get caught unless someone like me were to

call Immigration about him. Workers do indeed occasionally get caught, but it is quite infrequent. By and large, police in Chungking Mansions operate under the principle of laissez-faire neoliberalism: as long as the Hong Kong public is not harmed, let business go on unimpeded, since business is the foremost priority of Hong Kong. This attitude is what makes Chungking Mansions possible.

Visas and Residence Rights

A concern that unites most of the people who stay in Chungking Mansions is that of visas and residence rights, in both Hong Kong and China. A significant number of the traders one encounters in Chungking Mansions are based in China and are in Hong Kong to renew their visas. This was most obvious in 2008 when China tightened its visa policy before the Olympics, as we saw in chapter 3, but the matter is never far from the minds of most traders, since their futures depend upon the willingness of Chinese and Hong Kong officials to grant them visas.

Traders who work out of China have often worked out techniques for how to get the longest possible visas. One Kenyan trader was convinced that he could get the best possible deal by ignoring the many travel agents in Chungking Mansions and elsewhere offering a China visa and going to the Chinese consulate in Hong Kong himself. He is direct, he told me, with the Chinese officials there: "I say to them, 'I need a tourist visa, but I'm not a tourist. I need it to do business. . . . I don't ask for too much. If you ask for two weeks, they'll give you two months. But if you ask for three months, they'll give you three days."

Once traders are in China, they must register with police, which many forget, requiring a police pay off. As one trader told me, "They decide everything on their own: you pay them off right there, 100, 200, 500 yuan." Even if an African trader is married to a Chinese woman, he cannot remain in China, I have been told over and over by distraught African spouses, but can only obtain a business visa for up to three months, with no guarantee of permanency.

Many traders feel bedeviled by the Hong Kong government's increasingly strict visa regulations. A Ghanaian trader related how difficult it is for him to get a Hong Kong visa in Ghana, unlike in earlier years when he could simply show up at the Hong Kong airport. To get a Hong Kong visa now, he must go through the Chinese embassy in Accra, who then fax everything to Hong Kong Immigration. He said that he had to go to the Chinese Embassy every day, and the entire process took him a month in all. The Chinese Embassy, he said, invariably blamed Hong Kong, saying that "the Hong Kong officials haven't decided yet." As a store proprietor in Chungking Mansions told me, "The Hong Kong government has to take merchants like me into account when they set such a strict visa policy. Otherwise, I'll go broke and have to get welfare."

A Pakistani phone seller told of how he repeatedly went to the Immigration Department in Hong Kong on behalf of three Pakistani customers to ask if their application for entry visas had been granted; the official reply was "still on the waiting list." Their absence would affect his business, and he was left furious and helpless. A Chinese watch seller called up Immigration on behalf of his long-term Ghanaian customers who are stranded in Ghana and cannot do business with him; he said that while they can get a visa into China, they can no longer get a visa to come into Hong Kong. Increasingly, in 2008 and 2009, these complaints came to be heard from many Chungking Mansions merchants, but invariably, Hong Kong Immigration told them nothing when they enquired.

The ability to be granted at the airport a long stay in Hong Kong accounts for many of the nationalities one sees most predominantly at Chungking Mansions. To take just one example, there are often some thirty sex workers from Kenya and Tanzania at work in the building. They are able to engage in this trade, unlike women from most other African countries, because the ninety-day visa-free entry they receive at the airport makes such work possible and profitable. Few if any women ever desire to be sex workers, but for those who practice the profession, a long stay makes it eminently more practicable. Some also become asylum seekers, giving them an even longer period in which to stay in Hong Kong. Asylum seekers—whom we will shortly discuss at length—cannot return to their home countries, unlike temporary workers who must return periodically, or else their claim will be ended; they remain in Hong Kong indefinitely.

For those nationalities who cannot get visa-free entry into Hong Kong, one can obtain a business visa for Hong Kong, and some Nigerians, in particular, have made an art of this. Business visas are typically obtained through a letter from a Hong Kong company, which may be hard to get for one's initial journey to Hong Kong. Some Nigerian traders get around this difficulty by hiring agents, experienced traders who already have personal connections with sponsoring companies, to provide them with the letter from a Hong Kong company, for US$50 to US$400 depending on how close the new trader is to the agent. Once they are in Hong Kong, they ask a Hong Kong trading company to sponsor them, which these companies are generally willing to do in order to enlarge their customer base. This is also the case for gaining entry into China. Factories in south China can offer a "letter of invitation" for US$300 to US$500; since factories can issue a very limited number of these—one a month is what I have heard—Nigerian traders in particular scramble for them, and in some cases, I have heard, forge them. Another common Nigerian practice to overcome the problem of not being allowed into Hong Kong is to get a passport from another country—Zambia and South Africa are common choices—which are allowed freer access into Hong Kong. By several accounts, this is easy to do for a few hundred US dollars.

Another category of people in Chungking Mansions who must constantly worry about visas are the tourist-visa workers, predominantly from India. It has apparently become a bit more difficult in recent years for these temporary workers to extend their stays in Hong Kong; one worker I know tells me that he used to be able to be in Hong Kong for forty-two days, but in 2007 it was just twenty-five days. Later he was again given forty-two days, but the arbitrariness of not knowing how many days he will be given to stay in Hong Kong makes his situation difficult.

Some of these workers too have begun to claim themselves as asylum seekers. I said to one new worker/asylum seeker, "But you can't go home if you're an asylum seeker." He looked at me blankly and said, "That doesn't matter. Money is what matters. My family cares more about the money I send home than about seeing me." Those who choose to become asylum seekers make the same or slightly lower wages than they did as temporary workers, but do not have to pay for the flights back home, even if those flights were mostly subsidized by the goods they carried back and forth.

An additional strategy for staying in Hong Kong is marriage to a Hong Kong permanent resident. I know one worker who is married in Kolkata and has a happy family, he says—he showed me pictures of his two grade-school sons—but was going through a paper marriage with a Hong Kong Chinese woman, a friend of his, in an effort to get Hong Kong residency. Several of the South Asian temporary workers I know who are single have Hong Kong Chinese girlfriends whom they seek to marry, and thereby obtain, if not Hong Kong residency, at least an implicit assurance that they can stay on in Hong Kong indefinitely.

For those South Asians or mainland Chinese who already have residence rights in Hong Kong, their concern may instead shift to bringing family members to Hong Kong. I have frequently heard of Chungking Mansions managers with children or siblings in Pakistan they seek to bring to Hong Kong; as one older man told me, "I have four sons in Pakistan, two in Lahore, and two in Karachi. I've applied to get them to come to Hong Kong; I think two will come. But the papers take a very, very long time." I also know of cases where one Pakistani brother has Hong Kong residency while the other does not: the brother with residency makes HK$7,000 a month, while the one without residency makes only HK$3,000 per month, an enormous gap in pay.

There are also the visa overstayers. These people are officially illegal, not just because they may work, but more, because of their very presence. It is difficult to catch an illegal worker in Chungking Mansions, because they can always claim to be "helping out a friend for a minute." However, overstayers are comparatively easier to catch, since their passports, or in some cases their lack of passports, give them away as illegal.

I am told that there are perhaps no more than a hundred overstayers in Chungking Mansions at any given time. One group of overstayers is Nigerian. They may come to Hong Kong to work legitimately as entrepreneurs and then, after several months, go to the Nigerian embassy claiming that their passports have been stolen. An occasional practice is for Africans, as well as South Asians, who bear a degree of facial resemblance to share a passport on their different trips home. "To Chinese most Africans look alike," I'm told, apparently giving this practice an excellent chance of success. Dodges change every few months, but generally speaking, these nimble entrepreneurs seem to manage to stay a step or two ahead of the police and the law.

Guangzhou has far more overstayers from Nigeria and other African countries than does Hong Kong and Chungking Mansions, both because there are many more Africans there, and thus safety in numbers, and also because police enforcement is less thorough and more arbitrary. Apparently it is more plausible in Guangzhou than in Hong Kong to make a living for years as an overstayer. But this is fraught with peril, in that one may get caught and deported and lose everything, returning home in shame with nothing to show for one's years of effort overseas.

In July 2009, an overstaying Nigerian in Guangzhou jumped out a window fleeing a visa check and was rumored to have been killed; there was a protest, with several hundred angry Africans surrounding a police station and demanding justice.[3] One key difference between China and Hong Kong in this regard is that in Hong Kong one can claim to be an asylum seeker, something that is impossible in China. I know of one overstayer in Chungking Mansions who was caught by the police working in a guesthouse and placed in detention for several weeks. He declared himself an asylum seeker and then went back to work at the guesthouse once more, gambling that he will not get caught again. Last I heard, he was still working there, sending his money back to his family in Nepal every month.

Asylum Seekers and the Law

Let us now turn to asylum seekers, to whom we will devote the rest of this chapter, not only because they make up a significant proportion of the population of Chungking Mansions, but also because they are those who are most obviously trapped by the law—trapped between states and generally unable to get out. Asylum seekers are those who have fled their home countries because of political, ethnic, or religious persecution and seek new lives in another society. Some asylum seekers seek a new life primarily for economic reasons, although this cannot be publicly admitted. Asylum seekers wait in Hong Kong for their cases to be decided, often after years; meanwhile they make whatever lives they can for themselves in their impoverished and more or less subterranean existences.

There is a vast literature on asylum seekers worldwide, with compelling recent books describing the treatment of asylum seekers and refugees in the United States, Western Europe, and Australia.[4] These portrayals reveal that Hong Kong uses the same strategies as many of these other societies in seeking to curtail the number of asylum seekers coming to its shores. Hong Kong differs from these other societies in allowing virtually no asylum seekers to permanently remain in Hong Kong, but rather insisting that they resettle in a third country. Hong Kong also differs in having a relatively more open visa regime than most of these countries.

There are clearly a fair number of asylum seekers in Chungking Mansions, but exact numbers are impossible to come by. Only a minority of asylum seekers go to NGOs such as Christian Action, on Chungking Mansion's six-teenth and seventeenth floors (E Block), set up specifically for asylum seek-ers. Many more work on the ground or first floors, or throughout Chung-king Mansions, but do not make their identity as asylum seekers known.

I occasionally ask shopkeepers how many of the people passing through Chungking Mansions are asylum seekers. One estimate I've heard is this: "Of 10,000 people passing through Chungking Mansions, 2,000 are asylum seekers, 4,000 are working illegally on tourist permits, and the other 4,000 are traders or legal workers." These figures are exaggerated, but do reflect commonly held beliefs about the ubiquity of asylum seekers. My own rough guess, based on all the people I know in Chungking Mansions, would be that there are 300 asylum seekers and 500 tourist-permit workers in or around the building at any given time during the day: still a quite significant num-ber, but much less than the number guessed at by some of the people I talk to. Traders and tourists are the bulk of people one sees in Chungking Man-sions, and the overwhelming majority is legally in Hong Kong, even if the traders, admitted as tourists, technically should not be engaged in business. A number of shop clerks on the ground and first floor, as well as in guest-houses and other businesses on higher floors, are indeed working on tourist permits or are asylum seekers, although many more, probably the majority, are legal Hong Kong residents.

Asylum seekers, as earlier noted, have the advantage of never having to go home to renew their permission to stay in Hong Kong. Thus there is signifi-cant temptation to hire them, particularly South Asian asylum seekers, who can blend in without being conspicuous. However, many asylum seekers do not work, following the legal rule that they are not allowed to work in Hong Kong. Once they have surrendered themselves to immigration authorities and emerged from detention, asylum seekers can obtain HK$1,000 in rental assistance each month paid directly to their landlord and HK$900 in gro-ceries each month through International Social Services, an NGO commis-sioned by the Hong Kong government. On this amount it is possible to sur-vive in Hong Kong, barely.

The aim of asylum seekers is to be accepted as refugees and then admit-ted to a third country to live, such as Canada or the United States. How-

ever, only a small number of asylum seekers—most often from countries that are in chaos, such as Somalia—ever attain this aim. Some asylum seekers do indeed attain refugee status; some manage to marry Hong Kongers or other foreigners and obtain residence rights that way; some return home; and some are deported. But most I know continue to eke out lives year after year in Hong Kong, unable to travel outside the territory, waiting interminably to have their cases decided.

Some asylum seekers—often although by no means always those who do not have legitimate cases to make—work and send their money home. Most struggle on extremely low wages, but a few have managed to make significant business niches for themselves, often in exporting goods to their home countries or in serving as middlemen between traders and shops, or retailers and wholesalers of goods, and manage to build new houses for their families back home.

Other asylum seekers—those who are idealists, strict abiders of the law, or in some cases simply lazy—do not work, except sometimes in the service of charity groups that do not pay them. Some of those who do not work are those who, paradoxically, could benefit Hong Kong the most if they did—they are political leaders and dissidents in their home countries and are remarkably intelligent and insightful. But they also are those who most insistently seek to follow the letter of the law, because if they worked and were caught, they might be sent back to their countries and face imprisonment, torture, and perhaps death.

Most asylum seekers do not live in Chungking Mansions,* but come intermittently to the building, although Chungking Mansions and the surrounding area remains the social center for many. In May 2006, there were some 1,600 asylum seekers in Hong Kong waiting for a decision in their asylum applications. By 2007, the number had jumped to 2,600.[5] At present, the number has shot up drastically because so many asylum seekers are now making their claims with the Hong Kong government through the Convention Against Torture (CAT), as I explain later. By the end of August 2009, there were 5,638 outstanding torture claims received by the Hong Kong Immigration Department,[6] and several thousand outstanding claims also being processed by the UNHCR. Most claimants go through both. At present there are probably over 6,000 asylum seekers in Hong Kong. Most are from

*In 2009, International Social Services began a policy of denying monthly rental assistance to those asylum seekers who were living in Chungking Mansions, insisting that they move elsewhere, perhaps in order to deter illegal workers.

South Asia, with a significant minority from Africa and a smattering from other countries—although there are none from China, since Hong Kong is itself part of China.

Hong Kong's population is largely made up of those who fled China at some point over the past sixty years, to some extent resembling in spirit today's asylum seekers.[7] However, African and South Asian asylum seekers are quite new in Hong Kong. Hong Kong has long suffered from panics over illegal immigrants. There were many outcries over Vietnamese boat people in the 1980s and 1990s;[8] more recently there have been worries over mainland women seeking to deliver their babies in Hong Kong and thereby make them Hong Kong residents.[9]

The current wave of South Asian and African asylum seekers began coming to Hong Kong only quite recently, in the early 2000s. I am told by asylum seekers that the biggest reason they began coming to Hong Kong is that in the wake of 9/11, other nations tightened their visa policies, making Hong Kong an appealing destination.[10] As word spread that African and South Asian traders could be admitted to Hong Kong without visas, potential asylum seekers took note.

Despite the great sufferings that some asylum seekers have gone through, they tend, like the other denizens of Chungking Mansions, to be middle-class in background and are among the well-off in their home countries, as shown by the fact that they were able to come to Hong Kong. While some traveled overland through China, and others arrived by boat, the majority were able to pay the price of airfare from their home countries. The Somali asylum seekers and refugees I know tend to have the calm, even fastidious deportment of the teachers and accountants they were in Mogadishu. Unlike some of their fellow countrymen and women who, fleeing the violence of Somalia, drowned in capsized boats in the Gulf of Aden, they were able to buy the services of brokers who put them on commercial airplanes and got them to Hong Kong. As noted in chapter 2, for several years I have held a weekly class on current events and other matters for asylum seekers, and it is like a lively college seminar, replete with vociferous arguments about African colonialism, homosexuality and heterosexuality, the possibility of life on other planets, the future of the Internet, and the nature of God.*

These asylum seekers must convincingly claim to have been persecuted

---

*Some of these asylum seekers come to my undergraduate classes at the Chinese University of Hong Kong. I have been in passionate classroom debates with them on issues ranging from imperialism to witchcraft; while we debate, many Chinese University students look on intimidated, unused to such vibrant discussions.

ethnically, religiously, or politically if they seek refugee status through the UNHCR, or to have been tortured or face the threat of torture if they seek protection through CAT. The organizations they appeal to must decide whether their cases are valid or not, but often this is extraordinarily difficult to do. Torturers and persecutors in developing countries may not leave paper trails documenting their actions: these are reaches far beyond the light that Google may shed.

Interviewers thus look for internal consistency in asylum seekers' accounts, but one who has been tortured or persecuted may not or may no longer have the logical or oratorical skills to meet the interviewers' criteria. Who is valid and who is not becomes a game gambling with asylum seeker's lives hanging on the balance of a scant few hours or minutes of interviewing.[11] Remarkably few win this game. In 2008, of 1,547 refugee claims evaluated by the UNHCR, only 46 were recognized as valid,[12] a bit less than 3 percent. The Hong Kong government has recognized only one torture claimant thus far, with the growing thousands of others still waiting.

"Real" and "Fake" Asylum Seekers

The words "real" and "fake" are occasionally used in discussing asylum seekers, sometimes by asylum seekers themselves and sometimes, in derision, by shopkeepers in Chungking Mansions. One asylum seeker, himself manifestly genuine in his claims, told me that probably 80 percent of asylum seekers are bogus in their claims.

That is a huge percentage; however, the longer one looks at the issue of "real" and "fake" asylum seekers (in a sense like the "real" and "fake" goods discussed in chapter 3), the more complicated the matter becomes[13]—the line between "real" and "fake" is so blurry as to be all but indistinguishable.* There are some asylum seekers who are manifestly genuine. There are others who have left their home countries not because they have been threatened or persecuted, but rather for the sake of economic gain: they have claimed asylum-seeker status because it enables them to make money in Hong Kong. Many asylum seekers fit neither of these types, but are in the middle between them.

It is often very difficult to meet the requirements of the UNHCR or CAT

---

*One asylum seeker who read this chapter has strongly advised against the use of these terms, since the line is so unclear: "You're saying that some people are entirely genuine and other people are entirely not, but that's not the way it is." His point is valid; however, because these terms are so often used in Chungking Mansions, I retain them, albeit in quotation marks.

even if one has experienced or been threatened with violence. A Ghanaian asylum seeker told me that a neighboring family was after his family's land; one member of this family had threatened to kill him after an acrimonious argument. A Senegalese asylum seeker said that he was running a boat, and it crashed and people drowned—the husband of a woman who died vowed to kill him. A Pakistani man, whose account we later hear, told me of how his marriage had been a disaster, but his relatives had threatened to kill him if he sought a divorce, since it would shame the family. An Indian man said to me, "I lost my business selling T-shirts.... My creditor said, 'If you don't give me my money, I will kill you!' My mother said, 'You are my only son. Go somewhere else, anywhere!'"

It makes sense that these people would flee—their lives seem to have been in danger. However, although these cases involve death threats, they do not involve torture or its threat, or political, religious, or ethnic persecution; rather, they are personal disputes. In a developed-world context, one so threatened might seek a restraining order, or use some other legal means to escape the situation, but this isn't available in the developing countries from which these people come. Their cases will probably fail, unless they can make up different stories, because they don't fit the criteria through which refugee status is granted.

I know several asylum seekers who wear their claims directly on their bodies. One is a South Asian man with a bullet lodged in his femur. He showed me the x-rays, which he always carries with him—he was shot by government forces and remains in grave danger, he claimed. Another, mentioned in chapter 1, always wears dark glasses; he was blinded in prison, he says, when prison guards forced him to stare at the sun for hours by taping open his eyelids. However, these claims will not hold up without corroborating evidence. How can the first man prove that he was shot by government forces rather than in an accident? How can the second man prove that he was blinded in prison? The claims of these asylum seekers are on their bodies, but this is not enough. They can only hope that there is some public record (at best accessible through Google) that will corroborate their bodies' claims.

Some asylum seekers are flamboyantly lying. One West African told me this story. When he was small, he was forced to join a religious sect; when he was twenty, he found out that the sect planned to castrate him on his twenty-first birthday, so that he would not be attracted to women but would unconditionally love God. He hurriedly escaped and fled deep into the jungle. In hiding, he met two Australian men who, after he showed them a vial of diamonds his late mother had given him, agreed to help him. They gave him a drink, drugged; he lost consciousness. For an indefinite period, he drifted in and out of consciousness in a dark enclosed space, a ship's hold, he surmised; they continuously gave him more to drink. Eventually, his head cleared, and he woke up: he was in a vacant lot in Hong Kong, with no diamonds, no money, no passport, and no idea how he'd gotten there. I told him that no one would ever believe this story; he had seen too many bad adventure movies. But he was adamant.

I had trouble suppressing my laughter when I heard this story, and indeed, UNHCR personnel have told me that one problem they face is that of interviewers keeping a straight face before the outlandish stories asylum seekers may tell. There is, a UNHCR official told me, a standard story from Nigerians and other West Africans: "My father was a king, and I was supposed to eat his heart after he died so that I would inherit his mantle. My mother was Christian and refused to let me eat his heart. Not only my community, but also the spirits hate me for this; my life is being threatened, and so I can't go back." This story is told over and over again, this official said: "We have to work hard not to laugh out loud when we hear one more story like that."

However, even for a story such as this, one cannot be sure what is genuine. A West African asylum seeker showed me a detailed account from the Internet concerning sons of chiefs and the pressure they are under, and how some of them are persecuted, particularly if they have embraced Christianity—this Internet story mirrored his own personal story. His case was rejected by the UNHCR—possibly to their stifled laughter?—and he turned to the CAT to make his claim, whose verdict he still awaits. Recently, he showed me several letters that he had received from academic specialists in the United Kingdom and elsewhere attesting to the plausibility of his claims. He may have been a victim at the UNHCR of having a true story that ran too closely to the false story that others tell.

The asylum seekers I know occasionally discuss when it is appropriate to lie to the UNHCR or Hong Kong authorities. I consistently hear that it is wrong to make up a story that has no truth, but very often one must to some extent distort reality simply to have a clear-cut and easily comprehensible story line: "The situation is actually so complicated that you must make it plainer and simpler for them." This is particularly felt to be necessary because the UNHCR personnel are often seen as callow and ignorant: "She didn't even know where my country was! How can she judge my case?" In a larger, procedural sense, because the UNHCR, unlike the Hong Kong government, has not allowed asylum seekers to correct or even see the transcripts of interviews written up by its caseworkers, there is potential for mistakes to be made—making lying all the more necessary in some asylum seekers' views.

However, embellishing or simplifying one's story carries its own risk. The UNHCR and the Hong Kong authorities greatly emphasize consistency in asylum seekers' accounts; the danger in lying is that one may slip up and say something inconsistent with one's earlier account, dooming one's chances of becoming a refugee.[14] This is something that has severely hurt the credibility of several asylum seekers I know.

I noted earlier that "fake" asylum seekers are sometimes thought of as those who work, while "real" asylum seeker are thought of as those who do not work, in that if one works and is caught, one may be sent back home and imprisoned or killed. There is considerable truth to this, but here too there are many shades of gray. Some asylum seekers are consumed with worry about their families and are willing to take considerable risks to be able to send money home.

Some kinds of work—for example, arranging to send goods to trusted confederates back home for subsequent payment—are difficult for any authorities to trace, as long as certain precautions are used, such as having money wired under a friend's name. However, to engage in such work, one needs to have reliable African connections, which may be difficult, given the fact that the asylum seeker is indefinitely stuck in Hong Kong. People back in Africa, I'm told, often believe that asylum seekers in Hong Kong are wealthy ("They give asylum seekers a lot of money just to live!"), and so the money asylum seekers send back home for investment may simply be spent by family members or friends who have their own pressing needs.

Asylum seekers who cannot manage to engage in trade may try other kinds of low-risk work, such as guiding African traders newly arrived in Hong Kong for a hoped-for commission. At one session of the class for asylum seekers, a working asylum seeker declaimed at length about how asylum seekers should "get off your asses and work." He described how he went to a junkyard and photographed car parts with his mobile phone, then went back to Chungking Mansions and showed African traders what was available, for a cut of the profits. "Anyone can do this," he said. The response of some asylum seekers in the class was to declare, "That's illegal! I won't do that! I believe in obeying the law." Others said, after he left, "I don't believe him—I think he's working for the Hong Kong government and trying to entrap us."

Some asylum seekers may, out of desperation, engage in work that renders them highly visible and potentially subject to arrest, such as selling copy watches on the sidewalks surrounding Chungking Mansions. Some of those engaged in such work are indeed more or less "real," from all I can tell. On the other hand, there are asylum seekers who do not work but rather use their charm to relax and drink Chungking Mansions' very cheap liquor month after month. The working asylum seeker in the preceding paragraph later exclaimed to me, "Most asylum seekers are lazy. They don't want to work! They'd rather get a handout than work for themselves. This is why Africa is so poor and controlled by white people!" (As we've seen, however, most asylum seekers in Hong Kong are South Asian rather than African, and many do indeed work.)

It is interesting that while among "real" asylum seekers, "fake" asylum seekers may be looked down upon because they are in Hong Kong for economic reasons, among Chungking Mansions merchants and traders, it is those asylum seekers who don't work who are scorned. An East African trader asked me if there were any asylum seekers in Chungking Mansions. I told her that there were, and she sneered, "Those people are all fake! They're just lazy! They just want to live off the government! They have a better life than I do, because they can relax, but I have to work!" Others expressed a broader resentment: a shopkeeper told me, "It's because of so many asylum seekers that the government restricts the visas of African countries, preventing African people from doing business here.* They cost us money. All of them should be outlawed!"

I know well a number of admittedly "fake" asylum seekers who have come to Hong Kong for largely economic reasons. A Pakistani man, whose account we will shortly read, was asked by his family to join his uncle, a longtime resident of Hong Kong, to help run his business. If his Hong Kong relation had been his father, then getting Hong Kong residence would have been possible for him, but because it was his more distant relative, there was no such possibility. Thus he felt little choice but to declare himself an asylum seeker and manufacture a claim. This pattern particularly holds true among South Asians, who may come to Hong Kong to join a relative's business in Chungking Mansions and declare themselves as asylum seekers to enable them to legally stay in Hong Kong, if not to legally work.

An asylum seeker once told me that if a person is tortured, or has seen someone in their family killed, they will always have that in at least the back of their minds; it never goes away. He acknowledged that he himself has recurring nightmares of the terrible things he saw in Somalia. He maintained that many of the asylum seekers from West Africa or South Asia must necessarily be "fake" asylum seekers, economic migrants, because they seem too happy.

---

*I cannot verify this, but given the rapidly expanding number of asylum seekers in Hong Kong, he is probably correct in this claim.

I do not know how true this may be. One asylum seeker spoke in a re-markably light-hearted way in my class about torture, making me wonder if he could really have experienced intense suffering in his own life, but then I learned that he had recently been released from a mental hospital in Hong Kong—he too had demons, although not demons that he chose to show to me. How many of the asylum seekers I know have indeed experienced awful things and hide those in their public faces, and how many have never gone through such experiences? I don't know, and perhaps it is obscene to even ask, but I can't help but wonder. I remember one extraordinary night in which, alone long after midnight, an asylum seeker from Central Africa confided to me that he had adopted his brother's name because he himself was responsible for his brother's death. The authorities had been looking for him, and he had hid: they killed his brother instead. He sobbed inconsolably for half an hour. After that night, I never saw him again.

The Lives of Asylum Seekers

One of the biggest difficulties in asylum seekers' lives in Hong Kong is the potent combination of uncertainty, boredom, and drift: a sense of their lives being stalled. I occasionally give a little moral lecture to the asylum seekers I know: "Yes, you've suffered. But you've been given time. Don't work if you don't feel it's right, but at least study. Go to the library and read every day!" Some have more or less followed my advice, but the capriciousness of their existences make this hard for most.

Many asylum seekers wound up in Hong Kong largely by happenstance. One asylum seeker I know told me that he had investigated over the Internet where in the world he might be able to go to live that would require no visa. Samoa is what he found. But by the time he got to Hong Kong, he found that he would indeed need a visa to get to Samoa, and so he found himself indefinitely stuck in Hong Kong. The standing joke among many asylum seekers is that Hong Kong is a very strange place, because it's so easy to get in and so hard to get out (unless the asylum seeker agrees to return to his home country).

Because it may take months for asylum seekers to receive the requisite pa-perwork enabling shelter or rent assistance, some have experienced extended periods of sleeping outside, often in the vicinity of the Star Ferry Terminal, one of Hong Kong's touristic icons. When the paperwork comes through, which in some cases may entail many phone calls and repeated entreaties, the basic physical necessities of life are more or less taken care of, but other worries remain. Some asylum seekers are convinced that secret police from home are after them, a fear that in some cases may be far-fetched, but in other cases is not. There are businesspeople in Chungking Mansions from almost all asylum seekers' home countries, and some asylum seekers fear that these businesspeople will recognize them and report them back to the government, which may in turn torment their families.

Some of the asylum seekers I know have trouble comprehending that their lives have come to this strange current state. I had a long conversation with a Bangladeshi man who said that until very recently he was a wealthy businessman, but he had supported the wrong political party—supporters of a different party came and beat him up. He eventually left Bangladesh, leaving his wife and daughter behind. He showed me his Global Visa credit card, expired less than a year before, once his ticket to all the globe, but now only a worthless reminder of who he once was.

In Chungking Mansions, I know of a number of asylum seekers who are ashamed to wait for the E-Block elevator at lunch or dinner time, when two Christian charity organizations in the block offer meals for asylum seekers; instead they walk up the long flights of stairs so that no one will see them going to accept free meals. I know of another asylum seeker who feels guilty because, even with the tiny allowance he gets from the Hong Kong government, he is able to lead a better life than the Chinese family leaving next door to him: "They have terrible bedbugs. I can tell from the laundry they hang out." He hopes that they will never find out that he is aided by the Hong Kong government, as they are not, even though he is utterly poverty-stricken by most Hong Kong standards.

And what might these asylum seekers become? On the one hand, there are those fortunate souls who are granted refugee status. A number of the Somalis I know have been granted such status; one mused to me about how terrible Somalia was but how lucky he himself was, paradoxically, to be from a country in such turmoil. I asked him about his family, if he phoned them often, and he explained that no, he's never phoned them—they've vanished. Everyone fled because of the terror; he has a rough idea where they are now, but he has no way to contact them and doesn't know if he'll ever see them again, since going back to such chaos would be a death sentence for him. He, on the other hand, would soon enough be a new man in a new country with a new life.

On the other hand, there is the far larger number of people who are refused. I once asked two of my students what they would do if they weren't granted refugee status, and they said they would kill themselves: "I'd spend my last dollar on a ferry ticket and jump off when no one was looking," in one's words. "I'd go to my room and die," another said. I know no one among the asylum seekers who has actually committed suicide, but these comments do show the depths of despair that refusal of their claims may lead to. Even if they are not repatriated, as most are indeed not, their lives remain in limbo.

It is not surprising that asylum seekers do anything they possibly can to gain refugee status. Once, a Nepalese asylum seeker, a Christian, came to me in a state of fury. "A pastor baptized a bunch of Nepalis today even though they'd only been in Hong Kong five days. They don't know anything about the Bible. They don't know Christianity. They just want to become Christians so that they can get refugee status somewhere!" Western countries, it is commonly believed, more readily accept Christians than those who are not Christians. He was offended because he had been constantly studying the Bible himself and resented those who embraced the faith opportunistically—and those, like the pastor, who abetted this.

Another way to break out of the limbo of being an asylum seeker is to find a girlfriend with Hong Kong residence and marry her; as long as the marriage continues, these asylum seekers will not be deported. Many of the girlfriends of asylum seekers are Filipina or Indonesian domestic helpers, who by the terms of their contracts are forbidden to marry. Other relationships are much harder to form, since they typically require money, something that most asylum seekers do not have. One asylum seeker I know indeed has a Hong Kong girlfriend, the holy grail sought by so many, but refuses to marry her. "What if you marry and the relationship doesn't work out? For the first four years, the wife has to write to Immigration once a week to say that they're still married. I'd rather try to get refugee status on my own." Asylum seekers sometimes lie about who they are to their girlfriends. One case involved an asylum seeker who suddenly died, apparently of a heart attack; his well-dressed Filipina girlfriend was seen crying out, "He's been lying to me all this time! He said that he was in business!"

Underlying much else in the lives of asylum seekers in Hong Kong are the two very separate paths of those who work and those who do not. My own observation is that those who work tend to be better able to deal with all the psychological difficulties of being an asylum seeker, in that they have something to keep them occupied day after day. A well-situated asylum seeker from Pakistan said, "Whatever the Hong Kong government does to me is no problem, because I have made enough money. I'm satisfied. I can go back to Pakistan." He had begun by working for a very small wage, carefully saving up his money, and then invested several thousand Hong Kong dollars in a business venture that fortunately paid off with enough of a profit for him to continue and expand.

To get started in business is, however, perilous. I know one asylum seeker who carefully saved his money over the months and bought eight motorcycle helmets that he sent to Nigeria to sell, just as a new law went into effect in January 2009 requiring that all motorcycle riders wear helmets. He expected to make a profit of US$100, enough to finance his next deal, but as so often happens, there was a miscalculation of government regulations, and his Nigerian partner absconded with the money—he wound up with nothing to show for his troubles.

Those asylum seekers who do not seek to make money have wholly different concerns. As one asylum seeker told me, "I'm real, unlike most other asylum seekers, and yet the UNHCR keeps asking me to jump through all these hoops"—they only seem to sneer at his efforts to prove his legitimacy, he felt, and he stewed endlessly over this situation. "Why won't they listen to me? Why can't they understand that I am real?" An asylum seeker once pointed at the Nepalese drug addicts in the back alley behind Chungking Mansions and said, "I don't understand it. They get paid welfare by the Hong Kong government, HK$4,500 a month, and don't work because they don't feel like it. I get almost nothing from the Hong Kong government and would love to work, if only the Hong Kong government would let me."

But of course, the Nepalese drug addicts are the sons of Gurkhas stationed in Hong Kong and have the all-important Hong Kong identity card. The asylum seekers are being shut out from the opportunity ever to attain such a card. They are being treated with a degree of limited humaneness by the Hong Kong government, but are absolutely kept at arm's length: short of marriage to a Hong Konger, Hong Kong will never be their home.

This is wholly understandable from the government's perspective—Hong Kong cannot afford a flood of refugees—but is deeply tragic in a personal sense. There is enormous talent among these asylum seekers, talent that Hong Kong can hardly afford not to recognize and utilize. Some of these asylum seekers keep themselves more or less busy through volunteer work of various sorts, others go to the library, and others only stew. Many of these asylum seekers, scorned though they may be, form the intellectual class of Chungking Mansions.

Here are the accounts of several asylum seekers:

John Mukasa

I was born in central Africa (it's too dangerous for me to tell you the country) in a family of seven—I'm the youngest boy. My mother was a politician. In the 1970s, people of my tribe were being killed by the government. My mother was well known. She was secretly sponsoring a rebel group and the government got wind of it. Friends had come to our house urging her to leave, but she refused and said that she would die for her country. A few days later, she was arrested. They picked her up and put her in an open vehicle, driving it through the whole town for everybody to see. I was too young to understand, I didn't know why people had come to my home. But to see my brothers and sisters crying.... They took her away and killed her. I never saw her again.

After that, my grandmother took us away to her village. My father never contributed anything, but my mother had two brothers and two sisters, and they all contributed to our upbringing. My eldest brother knew everything about what had happened to my mother—he could not study, started drinking heavily, and died....

There was a large family dispute over whether my mother's side of the family or my father's side would take care of us. It was really a dispute over who would get my mother's property—the police had to be called in. I was sent to my father's side, a very rural area. I realized it wasn't my home; I cried every day and night, and they had to take me back to my mother's family.

I grew up not knowing that my mother had been killed; I only learned the real story later. I went to school in the village; I used to get up early and look after the goats, take them out, tie them, and then run to school, three or four kilometers away from home. When I did well on exams, my uncle brought me to the city to compete with secondary school students there. But another rebel group seeking to overthrow the government came and chased us away from our house. So many people died; so many people were killed. My auntie drove us to her home that night; they squeezed us in....

My older brother was given a scholarship in America to study aeronautical engineering. He said, "I want you to be a pilot like me." I applied to flying school in South Africa and was admitted, but then I was in a motor accident. My elder sister had AIDS, and I was riding a bicycle thinking, "I'm going to lose my sister," when a car ran over me. I was not supposed to survive. That's the time I realized that people loved me. I broke my clavicle and many other bones. I knew that I could never be a pilot after that. I was disqualified.

At this time more rebels emerged. If you are a member of my tribe in my country, no house, no job, no nothing. If the government supporters find you on the street, they put a tire over you, pour paraffin, and burn you alive. Right now, there are hundreds of thousands of people of my tribe in the refugee camps.

I first became involved in politics in 2001. I grew up knowing that politics is a bad thing, but I joined politics because ... well, I believe that we have to work to change the government! I was elected campaign chairman of a place where I didn't even speak the local language; I was going to the office of the presidential candidate and mobilizing people on the ground. Even now, people call me "chairman." The government agents came looking for me, because my style was different—I could move the people well. They wanted to intimidate me; they wanted me to join them. The man who was my direct boss was arrested; up until now, we still don't know where he is. . . .

My relatives were telling me, "Please. Don't do this. Get out of politics. You lost your mother because of this. The government has a long arm." In my constituency, the opposition won. And after that, they started to come looking for me at night. I went to a pub once, and I could see them pulling out their pistols and putting them on the table. Why didn't I get out of politics? With people power, we can change the government. I knew that with a new government, my people in the camps would be allowed to go home. . . . After that, my uncle called me and told me quietly, "Your life is at risk. You'd better leave this place." He himself took money from his pocket and paid for a place for me, far from where I was staying, and sent a car to come and carry me there. The UNHCR completely failed to understand this! They have no proper background—they think that the politics of my country is like the politics of the developed world. But it's not like that at all.

I realized that I had better leave. I received a conference invitation to the United States. This was my chance to seek asylum, but I couldn't get a visa in time. I went to a travel agent and asked, "Where can I most easily go to get away from here?" and I was told China. I got off the plane in Hong Kong and talked to a black guy at the airport. He told me to go to Chungking Mansions, and there I was told that there is a UNHCR office in Hong Kong—I went and declared myself. This was in 2006.

Hong Kong is not bad—it's secure here, that's the best thing. You can walk anywhere without looking over your shoulder. When I first arrived, there was discrimination by Chinese against Africans, but I see it disappearing. Hong Kong has rule of law—whether you are a Hong Kong person or not, you will be treated according to law. Yes, I feel that I've been treated fairly in Hong Kong. I understand that if Hong Kong enabled asylum seekers to work, there would be fewer jobs for Hong Kong people.

My biggest disappointment since I've been in Hong Kong has been the UNHCR, because the process is not transparent. They say, "you said this," from your earlier interview, and they may be totally wrong, but there's nothing you can do about it. Because Hong Kong is not a signatory to the Geneva Convention, the UNHCR is independent. You can't touch them; you can't go with a lawyer to challenge them. The bottom line is that I want protection. I fled from my country because my life was threatened, but now the international organization that was supposed to protect me is saying that they cannot protect me. What am I supposed to do? The UNHCR is not credible. They sit in air-conditioned offices and know nothing about Africa. I hope that the people who work for that Hong Kong office become asylum seekers themselves. Then they will understand!

Once in a while, I talk to my brother by phone, and he can link me to my wife and children. No, I don't talk to them directly much. All the incoming telephone calls from overseas are tapped—there's a risk. I love my children and my wife; I miss my family each and every day. I love my people, too. But I cannot go back. I know what that government might do.

No, I've never worked in Hong Kong—it's illegal. A guy owning a factory in mainland China was looking for an African partner—he offered me the job. But I told him that I was an asylum seeker. I gave him the name of another East African, who could take the job, as I couldn't. Even as I talk to you now, I know that the government is aware that I am here. I heard two days ago that in Canada an asylum seeker was discovered to be undercover, to have been sent by my country's government. I'm very careful—they may seek to poison me. I don't eat and drink with people I don't know well.

If I could go back ten years, would I still join politics? If I see people suffering, I would still join. No, I have no regrets. It didn't work out. But people suffer every day—if you try something and it doesn't work out, what can you do?

Muhammed Hasan

When I was a child, I did not want to leave Pakistan. Pakistan is my motherland. I studied in college, but I was very fond of cricket. I was a great cricketer—I could have made my name on the Pakistani national team. My father wanted me to study only. He was an old-thinking man—only if I studied could I make progress in my life, he believed. If he had put some money on me, for one season only, I could have excelled. But in Pakistan, you must fulfill your family's wishes. I finished college and began to run a sporting goods store in my city.

When I was in college, I used to go to my uncle's house each day, and I would see my cousin there. I was not interested in her. But my auntie was telling me all the time, "You should marry her. You have seen her today? She was looking very beautiful." If you tell a man about a woman's beauty all the time, the day will come when he will start taking interest. This happened to me.

My cousin was so deceptive: she told me that she loved me, although she loved someone else. She was trying to make way for her brother. She belonged to a very poor family. Hong Kong was a big dream for them. My cousin in Pakistan was trying to get me to marry her, so that her brother would be able to marry my other uncle's daughter in Hong Kong, who has a Hong Kong ID. Otherwise, I would have married that uncle's daughter, and I would have gone to Hong Kong myself. My uncle there was going to give his daughter to me—he came back to Pakistan and he insisted. But that didn't happen, because I married my other cousin instead. I fell in love with her; I was very stupid.

I knew immediately that I had made a mistake. Before the marriage, she had had another boyfriend, and she still loved that boyfriend, I found out. She told me, "I married you so that my brother can advance in his life. So don't ever touch me." I was stunned. I told her, "Now you are telling me 'don't touch my body.' You will tell people that 'this is not a man.' So I will do it anyway." So I did. That's why I have a six-year-old daughter now. She was born in 2002.

I haven't divorced my wife—I cannot, because of my relatives, who threaten me with death if I divorce her. She also wants to divorce, but the relatives also pressure her not to, because it would dishonor the family. I cannot fight in courts—these relatives are the landlords there! In Pakistan, my family will die out if I don't have children. From a Pakistani point of view, I should have a son. I loved that girl! But she was playing with me. . . .

After this, I was too depressed to take care of my business. My father died in 2004; I decided to leave and go overseas. I could not survive in Pakistan—my uncles, the landlords, would cause me problems even in the big cities if I went there. I wanted to go overseas because I wanted to marry and make a family. I traveled from Pakistan through Iran to Turkey to Greece, taking buses and walking whenever we got near borders, because the army was covering the borders.

It took four months in all, before I was caught. In Greece, the border police said, "Run!" to go back to Turkey. I managed to hide in a sunflower grove. I went to Istanbul, but someone called the police, and I was put in detention. Then they sent us to Iran, and we were set upon by thieves, kidnappers—Kurds—we fought with them, and two of us were killed, shot dead. But we were eighty and they were ten; we rushed them, captured them, broke their bones, and threw them down the mountain. After that, we were in great danger, since Kurdish tribes would come after us—we ran the whole night, searching for an army station to surrender to.

Back in Pakistan, I was in terrible physical shape—I was standing in front of my mother and she didn't even recognize me. I recovered and worked, but the whole responsibility for my family—my mother and my disabled brother—was on my shoulders, and I couldn't earn any money in Pakistan. So, in September 2006 I went to Hong Kong to work. My uncle called me and said, "You apply for a China visa and come to Shenzhen. Then I'll get you a Hong Kong visa." But then, in Shenzhen, he told me, "Don't tell anyone that you are my nephew. Tell everyone that you are my brother. This way, working in the shop, nobody can disturb you." My uncle took me to the UNHCR office—I had to become an asylum seeker.

Then my uncle brought the brother of my ex-wife in Pakistan into the shop. They gave my ex-wife's brother a Hong Kong ID card and were planning to send me back to Pakistan. So I went to the police in Hong Kong and surrendered myself. I turned to the police because that was the only way I could stay in Hong Kong and not return to Pakistan. I will return to Pakistan only when I have enough money to fight these people!

I was put in detention in Hong Kong. There are four people to a cell; there's only one toilet, and you have to use it in front of everyone. The most shameful thing in Hong Kong is this: you won't face physical torture, but they'll make you take off your clothes many, many times before everybody. This is how they make you feel ashamed that you have crossed your country's borders. They have the right to do this, because you have illegally entered their home.

When I got out of detention, my uncle took away my phone and half my money—HK$400 of HK$800—and even a jersey I'd borrowed from him. But I felt in my mind that this is the blessing of God. At least I can do my own work now, dying through fighting—in the shop I could not fight. I was in a very bitter situation for a month—I had no money. Then I begin to make money little by little. I am careful about where I keep the money— I live with several other people, and I cannot fully trust them. I send money back home to my mother. I have managed to send HK$1,500 back home over each of these past two months. That I am sending the money back to my family makes me feel proud. *Inshallah*, I will succeed! I have told the UNHCR that the Taliban seeks to kill me. This is true.

I still can't earn much; it will take time. I am the one who has to feed my family. I am trying my level best.... Yes, my regret now was not marrying my Hong Kong uncle's daughter—I was deceived. They were all planning fifteen years ahead as to who should marry whom: they had planned out my marriage many years before. Of course my ex-wife knew this plan; she was a major part of it. She used to call me every day for two or three hours—it was all fake. I loved her! From her standpoint, she sacrificed her earlier love and pretended to love me; she did this for the sake of her brother's Hong

Kong ID card. She sacrificed her love, but she could not accept that she had to go with me.

Had she accepted that sacrifice, it would have been a better situation for herself and for me. I might then be living in Pakistan with a happy life. I would never be here in Hong Kong. But after what happened, I can no longer live there. I was crushed by my relatives—I knew I had to go abroad to live.

Hasid Adan

I was born in 1981; I left Mogadishu, Somalia, March 28, 2006—always there was fighting of family clans. Yes, I had many family members killed. Anyone in Somalia after 1991 has had at least one or two members of their family killed, maybe right in front of them. People in Somalia now—they kill for no reason. You can do nothing because those people belong to the clan that has the most power. If you fight back, kill the killer, they will finish off the rest of your family. My big brother and my mother are still in Mogadishu. God bless them. I want to cry. But even if they die today, I cannot feel too sad, because it's like they are dead already in my heart. It's because there, anything can happen at any minute. I pray to God to help me do something for them. My mother, she's the one who helped me go outside.

In 1994, I was a child—I remember well the day when my father and one of my big sisters died. They killed my father because they said that he was an informer, and my sister too. I know the three guys who killed him—two of them have been killed since. I've never held a gun—I won't touch one. My family didn't have power; we were just businesspeople. Some of the things you see, you just don't want to say to anybody—you just keep it inside. Some people there, if you don't pray, they kill you; if a woman doesn't wear a *hijab*, they kill you; if you read the Qur'an and make a mistake, they kill you. They are not true Muslims, because they kill.

Two more of my sisters were killed in 1996; a bazooka shell blew up their house. My older brother was taking drugs and wasn't reliable; my uncle said to my mother, "You can send Hasid overseas." There are people who take care of you when you go overseas—you pay them US$6,000, US$7,000. They said to my mother that they'd bring me to the United States, but they brought me to Hong Kong instead. They explained about the UNHCR, that the government will pay your rent, and if you get asylum you can go to the US. I know Somalis who went directly to the US—until now, they can't work. I was in immigration jail for one month six days. I was so happy—

I knew that I would not die! And nobody will beat you there. You are respected—"yes sir, yes ma'am"—immigration treats you well. It's not like Somalia, where an eleven-year-old child might kill you.

Aside from that, I've been twice in prison here in Hong Kong. The first time—well, I never drank alcohol in my home country. After a month in Hong Kong, one night I drank whiskey for the first time. I don't know what I did—I lost my mind—I woke up in the police station. I said, "Please God, make this a dream," but it was true. They explained to me that I had gotten in a fight with some Nepalese: I apparently broke a bottle and hit someone over the head. Witnesses saw me, even though I don't remember anything. They gave me seven months in prison. Yes, I am lucky they didn't send me back to Somalia—the UNHCR helped me, and Immigration too, because they know the situation in Somalia. If you go back, they will kill you.

The UNHCR granted me refugee status, and helped me very much. Somali people can go to America, Canada, Europe, and work, although we cannot work in Hong Kong, that's what the immigration papers say. I have worked, though. In prison I met Pakistanis, Indians, Bangladeshis—they work, helping in shops and restaurants in Chungking Mansions and elsewhere. Some of them make HK$5,000 a month, others HK$9,000! After I left jail, I understood that if it is work that Hong Kong Chinese people will do, the police will arrest the foreigners. But Chinese won't work in Chungking Mansions, so the police don't care, I think.

The first thing I did, after I left prison, was to start working in a guesthouse in Chungking Mansions. They didn't pay much—HK$2,200 a month, and HK$40 a day for food. I worked there only one month and twenty days. Some customers complained. A white man said that he lost his wallet, but that guy came back at 6 a.m. Maybe he lost his wallet outside; but he complained and called the police—I ran away. A couple of weeks later, a Nepali complained that he lost his mobile phone in his room. I didn't take it. The man who lost the phone was Nepali, and the boss was Nepali, so I left. Maybe they arranged it with each other!

After that, I began working with some Malian guys on the first floor, sending mobile phones to Africa. They gave me HK$20, HK$50, for packing the phones into boxes. The phone dealers came to know me. If I brought in a customer, they might give me HK$1 per phone—if he bought fifty phones, I got HK$50. I began getting more—HK$3 per phone: if the customer wanted three hundred pieces, I got HK$900. Once people know you and trust you, it's easy to do this.

Then I started to make friends with Somalis—businessmen who go to Nairobi. They have Kenyan passports; they do business in Kenya—nobody can do business in Somalia, except for a container every month or two, with fifty gunmen to protect it. Somalis are very clever in business—some worked five or seven years in the US, saved up US$50,000 and then started trade in Nairobi. I help these kinds of people in Hong Kong. The most money I've ever made at this was HK$18,000, selling cars to traders from Madagascar. I did everything for them; they didn't speak English. I send money back to my mother in Somalia—I send this money to someone in the UK and they send the money back to Somalia through informal means.

Then I met some Namibian guys. They said, "We are black brothers; we need you to help us. We have diamonds, but we don't have the certificate for them, so we want to sell through the black market." My friend and I said OK; we didn't know anything about this business, but maybe we could get a good commission. We met in a coffee shop, and they showed us samples of the diamonds. I didn't know if they were real or fake, but I was sure that in Hong Kong no one would buy diamonds without testing.

My job was to find a buyer. I called my African friends who knew the business, and they said that nobody would bring seventy pieces of these kinds of diamonds if they were real. We found Chinese buyers. I told them, "Look, I don't have experience in these kinds of stones. I don't believe these people. Are you sure?" They said the diamonds were genuine. The commission was going to be US$150,000. The next day we brought the Chinese to meet the black people. The Chinese had already called the police. After five minutes, fifty police came down on us.

I was only the connection; I didn't know anything about the diamonds, but they arrested me. I was terrified. Finally, I went to the high court and there was a judge who was a good man; he let me talk. This was October 2008; the Hong Kong courts dropped my case and let me go free. They said, "If you want to file a complaint, go ahead. If the police arrested someone who is innocent, they will pay money for what they did." I said no, I don't want anything; I knew that I was wrong. I said, "If you release me, I say thanks to the police and the Hong Kong law." They gave me back my freedom!

After this matter, I have stopped working. I want to go to America. After my second interview with the American Embassy here, I explained to them that I have a criminal record in Hong Kong. They said that I might still be able to come, but the problem is that I always like to do something, and our time in Hong Kong is 80 percent empty. So now I study language. I want to learn Mandarin, or Cantonese, also Spanish or Italian. I used to put all my energy into working, but now I want to follow the rules. You know, God helped me two times in Hong Kong. If I mess up a third time, it means that I'm crazy or stupid!

The Changing Treatment of Asylum Seekers

Over the past several years, there have been significant changes in how asylum seekers are treated in Hong Kong. Before 2005, asylum seekers were
dealt with primarily through the UNHCR and its office in Hong Kong; the
Hong Kong government sought to leave the matter of asylum seekers to the
UNHCR, which was understaffed and unable to handle the flood of asylum
seekers that began to arrive in 2005 and thereafter.

For a period in 2006 to 2007, the UNHCR began providing not formal
letters, but merely appointment slips, which were not sufficient to give legal
protection. During this time, asylum seekers were regularly subject to arrest
by the Hong Kong police; when the asylum seekers I knew saw a policeman,
they would quickly scurry away, particularly because asylum seekers were
detained for an arbitrary and indefinite time, ranging from a month to six
months or more. Asylum seekers from Asia and Africa were relatively new
in Hong Kong, and it seems apparent that the Hong Kong government had
no set policy, except to lock them up indefinitely to discourage more from
coming. Many asylum seekers I knew, especially Africans, who are particularly visible as outsiders in Hong Kong, stayed in their rooms day after day
for fear of arrest.

Hong Kong mass media, especially English-language mass media, soon began discussing the injustice of this situation. As the *South China Morning Post* editorialized, "Hong Kong's Treatment of Asylum Seekers [is] Shameful."[15] Asylum seekers themselves engaged in protests, marching on the UNHCR headquarters. Some thirty African asylum seekers, locked up in detention for months, went on hunger strikes as a way of protesting their situation.[16] Various Hong Kong legislators came to visit them, as did too the Director of Immigration in Hong Kong.

Apparently as a result of these protests, the Hong Kong government made the stay in detention for asylum seekers more limited, generally less than a month and often little more than a week. After detention, which is meted out as punishment for breaking Hong Kong immigration laws, the asylum seeker is provided with identity papers—a laminated plastic sheet that all asylum seekers carry in lieu of a passport or Hong Kong ID card— that prevents them from being jailed again for immigration offenses, at least until their cases have been decided.

Beginning in 2007, asylum seekers, on the advice of human rights lawyers in Hong Kong, began turning to CAT as their avenue to gain refugee status, instead of or as well as the UNHCR. The Hong Kong government is a signatory to CAT, as it is not to the UN's Convention Relating to the Status of Refugees. Given the difficulties of the UNHCR in handling its backlog of cases and its perceived indifference toward the plight of many asylum seekers, it seemed to make increasing sense to go through the Hong Kong government—even if refugee status in a third country was impossible to get through the Hong Kong government and the Hong Kong government granted residence status to almost no asylum seekers within its own shores.

The UNHCR cannot be sued, unlike the Hong Kong government, as we saw in John Mukasa's account; the UNHCR has no one in Hong Kong that it must answer to, something apparently true not just in Hong Kong but worldwide. Harrell-Bond writes, "As one . . . UNHCR management consultant acknowledged, 'We work for no other organization in the political, governmental, or commercial world which has such an absence of mechanisms for determining citizen or consumer satisfaction.'"[17]

Through all my years of involvement with asylum seekers, it has been difficult to hear a good word for UNHCR, which is viewed by many asylum seekers as being incompetent and arbitrary in its judgments. On the other hand, the Hong Kong police and government are generally viewed favorably. A UNHCR official I spoke with said that one reason why the UNHCR is held in such low esteem is that asylum seekers tend to view the UN in highly idealized terms, and thus its mistakes are seen as unforgivable. But the Hong

Kong police are compared to the police in asylum seekers' home countries, and the fact that in Hong Kong the police do not take bribes and are relatively fair is seen as amazing.

Asylum seeker claimants as of 2009 still must go to jail to obtain papers enabling them to legally stay in Hong Kong until their case is decided, and to obtain rental aid and groceries from International Social Services, the charity organization commissioned by the Hong Kong government. Many asylum seekers have resisted this because they have viewed detention as a horrendous experience, as it apparently has been in past years. However, in 2008, when I asked several asylum seekers to tell me about their experience in detention, they said, "It's pretty good. Toilets are in separate stalls; they give out newspapers; there's a television." In detention, immigration violators from different countries are housed in the same facilities—except for mainland Chinese, the most common immigration violators by far in Hong Kong, who are housed in a different wing. Several times in Chungking Mansions, I have seen an African and a South Asian man embrace one another: they have become close friends in detention and now meet each other again outside and free.

Under both systems by which asylum seekers' claims are now adjudged, the UNHCR or the Hong Kong government, the chance of obtaining refugee status, whereby one can be resettled in a third country, is extremely low, as we have seen. But the consequence of being refused is generally not repatriation. Rumors have spread among asylum seekers that denied claimants may be sent home against their will: "If you appeal and lose, they can take you away right there. You'll be sedated and sent back to your home country with no one knowing." However, from all I've been told, the Hong Kong government does not forcibly deport asylum seekers whose claims have been denied, but seeks them to agree to be repatriated, a repatriation that the Hong Kong government apparently pays for. As one asylum seeker told me, "The police may put you in a cell and leave you there for months on end, but they won't get Immigration to deport you unless you yourself request it."

The only exception to this rule is those convicted of overt criminal acts, but even then, deportation is apparently rare. Because so few claimants gain refugee status and so few are deported, the number of asylum seekers continues to grow, with no resolution in sight. This situation—shaped in part by the ongoing stream of cases brought to the courts by human rights lawyers—cannot be sustained, and something must eventually give way.

What, then, will happen? Hong Kong seeks to minimize the number of asylum seekers by keeping their circumstances humane but barely tolerable. The asylum seekers I know in Chungking Mansions seek, above all, to be allowed to legally work in Hong Kong, but this would lead to many thousands of new asylum seekers flooding into Hong Kong.

Indeed, this is exactly what happened between March 2009, when a court ruling allowed asylum seekers to legally work, although their employers would still be prosecuted,[18] and November 2009, when work by asylum seekers again became illegal, punishable by a three-year prison sentence. The massive influx of new asylum seekers during these few months, many of whom were South Asians entering Hong Kong from China by small boat under cover of night, led the government to hurriedly revise the law.[19] Five hundred asylum seekers then staged a protest against the Hong Kong government.[20] As one newly arrived Pakistani asylum seeker told me, "People who steal or take drugs in Hong Kong only get put in prison for a few months. But people working without the right papers are jailed for three years! It's unfair!" He joined the protest, but, of course, to no avail—he eventually stopped working, for fear of being caught and prosecuted.

The Hong Kong government is deeply worried about asylum seekers, with a senior official calling the increasing number of claimants without ID a "ticking time bomb."[21] Hong Kong could no doubt assimilate many more thousands of asylum seekers than government officials admit, especially given the high intellectual level of many (who would make wonderful English teachers and cultural ambassadors in secondary schools). What might conceivably happen as a resolution to the fast-changing situation of asylum seekers in Hong Kong is that the government would allow those already here to work, while drastically tightening up entrance into Hong Kong. This would solve the problem of asylum seekers, but would shut the door on future claimants; it would also change the nature of Chungking Mansions, which exists in no small part because of Hong Kong's willingness to issue visa-free entry to people from many countries in the developing world and look the other way when these people engage in business or are employed.

It would be ironic if, in seeking to solve the problem of asylum seekers, the Hong Kong government in effect destroyed Chungking Mansions. At the time of this writing, the Hong Kong government is making plans to consolidate and speed up the processes by which asylum seekers are screened.[22] It is widely speculated that the Hong Kong government will within the next several years sign the 1951 United Nations Convention Relating to the Status of Refugees, which would cause Hong Kong to take full responsibility for asylum seekers, taking over from the UNHCR, something apparently sought after by the head of Hong Kong's UNHCR office.[23]

If this were to take place, it would dramatically change the situation of asylum seekers in Hong Kong: if Hong Kong government investigators can, after suitable training, speed up the decision-making process as to the fate of asylum seekers, then it seems possible that Hong Kong will no longer be a haven for economic asylum seekers. On the other hand, it may well be that Hong Kong government investigators will be no better able than UNHCR officials to determine who is justified and who is not among asylum seekers—and if an asylum seeker is sent home and is subsequently killed, the media outcry would be unbearable for the Hong Kong government. The resolution of the situation remains to be seen.

Chungking Mansions, as we've seen, is a contradictory place in terms of human rights, as is, in a larger sense, the developed world as a whole.[24]One key contradiction is the gap between political human rights and legal and economic rights, the former recognized as reasons for seeking asylum, but the latter not: why should this line be so salient? A second contradiction is that those asylum seekers who are most eloquent, most quick-witted, or most able to evoke the sympathy of their interviewers are those most able to win asylum seeker status. Both the articulate and the inarticulate may be tortured; but the intellectually and emotionally articulate retain a great advantage in being able to persuade others as to the reality of their experience.

A third contradiction is that almost as a rule the asylum seekers who break the rules and work are far happier than those who follow the rules and do not work. If an asylum seeker works illegally, then that person will be able to have a better life in Hong Kong and also be able to send money back home, to support family and to build up a nest egg for the future; the person will also be kept busy in their new enterprise. This opportunity does not exist for those principled (or lazy) people who refuse to work. All in all, to be an asylum seeker who strictly adheres to the rules is a terrible fate. To break the rules—particularly if one is savvy enough to go into private enterprise, as a middleman or entrepreneur—may lead to a reasonably good life.

And of course, as for asylum seekers, so too for everyone in Chungking Mansions. The law is made to be bent, and as long as one does not get too greedy or too obvious in flouting the law, one is unlikely to get caught. This is the rule of Chungking Mansions, as we have seen throughout this chapter. The tragedy of some of the asylum seekers I know is that, despite the time they have spent in detention for breaking the law as illegal immigrants, they are among the very few people in Chungking Mansions who believe that the law should be wholly adhered to.

This is the final contradiction: in following the law, these asylum seekers are not just the intellectuals of Chungking Mansions but also its outcasts.

future

We have examined Chungking Mansions as a place as well as the people within it, the goods and trade that define it, and the laws that circumscribe it. Let us now, in this book's last few pages, examine the changing imaginations of Chungking Mansions, the ultimate effect of the building on the people who live and work there, and the global significance and possible future of the building.

Changing Imaginations of Chungking Mansions

As has been shown throughout this book, Chungking Mansions is viewed in very different ways by different groups of people involved with the building. It continues to be imagined as a dark and evil place by many Hong Kong Chinese. Many tourists who come to Chungking Mansions choose their lodgings from the Internet on the basis of price alone and do not know where they are going until they arrive and may be shocked. For other tourists, Chungking Mansions is "the exotic third world in a safe first-world city," as we earlier saw, an image that may thrill, titillate, or terrify them.

On the other hand, Chungking Mansions continues to be imagined by many in the developing world of South Asia and Africa not as a hellhole of vice or a paragon of exotic otherness, but rather as a beacon of dreams, a place where one might make one's fortune and never again be poor—dreams that, for a few, come true, but for most remain dreams. For the Indian temporary workers, Chungking Mansions represents the attempt to become middle class, making far more money than one's white-collar peers back in Kolkata. For many young African traders, success in Chungking Mansions and, more broadly, in south China represents their transition to adulthood. If they fail, they are shamed and humiliated, but if they succeed, they are on their way to becoming respected members of their family and community. For many asylum seekers, Chungking Mansions symbolizes the allure and danger of home—it is not only where they can go to enjoy food and friends from the world they have left behind, but also where some feel they must protect themselves from potential spies among traders, who may bring word of their whereabouts back to their home-country governments.

These imaginations of Chungking Mansions are to some extent changing. For many African traders, Chungking Mansions has been replaced by mainland China as the cornucopia of their dreams. Chungking Mansions has instead become for them a sort of comforting way station, a place where they must renew their mainland visas but can otherwise relax, as is more difficult for them to do in mainland China given the tensions of their work lives there. Chungking Mansions, for many of these traders, is basically a mandated vacation spot. The fact that racial prejudice has apparently diminished in Hong Kong over the past several years, as it has not, by many accounts, in China, improves Hong Kong's attractiveness for some, less as a site of business than of relaxation. Chungking Mansions, for some African mainland-based traders, has become the developing-world equivalent of a gentlemen's club.

Views also seem to be changing among tourists. In 2009 I met a number of travelers who expressed their disappointment to me about Chungking Mansions. In one French traveler's words, "It used to be so crazy here, when I was here in the early 1990s. And now it seems so normal, so bourgeois." An American who had returned to Chungking Mansions after twenty years told me, "Chungking Mansions looks much nicer now than before, these elevators are so much better! . . . But you know, it was better before! Now it's middle class!" While the building has been cleaned up in recent years, no one would confuse Chungking Mansions with the bright, upscale stylings of Chungking Express, the mall on its second floor a world away. However, it nonetheless does look more spiffed-up than it was a few years ago, with television screens broadcasting cheery messages at points on the building's ground floor. Chungking Mansions continues to be an "exotic" mixture of peoples the world over. But maybe, bit by bit, it is indeed becoming "normal," as the world as a whole becomes progressively more "exotic" in the ordinary interactions of people of different cultures and religions from across the globe.

The biggest change in the imagination of Chungking Mansions over the past few years has been on the side of Hong Kong people. Mass media, in the years since I began studying Chungking Mansions has said little that is negative about the place, unlike preceding years when coverage, as a rule, was overwhelmingly negative. Mass media may acknowledge illegal workers and copy goods but tend not to play these up anymore: the dominant message is that Chungking Mansions is a more or less friendly place. Restaurant reviews in Chinese-language media in Hong Kong have given the impression that Chungking Mansions is a reasonable place to take one's family for a meal. The presence of Chinese security guards on the ground floor solidifies this view. Thus, increasingly, I have seen young Hong Kong Chinese walking through the building and on occasion casually talking with the South Asians and Africans there in a way that would have been difficult to imagine a few years ago.

Two examples from early 2009 demonstrate this point. On a Sunday morning I encountered a Hong Kong Chinese secondary school teacher with a flock of twenty or so students. She was asking her students to interview people from as many different countries as they could find, and so they had scattered throughout the ground floor of Chungking Mansions, asking questions of any and all who might answer their queries: fresh-faced and earnest Hong Kong teenagers asking, "What do people in your country eat for breakfast? What do they eat for lunch? What do they eat for dinner?" However inane these questions may be, this benign cross-cultural exchange in the erstwhile den of iniquity that is Chungking Mansions astonished me. Since then, I have occasionally seen several other teachers and gaggles of students following suit.

A second example I found even more astonishing. On Valentine's Day, I saw the West African clerk at a guesthouse finding, in the early afternoon, a shy young Hong Kong Chinese couple, perhaps in their late-teenage years standing before him. "Why are you here?" he asked. "Are you looking for a restaurant?" The young man, summoning up his courage, stammered, "We want a room," which was promptly provided and into which they promptly entered and shut the door. My subsequent enquiries at various guesthouses showed that this is becoming increasingly common. Unmarried Hong Kong couples, living with their parents, have no privacy and cannot afford expensive hotels, so increasingly they are coming to Chungking Mansions. A few years ago, the idea of young Hong Kong Chinese lovers using Chungking Mansions for their intimacies would have been unthinkable; any right-thinking young woman would have become enraged at the suggestion that her boyfriend take her to a place of dereliction and darkness for such a purpose. But today, for at least some young Hong Kongers, this is no longer the case.

Views of Chungking Mansions are changing, it seems, among the more adventurous young, but also, perhaps, among Hong Kong Chinese as a whole. These observations I make are tentative, since three-plus years of fieldwork are all too brief. A dramatic event in Chungking Mansions or in the world—whether a shocking crime, a global depression, or a property developer's plans—could change everything. Indeed, this may already be happening to at least a small extent. The crime novelist Michael Connelly has portrayed Chungking Mansions in a recent bestseller in a dark and unrealistic way, which may have an effect on perceptions of Chungking Mansions.[1] Ani Ashekian, a 31-year-old Canadian tourist in Hong Kong, vanished in November 2008 in a case to some extent echoing Connelly's novel,[2] but no evidence has been found linking her puzzling disappearance to Chungking Mansions, where she was staying; she was last seen in a shopping district miles away from the building. But for now, anyway, the popular image of Chungking Mansions remains as I have described it.

How Chungking Mansions Transforms People

If imaginations of Chungking Mansions are changing, so too are the imaginations of the people who stay in the building. How does Chungking Mansions change the people who stay there? Of course, there are huge differences in Chungking Mansions' impact on those who stay there a few days, such as the casual tourist, and those who stay there for decades. But cross-cutting these differences are those who are transformed by the cultural diversity of Chungking Mansions and those who are apparently unaffected by this diversity.

Some people are not at all changed by Chungking Mansions. A Nigerian trader, when I asked him if his experiences in Chungking Mansions, Hong Kong, and China had changed him in any way, replied, "No, of course not. My purpose in coming to this part of the world is to make money, not to make friends"—even if he did consent to talk to a foreigner like me for several hours about his life as a trader. He maintained that none of the new things he had experienced in these overseas places would have any bearing on his underlying understanding of the world. I mentioned in chapter 1 the Hong Kong Chinese who live or work in the building but who have few friends or acquaintances there and have never eaten South Asian food in their entire lives. They may well have more tolerance of ethnic diversity than almost all their fellow Hong Kong Chinese, simply in that they have shared tight physical spaces with people from a vast array of different countries. They physically encounter the world in a way that their fellow Hong Kongers do not, but psychologically they often claim it has had absolutely no effect on them in their lives.

For many of these people, the claim of being unchanged by their environment in Chungking Mansions, Hong Kong, and China is simply an assertion that their own rooted cultural identity as Igbo, Pakistani, or Chinese will not be altered by what they have beheld overseas. For others, however, there is a conscious rejection of Hong Kong and of China. The backdrop ethnicity around Chungking Mansions is, of course, Hong Kong Chinese, and it is not hard, as we have seen, to find antipathy toward them among the South Asians and Africans there.[3] A young trader from West Africa, somewhat drunk, angrily said to me, "Hong Kong people, they will all go to hell for their racism!" An Indian Muslim man told me in 2008 that he was leaving Chungking Mansions after one temporary employment spell and would never be coming back; instead, if he ever again was to be living overseas, he told me, it would be in Saudi Arabia, a place free of the sensuality that he felt had corrupted Hong Kong. I have never seen him since. For men like these, Hong Kong is not simply a neutral world that will not affect them in their lives, but an evil world that should be condemned and shunned.

However, there are many others, from similar backgrounds, who are not repelled by the new world they behold in Hong Kong and China, but rather enchanted (or from the viewpoint of the people mentioned in the previous paragraph, bewitched) by it. I witnessed two East African traders, one based in China and the other in Hong Kong, getting into a heated drunken argument in the alley behind Chungking Mansions over the two societies. One, who was staying in Chungking Mansions, shouted that "Hong Kong has more human rights than China. Hong Kong people look down upon Chinese!" and the other, who was living in Guangzhou, proclaimed that "Everything in Hong Kong is from China! If it weren't for China, Hong Kong wouldn't exist!" This is the kind of argument that Hong Kongers and Chinese might have in their more frank moments, but in this case it was two Africans, each vociferously defending his temporarily adopted home. I know of a few African traders who are completely enamored of China. I spoke with a Ghanaian trader who when he goes into Guangzhou stays with the factory owner he buys from and his family. I asked, "Is he your friend?" He said, "Well, no, he's really like my father."

Beyond like or dislike for Hong Kong or China, there is a broader sense of cosmopolitanism that Chungking Mansions may sometimes breed. A young Indian Muslim man newly arrived in Hong Kong in summer 2006 was working at a food stall where I often ate dinner; one night he beheld the bare backs and blond tresses of two young Eastern European sex workers passing just a few feet from him.* "Mister, they are bad women. You should not look," he told me when he saw me gawking, and covered my eyes with his hand to protect me from the sight, but, as I saw from the corner of my eye, he himself looked long and hard, if surreptitiously. A month later, these women returned; by then, he was accustomed to such sights. I asked him why he didn't cover my eyes this time, and he shrugged and said, "They must live, just like me." A month in Chungking Mansions had changed him, making him more morally tolerant or, by conservative Muslim standards, morally lax.

In Chungking Mansions, traders and asylum seekers from countries that have had hostile relations—Eritrea and Ethiopia, or Rwanda and Congo Kinshasa, for example—sometimes find themselves having personal friendships that transcend national or ethnic enmities. This is particularly true for South Asians from India and Pakistan. Some I know continue to dislike each other. I asked a middle-aged Indian who works for a Pakistani-owned business if he felt any dislike toward Pakistanis. He replied, after some thought, "I don't dislike Pakistanis. It's just their behavior that I hate!" He then went through a litany of bad behavior that he attributed to Pakistanis. Two years later, after the Mumbai terrorist attack had taken place in late 2008, a Hong Kong Chinese graduate student who was shortly to fly to Pakistan for fieldwork was asking for advice from the touts outside Chungking Mansions. An Indian restaurant employee said to her somewhat gleefully, "Don't go there! It's nothing but terrorists there! They'll kill you!" A Pakistani tout nearby glared at him in fury; all I could do to prevent a fistfight was to ask the Indian man to apologize to the Pakistani man, which he did, as I did as well.

However, others have their nationalistic antipathies changed by Chungking Mansions. One evening I saw several of my Indian and Pakistani ac-

---

* I don't think any Eastern European sex workers were working in Chungking Mansions at that time, although several were working in Mirador Mansions. These women were apparently in Chungking Mansions to buy phone cards, as well as, perhaps, to create a scene: they were followed by a dozen or more leering men everywhere they went in the building, of which they seemed smilingly well aware.

quaintances joking with one another and asked, "How can you be doing this?" I was told, "In India and Pakistan we hate each other, but here, outside of India and Pakistan, we are friends!" After the Mumbai terrorist attacks, I heard that the possibility of war between India and Pakistan was something many people in Chungking Mansions were worried about. But several people told me that this would have no effect upon human relations in Chungking Mansions and Hong Kong. One Indian manager said, "Wars are just for politicians!" His assistant, from Pakistan, said (perhaps under a degree of duress, although I couldn't detect it), "We'll still be friends if there's war. In Hong Kong, this would make no difference." Whether in fact this is the case, only a war would reveal. In any case, it does seem that the antipathy between Indians and Pakistanis that festers in their home countries occurs less in Hong Kong, because Hong Kong and particularly Chungking Mansions allows and indeed requires a degree of tolerance.

One evening in 2008 I went to the Kowloon Mosque for the meal marking the end of the day's fast during the month of Ramadan. I would normally not have gone into the mosque, but I was standing outside its entrance and was motioned to and then pulled in by a man who apparently knew me, so I went ahead. I followed him into the bathing room for ablutions and followed the motions he gestured to me, bathing my hands, face, and particularly feet. In fact I had been drinking a beer while working on my computer in a bar not far from Chungking Mansions in the two hours before I went to the mosque. If anyone from the mosque had seen me earlier in the bar—a bar open to the street—I might have been seriously harassed, I worried, but such a thing did not happen. Instead, during the meal of lentils and fruit and other foods, while I sat at a table of frowning Pakistani strangers, several Pakistani and African acquaintances approached and effusively welcomed me.

I later asked a Pakistani friend, "Why were people so nice to me in the mosque?" He said, "They are broad-minded here. In Pakistan, they are a pure form of Muslim. You have to be broad-minded when you are here in Hong Kong. In Pakistan, you might have been killed for what you did." In September 2009, I went to the mosque to break the Ramadan fast with a number of Pakistani friends from Chungking Mansions who welcomed me effusively every step of the way.

I have never encountered religious intolerance from Muslims in Chungking Mansions. One day I spoke at length to the proprietor of an Islamic bookstore on the first floor of the building. I told him that in my experience the Muslims in Chungking Mansions were more tolerant than the Christians or nonbelievers and seemed to have a higher moral standard: "The people who drink and go with prostitutes are generally Christians and not

Muslims," I said stupidly, trying to make friends with him.* He looked horrified and said, "Sir, you are mistaken. The first rule of Islam is to never criticize any other religions. All religions are sacred in their own way." Chastened, I apologized; he was right. The greater tolerance of Muslims than of Christians that I have experienced in Chungking Mansions (African Christians have occasionally proselytized me, warning me of the dangers of hell were I not to accept God into my life) may be due to the fact that, as a white person, it was assumed that I would "naturally" be Christian.

All in all, Chungking Mansions, as well as Hong Kong at large, does indeed function as a force for greater tolerance of difference in the world. Chungking Mansions does so because there are so many different nationalities and religions within its narrow confines that intolerance becomes all but impossible. Without at least an implicit acceptance of a vast array of different cultures, creeds, and moral codes, one cannot survive and do business in Chungking Mansions. Hong Kong as a society does so through its ideology of neoliberalism, as we will later discuss, emphasizing the pursuit of money over all else. Whether this tolerance can extend beyond Chungking Mansions in these people's lives is another question, but at least within Chungking Mansions, this is the dominant attitude to be found.

Cultural Identity

The transformation of attitudes among some residents of Chungking Mansions may ultimately involve their senses of cultural identity—who they think they are, culturally, and where they think they belong. I often asked the traders I interviewed, "Would you rather live in your home country or in Hong Kong?" I received a variety of different answers.

I spoke, for example, with two traders in their twenties from West Africa. One said, "I like my country, because my family is there. But I like Hong Kong because it's a very safe place. You can use your money here, and you don't have to worry. Yes, I'd leave my country and move to Hong Kong if I could." The other said, "I couldn't do that. I love my country! I want to live in my country. Maybe it's not safe sometimes, but it's home!" Variations of this

---

* This is not only my view. One Chinese shopkeeper, echoing others, said that Muslim customers were preferable to Christians because the former believed that they should not cheat according to their religious faith, but the latter were infamous for late payment. However, there are many Muslims in Chungking Mansions who drink and go to sex workers and engage in a range of other vices; certainly not all follow the moral strictures of Islam.

kind of disagreement I have heard many times, between those who would gladly leave their countries for a wealthier society such as Hong Kong, and those who would stay in their home countries out of love for home. For many of the former, Chungking Mansions in its cosmopolitanism was wonderful; for most of the latter, it was a necessary evil. In the above statements this was couched in terms of security: where can you live safely without fear that your gains will be taken from you? But where, too, is home, where you feel you belong?

Some of these traders based their answers on purely practical considerations—business. A trader from central Africa said, in a common Chungking Mansions refrain, "I love my country, but my home is really anywhere I can make money." A Pakistani businessman gave another typical answer when he said that he didn't like Hong Kong because everything was always work and so frenetic, but he could make much more money in Hong Kong than in Pakistan, so it made sense for him to work in Hong Kong. This strategy is to make one's money overseas but ultimately go home, where life is easier and more familiar because it is home—but of course, after decades of absence, whether home will still be home is another question. I would guess that not a few South Asians dreaming of eventually going home find upon return that home has been transformed beyond recognition, and is home no longer.

Many of the people I spoke with felt a sense of love for their home countries that bound them despite their world travels. This attitude was most surprising when I spoke with asylum seekers, those who had often been persecuted and driven from their countries. In one Pakistani woman's words, "Yes, some Pakistanis hate Ahmadiyya Muslims like me,* but I still love my country very, very much—those who hate us are just some people in my country, not my country as a whole." Perhaps it is the fact that many have been forced to leave their countries and may never return that leads so many of them to feel such a high degree of love for their countries in compensation. They love their countries even though, for at least some, it is their countries' governments that have been trying to kill them.

For others, love for country seems to stem from less exalted feelings. One African trader I spoke with at length seems to love his country because of the wealth and power he enjoys there, enabling him, among other privileges, to apparently abuse women with impunity and enjoy the power brought by his money:

Me: Would you like to live in Hong Kong if you could?

B: How can I stay in Hong Kong? In my country I have my family. I have my house, my car, everything's there—how can I leave that?

Me: Let's say I could give you a visa to bring your whole family here.

B: No, no, I wouldn't do it. I cannot live here—it's so expensive. . . . It's better to be in my country; I can speak my language. . . . My country has freedom. Unlike Hong Kong, in my country you can slap the ladies.† You can kill the ladies. Nobody cares. Here I cannot! If a girl slaps me at home, the police beat the girl! Yes, it's better to be in my country, I can do what I want. . . . I love my family, I love my country. Nobody can touch me. I have power. No, the police don't know me, but the police know money! If you have money you have power! Yes, because I have money in my country, I want to live there, that's my home.

---

*Ahmadiyya Muslims are followers of a nineteenth-century religious movement. In a broad sense, the relation of Ahmadiyya to Islam parallels the relation of Mormonism to Christianity. Pakistan has declared Ahmadiyya believers to be non-Muslim and has persecuted them.

†He was speaking shortly after we had witnessed a Filipina slapping an African man outside the 7-Eleven around the corner from Chungking Mansions—one of several such slapping incidents that I have witnessed there over the years—an event that profoundly shocked him.

I discussed in chapter 3 how many African traders are among the upper classes in their home countries. The above words show how, for at least some traders, this privileged position and ability, at least potentially to "get away with murder," is a large part of what makes one's country seem so attractive.

Other traders from Africa and South Asia feel less tied to their countries; they are cosmopolitan, as touched upon in the last section. An Indian temporary worker, who has been coming to Hong Kong for several years, talked with gusto about how his boss has taken him to Chinese hot-pot restaurants and Japanese sushi places. "I wish I could live in Hong Kong. I could do new things all the time!" he sighed. "I love Chungking Mansions! So many different kinds of people! Whenever I'm in India, I want to come back to Hong Kong and to Chungking Mansions. I want to keep learning new things."

A Nigerian trader I met in Chungking Mansions said, "I don't want to stay in one place." A young Ghanaian trader said, "I love traveling and visiting different places. I've been to Spain, Italy, the United States, and India, only partly for doing business. . . . It's not about having money. People who travel all over the world have different visions about life." The Nigerian trader Abraham Idowu, whose account we saw in chapter 3, proclaimed himself a "black Chinese" who would be happy to be living in China twenty years from now: "I could adjust to anywhere!" People such as these—a fairly small minority in Chungking Mansions, I think—find their senses of cultural identity in being citizens of the world.

Cosmopolitanism is not necessarily a choice. A Somali trader in his late forties who had left his country to live in Sweden and now lived in China told me, "My identity is fifty percent Chinese, twenty-five percent Swedish, and twenty-five percent Somali. . . . Every time you move from place to place, you lose your old identity. It's been twenty-six years since I left Somalia. I am rootless. I don't know where I belong." He recounted how he had left Somalia to go to a university in China in 1982:

> When I was in China, my home country went into civil war. After I got my degree, I registered in a refugee camp in Sweden. Sweden didn't recognize my Chinese degree. So eventually I left and came back to China. . . . The best thing in China is that everybody wants to make money. My sister lives in Minneapolis, so yes, maybe I could go there if I wanted. But she's rootless too! Being rootless is not a good thing. I'd rather have roots. I'd rather live in my home country, among my friends, helping my people. But I can't go back. Since 1982, I've never been back. It's chaos back there, a hopeless situation.

For him, unlike most other traders I have spoken with, cosmopolitanism and rootlessness are an unwelcome condition of life—at present, he feels that he has no home to which he could return.

This sense of forced rootlessness may also be true, albeit in a less tragic sense, for many South Asians in Chungking Mansions, such as those who are permanent residents of Hong Kong and yet still feel that Hong Kong is not their home. Some remain immersed in the home of their origin through mass media, as mentioned in earlier chapters, particularly through Chungking Mansions and its holiday festivities and television channels. I once found a Punjabi shopkeeper crying in front of a TV report about a bomb attack in his home province, a place he has not lived in for several decades. Hong Kong has been his physical home, but his heart, abetted by his choice of mass media, belongs to India.

Other South Asians feel that they cannot go back to their homes in India or Pakistan to live and now feel that they belong to Hong Kong. I know a young Pakistani merchant who hopes to marry his Hong Kong Chinese girlfriend and is wrestling over whether he should give up Islam for the sake of his girlfriend, since her father so stoutly disapproves of his religion. He may yet be willing to sacrifice the most pivotal part of his cultural identity for the sake of love in Hong Kong.

Many more South Asians in Chungking Mansions, as we saw in chapter 2, view themselves as more or less living temporarily in Hong Kong, despite having permanent Hong Kong residence, because Hong Kong is Chinese and thus, in their view, not home; they may dream not of return to their South Asian country but of immigration to a new country. This too is a kind of forced cosmopolitanism: these people may feel that they are global citizens not as a matter of cosmopolitan choice but bitter cultural necessity.

The cosmopolitanism of many Chungking Mansions residents is in distinct contrast to the lack of cosmopolitanism that they may sense among Hong Kong people. Ironically, Hong Kong people themselves have often complained in recent decades about having nowhere to belong to, of belonging neither to China nor to "the West" but being homeless.[4] Few South Asians in Chungking Mansions, focusing only on discrimination from Hong Kong Chinese, recognize that they and Hong Kong Chinese at large may suffer from quite parallel senses of forced cosmopolitanism.

What we thus see, overall in Chungking Mansions, is a range of views concerning cosmopolitanism. There are those who assert their love for their own cultural home and seek to avoid cosmopolitanism. There are those who welcome cosmopolitanism as "global citizens," seeking to experience all the world that they can. And there are those who adopt cosmopolitanism because of the globalized world into which they have been thrust through little choice of their own.

For many of the people I have come to know in Chungking Mansions, their position toward cosmopolitanism reflects how they feel about what I have termed, in an earlier book, "the global cultural supermarket"[5]—the vast array of cultural elements the world over, from food to music to religion, from which individuals can pick and choose in shaping their lives. The cultural supermarket may be thought of as being opposed to the culture of one's upbringing—one's roots—as one experienced it or imagines it. Throughout the world, some people welcome the cultural supermarket while others spurn it, and this seems no less true in Chungking Mansions than anywhere else. Those who are comfortable within the global cultural supermarket welcome Chungking Mansions in all its cosmopolitan cultural mix; those who are not comfortable may despise the building for its immorality and seek to return to their religious and cultural roots by departing the building or by sealing themselves off from cultural differences within the building.

Chungking Mansions illustrates how the global cultural supermarket is not necessarily most fully enjoyed by the developed world's affluent consumers, but extends to the developing world as well—some of the traders and temporary workers in the building delight in the cultural cornucopia they behold, and let this cornucopia shape their identities, while many more resist, just as is the case elsewhere in the world. Chungking Mansions illustrates how the global cultural supermarket extends from the world of high-end globalization to the quite different world of low-end globalization. It is part of the world as a whole—although most in the building do seem to keep the global cultural supermarket of cultural identity choices more or less at arm's length.

Global Significance

Chungking Mansions' significance lies not only in those whom it changes but also in how it helps us comprehend the world of low-end globalization, of which Chungking Mansions is a central node. The buyers and sellers of goods in the building have been drawn to it by the newly emergent industrial might of China and particularly by the fact that goods made in China can be bought so cheaply, as filtered through the more secure trading environment of Hong Kong.

To more fully understand the global positioning of Chungking Mansions, we can turn to world systems analysis.[6] World systems analysis considers the relation between the world's economic core of the United States, Western Europe, and Japan, the top end of economic powers; the semiperiphery of China, India, and Brazil, the rising middle aspiring to reach the top of the economic pile (and perhaps in a few decades rivaling or replacing those societies now at the top); and the extreme periphery, the poorer societies in the developing world. Much of Africa represents the extreme periphery, along with a number of South Asian and other societies; it is "off all kinds of maps,"[7] particularly the map of globalization. China in effect puts Africa on the map again, as Africans go to China or to China's entrepôt, Hong Kong (and Chinese go to Africa as well, in even larger numbers), to buy manufactured goods that their fellow Africans can afford.

Chungking Mansions represents a Grand Central Station in the passage of globalized goods from China to the developing world at large. The particular accounts that have filled this book all take place against this world economic backdrop. World systems analysis can be rightfully criticized for its emphasis on states as the locus of globalization, leaving aside subnational and supranational processes of globalization that bypass states, processes that have been apparent throughout this book.[8] However, to give a sweeping general depiction, world systems analysis does enable us to fruitfully analyze the passage of goods and people through Chungking Mansions, and so I use it here.

We have discussed in chapter 3 whether traders, in bringing the goods of the world—goods of the core copied or discarded in the semiperiphery and sent to the extreme periphery—are helping or hurting their customers and countries. The evidence is mixed, but it does seem that the goods of Chungking Mansions are the closest their impoverished customers can get to enjoying the fruits of globalization, the only globalization that many inhabitants of the extreme periphery may ever experience. Finally, the quality of these goods, though important, may be less important than their very existence: the products and emblems, by the hundreds of millions, of low-end globalization.

Chungking Mansions in its economic activities does not fit much contemporary theorizing concerning global capitalism. It is sometimes argued that a major feature of contemporary capitalism is that capital moves from the core to the periphery, where cheaper labor enables cheaper factories.[9] This is certainly true in the world as a whole, with American and Japanese manufacturers having shut their doors to be replaced by factories in Mexico, China, Malaysia, or India. It is also a primary reason why Guangdong Province is such an economic powerhouse: Hong Kong's and Taiwan's factories of several decades ago have moved to Guangdong.

However, in Chungking Mansions itself, we see the opposite of this trend:

not producers moving from the core to the semiperiphery, but traders moving from the extreme periphery to the semiperiphery to buy cast-off, knock-off, or copy goods from the core. African traders from the extreme periphery, where virtually no manufacturing is done, come to Chungking Mansions to buy from the world's low-end manufacturing center, China.

It is also sometimes argued that we live in "an increasingly global economy in which capital, trade, and investment are mobile but people are held back within the confines of the territorial state."[10] This too is largely true around the world: money moves with the speed of a mouse click, while people stay home, monitoring it from their computer screens in their offices and living rooms.

However, Chungking Mansions attracts its traders and merchants from around the world exactly because in its low-end globalization, face-to-face relations are, for the most part, all that can be trusted. Reliable capital, trade, and investment demand the physical presence of the investor in Chungking Mansions: this is why traders travel halfway across the world to be there. In this case too, low-end globalization operates in accordance with distinctly different sets of rules than high-end globalization.

If the goods of Chungking Mansions are moving from core to semiperiphery to extreme periphery (as in the case of fourteen-day phones bought in Chungking Mansions and sent to Africa or South Asia) or from semiperiphery to periphery (as in the case of China-made goods, the great bulk of goods sold in the building), most of the people in Chungking Mansions have been moving in the opposite direction, from periphery to core—Hong Kong represents the core, as China does not, judging from per capita income. This movement from periphery to core is true not just for traders, but for most of the different groups to be found in Chungking Mansions.

The African traders who come to Chungking Mansions tend to be more or less among the middle- and upper-class aristocracy in their countries, as we've seen, but coming to Hong Kong may represent a real financial burden for them, as those counting their pennies in Chungking Mansions eateries and eating Cup Noodles in 7-Eleven for their dinner attest. Hong Kong also places their own society in a mirror: "Why can't my country be like this?" an East African trader asked me. "Maybe in a few years . . . maybe in a century" is how he replied when I asked him back. Hong Kong, for some of these traders, represents their first glimpse of the developed world, and the city may throw at least a few into turmoil when they compare it to the world from which they have come.

The Chinese owners of many businesses in Chungking Mansions moved from periphery to core in coming to Hong Kong but wound up in Chungking Mansions, Hong Kong's own ghetto of the periphery, albeit a place where many have earned substantial profits over the years. Pakistani and Indian managers, or their parents or grandparents, also moved from periphery to core, but in at least some cases, as we've seen, they seek to move further into the core, to Great Britain or the United States, in their family's ongoing multigenerational immigration.

The Indian temporary workers largely come to the core from peripheral Kolkata as laborers. The wages they make in Hong Kong far outstrip the wages they could make in their home country. Although it is humiliating, several told me, for educated Indians like themselves to have to come to Hong Kong to work as dishwashers, touts, or goods carriers, the comparatively high wages they make in Hong Kong as compared to Kolkata, as well as their status as "big men" back in Kolkata, make this journey to the core worthwhile for most.

Asylum seekers come to Hong Kong because they desperately seek to leave their home countries and can get into Hong Kong relatively easily as compared to other developed-world destinations to which they might go. The fact that they have come to Hong Kong, thousands of miles away from their home countries, rather than to nearby countries, as is the more typical pattern of asylum seekers the world over, testifies to their comparatively well-off positions. They have had the economic, social, and cultural capital to "know where to go." They have wound up not in squalid refugee camps, but in Hong Kong—however difficult it may be as a place of sojourn for asylum seekers, it nonetheless provides frugal developed-world benefits, as opposed to the far less salubrious situations of asylum seekers in the developing world.

And there are the tourists. The tourists from poorer countries seek to experience a wealthy core society for as little money as possible, by staying in its developing-world enclave. They are following the same path as the traders, temporary workers, and asylum seekers, but instead of gaining money from the core, they seek to spend as little as possible in the core while enjoying its pleasures. The tourists from wealthier countries, on the other hand, are reversing the path of all the groups we have earlier considered. They move not from periphery to core but, for many, from core to "imagined periphery," a place from which they may experience the thrill of the periphery from within the safety of the core. Despite the negative publicity that has accrued to Chungking Mansions over the years, Chungking Mansions' location in Hong Kong makes it a prime locale from which to experience South Asia and Africa at what may seem to be a suitably safe remove.

Chungking Mansions becomes easier to understand when we consider the passage of its different social groups between peripheries and core and back, in all their inequalities, in the context of world systems analysis. Chungking Mansions offers an extraordinary window into the multiple patterns of migration that may be seen in the world today between realms poor and rich.

Most of the people within these different groups we have discussed are making a difficult attempt to pass from a realm of the poor to a realm of the rich. Some may succeed, but the wealth embodied in the skyscrapers that surround them in Tsim Sha Tsui today will probably be forever denied them. Chungking Mansions offers for many a window to developed-world wealth and at least the possibility of attaining a degree of wealth, but the walls are high and the ceiling all but unbreachable. For most, although not all, they glimpse the wealth around them in Hong Kong, make a small amount of money, and more or less accept their lot in life. At this they have little choice.

A central concept at work in creating the contemporary global inequalities that we have been discussing is that of neoliberalism, the ideology emphasizing the market as the ultimate arbiter of value and advocating minimal restriction of the market by the state. Neoliberalism has become the central political-economic doctrine of the world as a whole.[11] The recent economic downturn notwithstanding, it has been taken up in specific situations not just by Western market democracies, but by a range of societies ostensibly hostile to it in their ideologies of state control.[12] Neoliberalism, for a number of complex reasons, not least of which has been the British colonial government's desire for legitimacy in the closing decades of its colonial control by emphasizing business, has long been the central ideology of Hong Kong. Let me now discuss how neoliberalism works in shaping Chungking Mansions.

Neoliberalism is most obviously apparent in the fact that Hong Kong can be so easily entered. The Hong Kong government, although becoming somewhat stricter in recent years, still does not play a particularly restrictive role in enabling visitors to enter the territory, as compared to most other developed countries. The traders and illegal workers in Chungking Mansions are allowed in Hong Kong as tourists. Given the multiple stamps on their passports, immigration personnel understand that this is unlikely, but they largely look the other way. Traders and temporary workers coming to Hong Kong and going to Chungking Mansions often admit their purpose to Immigration and are not penalized. Indeed, perhaps they should not be penalized, since they are not generally taking jobs from Hong Kong residents. Societies such as the United States are not nearly as market oriented in considering immigrants, despite the fact that, by numerous accounts, many industries in the United States would collapse if the labor of illegal workers was abolished.

Hong Kong is generally somewhat strict in curtailing the labor of illegal workers from the mainland; my sense is that in the Immigration Department's dealings with South Asians and Africans likely headed for Chungking Mansions, there is somewhat less concern for legality, since these people are not competing for jobs (touts, dishwashers, clerks, guesthouse helpers, or traders in Chungking Mansions) that Hong Kong people would be likely to take.* The apparently increasing restrictions on African traders by Hong Kong Immigration in the last two years to some extent threatens Chungking Mansions' economic viability, with many more African traders now going to China because they cannot get a visa into Hong Kong; but still, Hong Kong remains more free in its visa regime than are almost all other developed-world societies. The comparative freedom of asylum seekers to enter Hong Kong, despite the problems that this has caused Hong Kong as of this writing,[13] is testament to the territory's desire to maintain a largely open border.

Aside from this, there is the fact that the police don't much bother cracking down on illegal workers, or on copies, or prostitution, or on any of the myriad violations running throughout Chungking Mansions, as long as no one complains. We saw this in chapter 4, in police officer Billy Tsang's account where he said that the police will not concern themselves with the sales of copy phones if there is no complaint from companies or individuals based in Hong Kong. If the buyer and seller both know that phones are copies and are satisfied with their transaction, then the police by and large keep out.

As for illegal immigrants of various sorts, he said that police prefer not to be involved, as we've seen. An Indian friend told me that a policeman in Chungking Mansions said to him, "You're not doing anything bad, are you? Except working illegally. As long as you're not doing anything bad, you'll be OK." The police combat drug dealing, robbery, and violent altercations, and occasionally pursue those with expired visas, but in other areas, they stay out. It is business as usual, legal or illegal. The police make exceptions to this when mass media pressure or changes in the law force them to act, but my general impression is that they would prefer not to act within Chungking Mansions to enforce laws that are largely unenforceable, and would rather let it be.

*To my regret, I have not been able to find anyone in the Immigration Department in Hong Kong willing to speak to me about these matters.

A third indication of Hong Kong's neoliberalism is that borders are so porous in enabling the passage of goods. Many of the phone sellers I know in Chungking Mansions have in recent years sold copy phones that have been brought in across the Chinese border into Hong Kong. There are, of course, all kinds of illegal goods brought into Hong Kong, and copy phones pale in significance compared to drugs or other goods harmful to public health. Still, the Hong Kong government does seem to be remarkably lenient. This is partially a matter of necessity—Hong Kong's borders with China are the busiest in the world, and so strict surveillance of all goods brought from China into Hong Kong seems all but impossible. Nonetheless, this laxity of enforcement also embodies a philosophy. The Hong Kong government represents the essence of neoliberalism: let business go on unimpeded.

Anthropological literature typically depicts neoliberalism as a profound evil, representing the forces of rampant global capitalism destroying all possibility of resistance.[14] From a macroscopic perspective, it is no doubt true that neoliberalism adversely affects the world. But in the small world of Chungking Mansions, the effects of neoliberalism seem largely benign.

What may be the most globalized building in the world is generally nonviolent, as we've seen, due to the common pursuit of profit by all who sojourn there. In Chungking Mansions, a positive side of neoliberalism is apparent—people from more or less hostile societies the world over, such as India and Pakistan, do not typically fight with each other, a beneficent side effect of the pursuit of money unimpeded by much state control. "I don't have time to fight with anyone! I come here to make money!" is a statement I have often heard in Chungking Mansions, a statement that would warm the hearts of neoliberal economists the world over.

Chungking Mansions represents not just a third-world enclave but a middle- and upper-class third-world enclave of people with money and education far beyond that of most of their fellow citizens at home. The peacefulness of Chungking Mansions not only comes from the ideology of neoliberalism but also from the fact that almost everyone in Chungking Mansions is a comparative success in life, by the very fact that they are in the building. Most are successes, more or less, within the social-Darwinistic competition of neoliberalism. There are of course exceptions to this, such as the Nepalese drug addicts, but by and large, this is indeed the case. It is ironic that a building popularly viewed in Hong Kong as a cesspool of sleaze is in fact a staunch bourgeois enclave of chamber-of-commerce capitalism, albeit with a few corners cut.

Chungking Mansions is so cheap simply because the rich in poor coun-

tries are the poor in rich countries—this is all most can afford. Nonetheless, the bourgeois character of Chungking Mansions, beneath the exoticism
of its surface, is its most striking feature. Almost everyone in the building,
whatever their current sufferings, as in the case of asylum seekers or even sex
workers or heroin addicts, has been more or less a winner in life. Chungking
Mansions remains a ghetto because it is ethnically distinct from the rest of
Hong Kong and is looked down upon or feared by most Hong Kong Chinese, something that most people in Chungking Mansions are all too well
aware of. However, it is a distinctly bourgeois ghetto, and more, a cosmopolitan ghetto.[15] It is cosmopolitan beyond the imaginations of much of the
Hong Kong world that surrounds it.

We discussed at the close of chapter 2 one effect of Chungking Mansions'
neoliberalism: the massive gaps between the rich and the poor. This is the
gap between the paunchy Indian shopkeeper and his temporary worker employee, between the guesthouse owner and the maid who manages the premises, between the rich African entrepreneur and the asylum seeker from the
same country who has practically nothing. But the building does not erupt
into class warfare because everyone hopes and believes that they themselves
will someday become successful and wealthy. This seems, objectively, doubt-
ful, but this is their faith.

This faith, even more than Islam, is the faith that unifies Chungking
Mansions. It is the faith that in the capitalist ghetto of Chungking Mansions, within the neoliberal world of Hong Kong and the massive gaps of
global wealth and poverty that characterize the world's core and peripheries,
one can squeeze out enough profit to make a better life for oneself and one's
family. Considering the new houses that spring up in Kolkata, or in Islam-
abad, or in Lagos, or in Mombasa, paid for by Chungking Mansions's earnings, the power of such a dream is clear—even if the majority of people in
the building probably never will become rich and are perhaps deluded for
even hoping for such a thing.

Hong Kong's neoliberalism could go even further. Various writers of
late have discussed whether the global regime of national passport controls
should be abolished, to let the market alone decide where workers from
across the globe might go in search of opportunities for employment and
wealth.[16] If this radical step were taken, parallels to Chungking Mansions
would spring up around the world: international crash pads for the poor
within the cities of the rich. Because this has not happened—partly because
Hong Kong alone in the developed world has such a high degree of flexibility
in who it admits—Chungking Mansions has remained more or less unique
in the world.

This, then, is the global significance of Chungking Mansions. It is a build-ing of the periphery within a city of the core, a city located between the de-veloping world's manufacturing hub and its poorest nether regions. It is a ghetto of middle-class striving within a city of wealthier middle-class striv-ing, viewing its denizens with fear and scorn yet letting business as usual be the law of the day. Chungking Mansions is a place where the ambitious from the poorer places in the world come to try to get rich or richer, in the shadow of the skyscrapers of the truly rich, which they will almost certainly never be-come. Chungking Mansions is where the better-off from poorer nations and enclaves of the world mingle, in the hope of becoming as rich as the people just outside its doors. All the individual stories of this book can only be un-derstood within this larger focus, of Chungking Mansions' particular place in Hong Kong and in the world at large. Within this particular place lies this book and the tales within it.

The Future of Chungking Mansions/The Future of the World

What, then, is the future of Chungking Mansions? One thing that should be readily apparent from this book's various discussions is the fragility of its current socioeconomic situation, which could easily be destroyed. If, for ex-ample, the Chinese government continues to loosen visa restrictions on Afri-cans in mainland China, and more and more flights from Africa begin to go directly into mainland China, as has already been happening, then Africans buying goods in Chungking Mansions will continue to diminish and much of the current business in ground-floor and first-floor stores may come to an end. If, taking a longer view, Chinese companies sending representatives to Africa increase in number, then African traders in Hong Kong and China will perhaps significantly decline in number; Africans in China will diminish to the extent that China is in Africa, and this will certainly affect Chungking Mansions.

On a different front, if Hong Kong immigration authorities, as directed by the Hong Kong government, becomes completely weary of asylum seekers headed to Hong Kong's shores, then they may choose to implement visa policies more like those of Australia, Japan, or the United States, whereby those from the developing world will not be granted visa-free access but will be sent packing on the next flight home if they lack a visa. There is some evidence that this is beginning to happen, with the burden of asylum seekers apparently increasingly outweighing the benefits of tourists from the developing world in the eyes of Hong Kong Immigration. Immigration's crackdown on illegal workers in Chungking Mansions in November 2009 may be a harbinger of the future.

On still a different front, if the Incorporated Owners of Chungking Mansions decide to greatly upgrade Chungking Mansions, then prices may sufficiently rise to drive out African traders and South Asian shopkeepers, making Chungking Mansions into one more second-rate Hong Kong shopping mall. If enough mainland Chinese become convinced of the economic potential of the building, Chinese owners and customers may become predominant, driving out most others and making the building a mainland Chinese enclave. If the Urban Renewal Authority in Hong Kong, the city's all-but-omnipotent planning czar, decides that the property is too valuable to remain "Chungking Mansions," then the building may be in short order torn down to make way for one more grand hotel, each largely indistinguishable from another. These scenarios illustrate the precariousness of Chungking Mansions. Because change is inevitable, the place can't last—although what it eventually becomes very much remains to be seen. Chungking Mansions, as we saw in chapter 1, has changed at points throughout its history, and change will doubtless continue.

I asked many of the owners of property in Chungking Mansions about how they saw the building's future, and more specifically, how they would feel about the building being torn down. As one relative of an owner said to me,

If this building in the next twenty years were to get demolished, it would totally finish the culture here. It has to happen, over time, because the building is getting older. It's prime location; they may tear it down and make a big hotel. . . . Yes, it is hard to get all the different owners together. But I'm sure that if anyone gets a good enough price to sell, they will sell. No one hates money! It will happen eventually; it's inevitable.

As another owner said, "This property is so old that maybe someone will restructure it—I hope so! If they tear down Chungking Mansions, they'll pay us quite a bit!"

Hong Kong newspaper articles and blogs have over the years often expressed the desire that the building be torn down,[17] but given the ownership structure, this has been extremely difficult. Until 2001, the law was that no building in Hong Kong could be torn down without the consent of at least 90 percent of the property owners. From 2001 on, this law has no longer held sway, and the Urban Renewal Authority in Hong Kong may tear down a building without such consent if necessary.

However, the sheer size of Chungking Mansions diminishes the potential profit that can be made from replacing the building. As a scholar of Hong Kong real estate told me, "Chungking Mansions has not been torn down—and several larger developers have thought about it—because it's so big that in terms of floors and floor space, tearing it down would make no sense." Typically, buildings of five or six stories are torn down, to be replaced by twenty-story towers that massively increase the saleable floor space of a building. But Chungking Mansions already has seventeen stories, and thus tearing it down would not lead to a great increase in saleable space.

There is also the fact that the building, even in its more or less decrepit condition over the years, has been a great generator of revenue. A top Hong Kong government official said of Chungking Mansions in 1993 that it would not be redeveloped because "even in its current condition, the building is a gold mine for its owners."[18] This seems even more true today for most owners. Shops go out of business from time to time, but few remain empty for long, given the dream of profits just around the corner. The goldmine of Chungking Mansions, despite the complaints and travails of so many current owners, continues to glitter, with investors continuing to line up money in hand. The building will thus presumably continue as it has, at least for the time being, into the future.

I would guess that Chungking Mansions will probably remain, for at least another decade or two, as a center of low-end globalization, but it will even-

tually be torn down—this is inevitable. Already it is one of the oldest buildings in the Tsim Sha Tsui area, and despite periodic refurbishment, its end
will come sooner or later.

However, in a larger sense, Chungking Mansions will remain. There will,
in the future, be more and more nodes where the developed and the developing world meet, where all the world intermingles. This has already happened
in the present, in localities from Paris to New York to Nairobi, and will happen to an ever greater extent in the future. Given the increasing collision and
intermingling of people throughout the world, the increasing presence of the
developing world in the developed world, and the parallel expansion of the
cultural supermarket across the globe, I predict that what Chungking Mansions is today, much more of the world will be tomorrow.

Chungking Mansions, although perhaps unique in the world, is also the
world we will increasingly all live within. Low-end globalization is not the
world's past; it is, in at least some respects, the world's future. Chungking
Mansions, in all its particularities, will of course vanish, but in a larger sense,
the ghetto at the center of the world may become, by and by, all the world.

NOTES

Prelude

1. Norman 1895, 17; quoted in Sandhaus 2010, 17.

2. Smith 1883, 48; quoted in Sandhaus 2010, 121.

3. Welsh 1993, 378–86; Tsang 2004, 47–55; Ku et al. 2003.

4. Mathews, Ma, and Lui 2008, 32–39.

5. *Economist* 2009, 29, 132.

6. White 1994.

7. See also Knowles and Harper (2009, 116–31) for a discussion of Chungking Mansions in the context of Hong Kong migration.

Chapter One

1. Harper and Storey 1999, 171.

2. IrisC's Flickr page, "Chungking Guesthouse," February 4, 2008, http://www.flickr.com/photos/pahud/2242268104/ (accessed March 6, 2009).

3. Li-jing Zhu, Annie Gu's Blog, Chungking Mansions, June 28, 2008, http://anniegwj.spaces.live.com/blog/cns!503FF852A409141B!7073 .entry (accessed March 9, 2009).

4. C. C. Chiou's blog, Chungking Building/Complex, June 16, 2008, http://blog.udn.com/minfengchiou/1963100 (accessed March 6, 2009).

5. Lailing, "Chungking Mansions," 2007, http://lailing.motime.com/post/661599/重慶。大廈 (accessed March 7, 2009).

6. Hamish McDonald, "Vice HQ Gets Facelift, but It's Only Skin Deep," *Age*, May 11, 2005, http://www.theage.com.au/news/World/Vice-HQ-gets-facelift-but -its-only-skin-deep/2005/05/10/1115584956620.html (accessed September 27, 2007).

7. Karl Taro Greenfield, "Hope and Squalor in Chungking Mansions," *World Hum*, August 13, 2007, http://www.worldhum.com/features/travel-stories/hope_and _squalor_at_chungking_mansion_20070813/ (accessed September 27, 2007).

8. Anonymous comment on Gossip Café, July 11, 2002, http://www.securework .com/hk/viewforum.php?f=3 (accessed September 27, 2007; site now discontinued.

9. Merriam Webster's Dictionary, http://www.merriam-webster.com/ (accessed August 24, 2010).

10. Weber 1976.

11. Appadurai 1996; Hannerz 1996.

12. Inda and Rosaldo 2002, 2.

13. Fallon 2002, 198.

14. Blommaert, Collins, and Slembrouck (2005) discuss one such globalized neighborhood in Ghent, Belgium, no doubt one of numerous globalized neighborhoods worldwide.

15. Ribeiro 2006.

16. Marcus 1998; Hannerz 2003.

17. Velho 1978; Ring 2006; Bestor 2004.

18. Jäggi et al. 2008.

19. "Mobile Marvels: A Special Report on Telecoms in Emerging Markets," *Economist*, September 26, 2009.

20. Wordie 2007, 26.

21. Richard Cook, "Miles Apart," *South China Morning Post*, September 28, 1997.

22. Mathews, Ma, and Liu 2008, 27.

23. White 1994.

24. Xuxi 2002, 5.

25. Wheeler 1981, 47; italics in original.

26. Caroline Dewhurst, "Gold Smuggling Rings Exposed," *South China Morning Post*, February 8, 1987.

27. "High-Rise Menace Needs Urgent Action by Govt," *Hong Kong Standard*, August 30, 1988; Mariita Eager and Jimmy Leung, "Chungking 'To Remain a Fire Trap,'" *South China Morning Post*, June 18, 1992; Samantha Rosich, "Facelift Fails to Improve Fire Safety at Chungking," *South China Morning Post*, February 9, 1992.

28. "Chùhnghing daaihhah yuhngdihn yúhnchìu fuhhòh chúhngpòu dihnsin jaahmmòuh gùngsì sìhngjip" [Chungking Mansions Exceeds Power Load; No Company Agrees to Do Electrical Wiring], *Ming Pao* (Hong Kong), July 27, 1993.

29. "Guesthouses Feel the Heat," *South China Morning Post*, October 16, 1994.

30. Charlotte Parsons, "Court Told of Nightclub Bomb Plot," *South China Morning Post*, November 1, 1995.

31. Greg Torode, "Hong Kong Muslims Threaten Hindu Shopkeepers," *South China Morning Post*, December 9, 1992; Edward A. Gargan, "Smell It, Taste It: All the Spice

of Life," *New York Times*, August 30, 1997; Adam Luck, "Terror Gang Stalks Chungking Mansions," *South China Morning Post*, January 28, 2001.

32. *Ming Pao*, "Yùhkèih gèuilàuh dòng fèifaat lòuhgùng póupin dòngguhk sàu Chùhnghing daaihhah kàuchah 103 yàhn" [Illegal Workers Common in Chungking Mansions; Authorities Arrest 103 People], *Ming Pao* (Hong Kong), July 21, 1993; Magdelen Chow, "Police Raids Criticised," *The Standard* (Hong Kong), June 7, 1995.

33. Tommy Lewis, "Hostel Owner Found Dead in Chungking Mansions," *South China Morning Post*, July 28, 2001; Marcal Joanilho, "Stabbing Murder at Chungking Mansions," *South China Morning Post*, March 25, 2002; Sara Bradford, "Man Jailed for Lying to Protect Murderer of Woman," *South China Morning Post*, May 21, 2004.

34. Martin Wong, "Facelift Raises Chungking Mansions From Vice to Virtue," *South China Morning Post*, April 28, 2008; Chandra Wong, "Chungking Mansions' Facelift Only Skin-Deep," *South China Morning Post*, April, 29, 2005.

35. See also Incorporated Owners of Chungking Mansions 2008, 52.

36. Mathews, Ma, and Liu 2008, 63–66, 73–76.

37. Stone, Chen, and Chow 2010, 242.

38. But see Bodomo (2007), who does describe Chungking Mansions as a community.

39. Liam Fitzpatrick, "Best Example of Globalization in Action: Chungking Mansions, Kowloon, Hong Kong," *Time*, Best of Asia edition, May 7, 2007. http://www .time.com/time/specials/2007/best_of_asia/article/0,28804,1614524_1614473 _1614447,00.html (accessed September 27, 2007).

40. For an insightful discussion of the mobile phone trade between Chungking Mansions and Africa, see Peter Shadbolt, "Where Africa Goes to Buy Its Mobile Phones," *Financial Times*, January 31, 2009, http://www.ft.com/cms/s/2/4609e212 -eb64-11dd-bb6e-0000779fd2ac.html?ftcamp=rss (accessed February 12, 2010).

Chapter Two

1. See Le Bail 2009.

2. Evan Osnos, "The Promised Land; Letter from China," *New Yorker*, February 9, 2009; Yang Dingdu, Pan Wang, and Liu Wanli, "Burgeoning African Community Tests China's Engagement with World," *Xinhua*, October 5, 2009, http://news.xinhuanet .com/english/2009-10/05/content_12183718.htm (accessed January 17, 2010).

3. White 1994.

4. Niall Fraser, "Expat Population a Mystery," *South China Morning Post*, February 9, 2003.

5. See Tam 2007; Elaine Yau, "Minority Report," *South China Morning Post*, October 16, 2009.

6. Martin Wong, "Officers Go Undercover to Nab Illegal Workers," *South China Morning Post*, December 27, 2006.

7. Constable 1997, 1–3.

8. Nishika Patel, "Badlands on the Heart of the City," *The Standard*, December 4, 2007.

9. http://www.chungking-mansions.com/index.html.

10. See Goffman (1959, 1967) on the complexities of self-presentation in interactions. Goffman can be usefully used in analyzing Chungking Mansions' microinteractions (Mathews 2007).

11. This parallels what Stoller (2002) has found among African street vendors in New York: the common desire to make money and support one's family trumps political, ethnic, and religious differences.

Chapter Three

1. Ulysse 2007; Browne 2004, 56; Ribeiro 2006; MacGaffey and Bazenguissa-Ganga 2000; Stoller 2002.

2. Richard Ling, personal communication.

3. Nordstrom 2007, 117–22.

4. InvestHK, The Government of Hong Kong, Special Administrative Region, http://www.investhk.gov.hk/pages/1/163.html (accessed November 16, 2009; page no longer available). See also the Index of Economic Freedom, http://www.heritage.org/index/ (accessed July 16, 2010).

5. Philip Bowring, "Economic Freedom? It Depends Where You Stand," *International Herald Tribune*, January 9, 2006.

6. Mathews, Ma, and Lui 2008, 15–17.

7. Smart 1988.

8. This definition is from Nordstrom (2007, 93).

9. Sam Mukalazi, "Buyers Duped as Fake Goods Flood Uganda," *East African*, April 9–15, 1999.

10. Ghosh 2001.

11. "Chùhnghing daaihhah beihfùng yéhgwànfó hèuigìng chàhwohk wuhngeuih sáulàuhdáan seungún méihjihkhon chòhng móuhbei péihbouh" [Chungking Mansions sealed over false alarm; toy grenades and model cannons found—American arrested], August 9, 2008; Joyce Man, "American Jailed for Batons, Stun Guns, and Mace Stash," *South China Morning Post*, January 21, 2010.

12. Lo 2006, 52.

13. Rojas 2009.

14. Lo 2006, 53–54, 59–60.

15. See Chalfin 2004.

16. Alden 2007; Rotberg 2008; Tull 2006.

Chapter Four

1. Foucault 1995, 116–31.

2. Michael Connelly, "When Fact Meets Fiction, the Cases Are Harder to Solve," CNN, October 29, 2009, http://edition.cnn.com/2009/CRIME/10/29/michael.connelly.fact.fiction/index.html (accessed October 30, 2009).

3. Ivan Zhai and Fiona Tam, "Africans Protest in Guangzhou after Nigerian Feared Killed Fleeing Visa Check," *South China Morning Post*, July 16, 2009.

4. See Gibney 2004; Nyers 2006; Brennan 2003; Ong 2003; Moorehead 2005.

5. Davis Momphard, "No Man's Land: Asylum Seekers Endure a Grim Waiting Game as their Fate is Decided," *South China Morning Post*, July 20, 2007.

6. Hong Kong Legislative Council 2009.

7. Mathews, Ma, and Lui 2008, 25–26.

8. Chan 2003.

9. Daniel Altman, "Bypassing Barriers for a Passport," *International Herald Tribune*, Managing Globalization, February 7, 2007.

10. Frelick 2007, 45–55.

11. Essed and Wesenbeck 2004, 53.

12. Barclay Crawford and Yvonne Tsui, "Reopen Refugee Camps, Say South Asians," *South China Morning Post*, March 8, 2009.

13. See Daniel and Knudsen 1995; Wilson 2009, 214–15.

14. Knudson 1995, 22.

15. "HK's Treatment of Asylum Seekers Shameful," *South China Morning Post*, Editorial, July 7, 2006.

16. Kang-chung Ng, "Asylum Seekers on 3-Day Hunger Strike," *South China Morning Post*, October 17, 2007.

17. Harrell-Bond 2002, 53.

18. Yvonne Tsui, "Asylum Seekers Allowed to Work," *South China Morning Post*, March 3, 2009.

19. Clifford Lo, "Ruling Blamed for Influx of Asylum Seekers," *South China Morning Post*, May 14, 2009.

20. Martin Wong, "Asylum Seekers Protest Against Laws Forbidding Work," *South China Morning Post*, November 21, 2009.

21. Phyllis Tsang, "Torture Claimants 'A Ticking Bomb': Refugees Without ID Difficult to Remove," *South China Morning Post*, November 29, 2009.

22. Hong Kong Legislative Council 2009.

23. Phyllis Tsang, "HK Asked to Unify Screenings for Torture, Asylum," *South China Morning Post*, November 29, 2009.

24. See Englund (2006) for a glimpse into how human rights activism may paradoxically further the oppression of the poor; see Verdirame and Harrell-Bond (2005) on how human rights organizations and refugee relief policies in the developing world deny refugees their human rights.

Chapter Five

1. Michael Connelly, "When Fact Meets Fiction, the Cases Are Harder to Solve," CNN, October 29, 2009, http://edition.cnn.com/2009/CRIME/10/29/michael.connelly.fact.fiction/index.html (accessed October 30, 2009).

2. Christopher Shay, "U.S. Crime Writer Tackles a Real Hong Kong Cold Case," *Time*, November 10, 2009, http://www.time.com/time/world/article/0,8599,1937140,00.html (accessed November 12, 2009).

3. Wong (1997) depicts some of the negative ways in which Chungking Mansions' residents view Hong Kong people, a depiction that remains true today as well.

4. Mathews 2000, 121–65, 192–93.

5. Mathews 2000.

6. Wallerstein 2004; Arrighi 2005; Hall 2000.

7. Allen and Hamnett 1995, 2; see also Ferguson 2007, 25–49.

8. Sassen 2007, 57, 81.

9. For example, Santos 2004, 297.

10. Tehranian 2004, 22.

11. Harvey 2005; Saad-Filho and Johnston 2005.

12. Ong 2006.

13. Phyllis Tsang, "Torture Claimants 'A Ticking Bomb': Refugees Without ID Difficult to Remove," *South China Morning Post*, November 29, 2009.

14. Harvey (2005), to take just one example, largely holds this view.

15. See Nashashibi 2007.

16. Pecoud and Guchteneire 2004; Hayter 2004; Marfleet 2006; Bacon 2008.

17. For example, Kevin Sinclair, "A Disaster Lies Waiting," *South China Morning Post*, September 22, 1997; BWG, Chungking Mansions, April 16, 2002. http://www
.bigwhiteguy.com/archive/2002/04/chungking_mansions/ (accessed June 25, 2010).

18. Joshua Fellman, "Eason Calls for Faster Approvals," *Hong Kong Standard*, August 4, 1993.

REFERENCES

Alden, Chris. 2007. *China in Africa*. London: Zed Books.

Allen, John, and Chris Hamnett, eds. 1995. *A Shrinking World? Global Unevenness and Inequality*. Oxford: Oxford University Press.

Appadurai, Arjun. 1996. *Modernity at Large*. Minneapolis: University of Minnesota Press.

Arrighi, Giovanni. 2005. "Globalization in World Systems Perspective." In *Critical Globalization Studies*, ed. Richard P. Appelbaum and William I. Robinson. London: Routledge.

Bacon, David. 2008. *Illegal People: How Globalization Creates Migration and Criminalizes Immigration*. Boston: Beacon Press.

Bestor, Theodore C. 2004. *Tsukiji: The Fish Market at the Center of the World*. Berkeley: University of California Press.

Blommaert, Jan, James Collins, and Stef Slembrouck. 2005. "Polycentricity and Interactional Regimes in 'Global Neighborhoods.'" *Ethnography* 6 (2): 205–35.

Bodomo, Adams B. 2007. "An Emerging African-Chinese Community in Hong Kong: The Case of Tsim Sha Tsui's Chungking Mansions." In *Afro-Chinese Relations: Past, Present, and Future*, ed. Kwesi Kwaa Prah. Cape Town: Centre for Advanced Studies in African Societies.

Brennan, Frank. 2003. *Tampering with Asylum: A Universal Humanitarian Problem*. St. Lucia, AU: University of Queensland Press.

Browne, Katherine E. 2004. *Creole Economics: Caribbean Cunning under the French Flag.* Austin: University of Texas Press.

Chalfin, Brenda. 2004. "Border Scans: Sovereignty, Surveillance, and the Customs Service in Ghana." *Identities* 11 (3): 397–416.

Chan, Wai-kwong Ocean. 2003. "From Refugee Camp to City Street: The Different Lives of Young Vietnamese in Hong Kong." Master's thesis, Department of Anthropology, Chinese University of Hong Kong.

Constable, Nicole. 1997. *Maid to Order in Hong Kong: Stories of Filipina Workers.* Ithaca, NY: Cornell University Press.

Daniel, E. Valentine, and John Chr. Knudsen, eds. 1995. *Mistrusting Refugees.* Berkeley: University of California Press.

Economist. 2009. *Pocket World in Figures.* 2010 edition. London: Profile Books.

Englund, Harri. 2006. *Prisoners of Freedom: Human Rights and the African Poor.* Berkeley: University of California Press.

Essed, Philomena, and Rianne Wesenbeck. 2004. "Contested Refugee Status: Human Rights, Ethics, and Social Responsibilities." In *Refugees and the Transformations of Societies: Agency, Policies, Ethics, and Politics,* ed. Philomena Essed, Georg Frerks, and Joke Schrijvers. New York: Berghahn Books.

Fallon, Steve. 2002. *Hong Kong and Macau.* 10th edition. Melbourne: Lonely Planet.

Ferguson, James. 2007. "Globalizing Africa? Observations from an Inconvenient Continent." In *Global Shadows: Africa in the Neoliberal World Order.* Durham, NC: Duke University Press.

Foucault, Michel. 1995. *Discipline and Punish: The Birth of the Prison.* Trans. Alan Sheridan. New York: Vintage Books.

Frelick, Bill. 2007. "Paradigm Shifts in the International Responses to Refugees." In *Fear of Persecution: Global Human Rights, International Law, and Human Well-Being,* ed. James D. White and Anthony J. Marsella. Lanham, MD: Lexington Books.

Ghosh, B. N. 2001. *Dependency Theory Revisited.* Aldershot, UK: Ashgate.

Gibney, Matthew J. 2004. *The Ethics and Politics of Asylum: Liberal Democracy and the Response to Refugees.* Cambridge: Cambridge University Press.

Goffman, Erving. 1959. *The Presentation of Self in Everyday Life.* New York: Anchor Books.

———. 1967. *Interaction Ritual.* New York: Anchor Books.

Hall, Thomas D., ed. 2000. *A World-Systems Reader: New Perspectives on Gender, Urbanism, Cultures, Indigenous Peoples, and Ecology.* Lanham, MD: Roman and Littlefield.

Hannerz, Ulf. 1996. *Transnational Connections.* London: Routledge.

———. 2003. "Several Sites in One." In *Globalisation: Studies in Anthropology,* ed. Thomas Hylland Eriksen. London: Pluto Press.

Harper, Damian, and Robert Storey. 1999. *Hong Kong, Macau, and Guangzhou.* Hawthorn, AU: Lonely Planet Publications.

Harrell-Bond, Barbara. 2002. "Can Humanitarian Work with Refugees be Humane?" *Human Rights Quarterly* 24: 51–85.

Harvey, David. 2005. *A Brief History of Neoliberalism*. Oxford: Oxford University Press.

Hayter, Teresa. 2004. *Open Borders: The Case Against Immigration Controls*. 2nd edition. London: Pluto Press.

Hong Kong Legislative Council. 2009. "Panel on Security of the Legislative Council Torture Claim Screening Mechanism." LC Paper No. CB(2)2514/08–09(01). http://www.legco.gov.hk/yr08–09/english/panels/se/papers/se0706cb2–2054 –1-e.pdf (accessed November 16, 2009).

Incorporated Owners of Chungking Mansions. 2008. *The Thirteenth Management Committee: Special Brochure*.

Inda, Jonathan Xavier, and Renato Rosaldo. 2002. "Introduction: A World in Motion." In *The Anthropology of Globalization: A Reader*, ed. Jonathan Xavier Inda and Renato Rosaldo. Malden, MA: Blackwell.

Jäggi, Marcel, et al. 2008. *Chungking Mansions: 3D [In]formality*. Basel, CH: ETH Studio, Contemporary City Institute.

Knowles, Caroline, and Douglas Harper. 2009. *Hong Kong: Migrant Lives, Landscapes, and Journeys*. Chicago: University of Chicago Press.

Knudsen, John Chr. 1995. "When Trust is on Trial: Negotiating Refugee Narratives." In *Mistrusting Refugees*, ed. E. Valentine Daniel and John Chr. Knudsen. Berkeley: University of California Press.

Ku, Hok-bun, Kam-wah Chan, Wai-ling Chan, and Wai-yee Lee. 2003. *A Research Report on the Life Experiences of Pakistanis in Hong Kong*. Hong Kong Polytechnic University: Centre for Policy Studies, Department of Applied Social Sciences.

Le Bail, Hélène. 2009. "Foreign Migration to China's City-Markets: The Case of African Merchants." *Asia Visions 19*. Paris: Centre Asie IFRI. http://www.ifri.org/files/ centre_asie/AV19_LeBail_GB.pdf (accessed November24, 2009).

Lo, Christian. 2006. "Making It at the Chung-king Mansions: Stories from the Bottom End of Globalization." Master's thesis, Department of Social Anthropology, Norwegian University of Science and Technology, Trondheim, Norway.

MacGaffey, Janet, and Remy Bazenguissa-Ganga. 2000. *Congo–Paris: Transnational Traders on the Margins of the Law*. Bloomington: Indiana University Press.

Marcus, George E. 1998. "Ethnography in/of the World System: The Emergence of Multi-Sited Ethnography." In *Ethnography through Thick and Thin*. Princeton, NJ: Princeton University Press.

Marfleet, Philip. 2006. Refugees in a Global Era. Houndmill, UK: Palgrave MacMillan.

Mathews, Gordon. 2000. *Global Culture/Individual Identity: Searching for Home in the Cultural Supermarket*. London: Routledge.

———. 2007. "Chungking Mansions: A Center of 'Low-End Globalization.'" *Ethnology* 46(2): 169–83.

Mathews, Gordon, Eric Kit-wai Ma, and Tai-lok Lui. 2008. *Hong Kong, China: Learning to Belong to a Nation*. London: Routledge.

Moorehead, Caroline. 2005. *Human Cargo: A Journey among Refugees*. London: Chatto and Windus.

Nashashibi, Rami. 2007. "Ghetto Cosmopolitanism." In *Deciphering the Global: Its Scales, Spaces, and Subjects*, ed. Saskia Sassen. New York: Routledge.

Nordstrom, Carolyn. 2007. *Global Outlaws: Crime, Money, and Power in the Contemporary World*. Berkeley: University of California Press.

Norman, Henry. 1895. *The People and Politics of the Far East*. London: T. Fisher Unwin.

Nyers, Peter. 2006. *Rethinking Refugees: Beyond States of Emergency*. New York: Routledge.

Ong, Aihwa. 2003. *Buddha is Hiding: Refugees, Citizenship, the New America*. Berkeley: University of California Press.

———. 2006. *Neoliberalism as Exception: Mutations in Citizenship and Sovereignty*. Durham, NC: Duke University Press.

Pécoud, Antoine, and Paul de Guchteneire, eds. 2007. *Migration without Borders: Essays on the Free Movement of People*. Paris: UNESCO Publishing; New York: Berghahn Books.

Ribeiro, Gustavo Lins. 2006. "Economic Globalization from Below." *Etnográfica* 10 (2): 233–49.

Ring, Laura A. 2006. *Zenana: Everyday Peace in a Karachi Apartment Building*. Bloomington: Indiana University Press.

Rojas, Jose. 2009. "I'm in Hong Kong: I've Graduated: The Igbo Apprenticeship System and Hong Kong's Role in Informal Education." Paper presented at the American Anthropological Association Annual Meeting, December 2–6, Philadelphia, Pennsylvania.

Rotberg, Robert. 2008. *China into Africa: Trade, Aid, and Influence*. Washington D.C.: Brookings Institution Press.

Saad-Filho, Alfredo, and Deborah Johnston. 2005. *Neoliberalism: A Critical Reader*. London: Pluto Press.

Sandhaus, Derek. 2010. *Tales of Old Hong Kong: Treasures from the Fragrant Harbour*. Hong Kong: China Economic Review Publishing.

Santos. Boaventura de Sousa. 2004. "Transnational Third Worlds." In *Worlds on the Move: Globalization, Migration, and Cultural Security*, ed. Jonathan Friedman and Shalini Randeria. London: I. B. Tauris.

Sassen, Saskia. 2007. *A Sociology of Globalization*. New York: W. W. Norton.

Smart, Josephine. 1988. "How to Survive in Illegal Street Hawking in Hong Kong." In *Traders Versus the State: Anthropological Approaches to Unofficial Economies*, ed. Gracia Clark, ed. Boulder, CO: Westview Press.

Smith, J. J. 1883. *In Eastern Seas; or, The Commission of H.M.S. "Iron Duke," Flag-Ship in China, 1878–83*. Devonport, UK: A. H. Swiss. http://manybooks.net/titles/smithjj2792627926–8.html (accessed April 3, 2010).

Stoller, Paul. 2002. *Money Has No Smell: The Africanization of New York City*. Chicago: University of Chicago Press.

Stone, Andrew, Piera Chen, and Chung-wah Chow. 2010. *Lonely Planet Hong Kong and Macau*. Melbourne, AU: Lonely Planet Publications.

Tam Sin-yu, Ophelia. 2007 "South Asian Students in Primary School: Minorities and Education in Hong Kong." Master's thesis, Department of Anthropology, Chinese University of Hong Kong.

Tehranian, Majid. 2004. "Cultural Security and Global Governance: International Migration and Negotiations of Identity." In *Worlds on the Move: Globalization, Migration, and Cultural Security*, ed. Jonathan Friedman and Shalini Randeria. London: I. B. Tauris.

Tsang, Steve. 2004. *A Modern History of Hong Kong*. Hong Kong: Hong Kong University Press.

Tull, Denis. 2006. "China's Engagement in Africa: Scope, Significance, and Consequences." *Modern African Studies* 44 (3): 459–79.

Ulysse, Gina A. 2007. *Downtown Ladies: Informal Commercial Importers, a Haitian Anthropologist, and Self-Making in Jamaica*. Chicago: University of Chicago Press.

Velho, Gelberto. 1978. "Stigmatization and Deviance in Copacabana." *Social Problems* 25 (5): 526–30.

Verdirame, Guglielmo, and Barbara Harrell-Bond. 2005. *Rights in Exile: Janus-Faced Humanitarianism*. New York: Berghahn Books.

Wallerstein, Immanuel. 2004. *World Systems Analysis: An Introduction*. Durham, NC: Duke University Press.

Weber, Max. 1976. *The Protestant Ethic and the Spirit of Capitalism*. New York: Charles Scribner's Sons.

Welsh, Frank. 1993. *A History of Hong Kong*. London: HarperCollins.

Wheeler, Anthony Ian. 1981 [1975]. *South-East Asia on a Shoestring*. Victoria AU: Lonely Planet Publications.

White, Barbara-Sue. 1994. *Turbans and Traders: Hong Kong's Indian Communities*. New York: Oxford University Press.

Wilson, Richard. 2009. "Representing Human Rights Violations: Social Contexts and Subjectivities." In *Human Rights: An Anthropological Reader*, ed. Mark Goodale. Oxford: Wiley-Blackwell.

Wong, Eve F. Y. 1997. "Foreign Eyes on Hong Kong People: The View from Chungking Mansions." *Hong Kong Anthropologist* 10: 32–37. http://www.cuhk.edu.hk/ant/hkas/pages/old%20series.html (accessed May 2, 2010).

Wordie, Jason. 2007. *Streets: Exploring Kowloon*. Hong Kong: Hong Kong University Press.

Xuxi. 2002. *Chinese Walls / Daughters of Hui*. 2nd edition. Hong Kong: Chameleon Press.

asylum seekers (*cont.*)
82–83, 171–87, 194; and Hong Kong
government, 180, 181, 190–94, 216; and
Hong Kong Immigration, 79, 172, 212,
216; and the law, 81, 152, 169–73, 194;
lives of, 178–81; and low-end globalization, 13; and lying, 174–76; and marriage,
99, 180; mass-media discussion of, 190–
91; and NGOs, 31; number of, 78, 170–
71; and police, 159–60; "real" and "fake,"
80, 82, 173–78; and refugee status, 80,
169–80, 188–92, 205, 210; as sex workers, 81, 167; Somali, 28, 171–72; South
Asians, 27, 81, 172; as "ticking time
bomb," 193; and UNHCR, 79, 175–76,
190–94; upsurge in, 5, 18, 193; and work,
42, 80–81, 98, 162–68, 171, 176, 180–
84, 193
Australia, 18, 34, 94, 169, 216
Australian opals, 18, 109

Babri Mosque, 36
backpackers, 14, 17, 30, 34, 37
Bangalore, 124
Bangkok, 13, 20, 61, 65, 124
Bangladesh, 18, 110, 179, 188
Bangladeshis in Chungking Mansions, 18,
32, 37, 47, 71, 96–97, 179, 188
batteries for mobile phones, 117, 132, 148
Beijing Olympics, 119, 136–37, 140, 165
Bengali, 39, 96
Benin, 78
Bentham, Jeremy, 158
Bestor, Theodore, 21
Biman Bangladesh Airways, 75
borders: Hong Kong-China, 5, 6, 58, 59, 77,
120, 130, 133, 213; Hong Kong borders
as open, 79, 130, 212–13
Boss, 130
Brazil, 20, 208
bribery: of customs officials, 59, 63, 129,
138–39, 141, 144; of police, 159, 192
British in Chungking Mansions, 34–35, 39,
44, 68, 89, 91, 116
Brixton, 19
buildings, anthropologists' study of, 21

cameras, 27, 113, 124, 126, 155; closed-
circuit, 37, 39, 40, 42, 158–59

Cameroonians in Chungking Mansions, 96–
97, 121
Canaan Export Clothes Wholesale Trading
Centre, 119
Canada, 68, 80, 94, 170, 184, 188, 198
Cantonese (language) in Chungking Man-
sions, 24, 31, 38–39, 48, 53, 68–69, 71,
73, 85, 91, 189
Caribbean, 105
car parts, used, 5, 58, 59, 176
cars, used, 58, 125, 143, 189
caste, 49
CAT. *See* Convention Against Torture
(CAT)
Cathay Pacific, 23
Central Africa, 97, 128, 178, 181, 203
Central America, 125
Central District, 13, 83
Chan, Ocean, 89
Chennai, 86
Chikyū no arukikata, 90
China, 24, 61–63, 91–92, 108; business
practices in, 57–58, 118; companies in,
118, 123, 135, 137, 150, 216; factories in,
107–10, 118, 147, 167, 208; and Hong
Kong's history, 1–5, 172; immigrants
from, in Chungking Mansions, 39, 66;
lack of law in, 12, 108, 145; language barrier in, 143, 146; low-end globalization in,
20; lure of, 44, 58, 135–37; as manufacturing powerhouse, 18–19, 118; racism
in, 142; relations with Africa, 65, 150;
traders in, 11–12, 17–18, 44, 57–61, 63,
66, 70, 77, 112, 118–19, 123–37, 142–
47, 150, 166, 196, 205, 212, 215–16; visa
policies of, 31, 58, 77, 112, 165–67
China-made goods, 41–42, 58, 63–66, 118,
149, 209; clothing, 118, 139; copies, 41–
42, 64, 72n, 111, 114–17; impact of, 149;
phones, 63, 72n, 93, 111, 114–17, 121–
23, 132
Chinese mainlanders in Chungking Mansions, 9–10, 30; business investors, 44,
72, 108, 216; customers in guesthouses,
30, 37, 85, 91, 101; guesthouse owners,
100–101; sex workers, 86; store owners,
27, 44; tourists, 44, 52, 91–92, 94
Chinese mainlanders in Hong Kong: immigration violators, 192; in Mirador Man-